The Economic Legacy of the Reagan Years

The Economic Legacy of the Reagan Years

Euphoria or Chaos?

Edited by
Anandi P. Sahu
and
Ronald L. Tracy

 PRAEGER

New York
Westport, Connecticut
London

Library of Congress Cataloging-in-Publication Data

The Economic legacy of the Reagan years : euphoria or chaos? / edited
by Anandi P. Sahu and Ronald L. Tracy.
       p.   cm.
       Includes bibliographical references.
       ISBN 0-275-93596-5 (alk. paper)
       1. United States—Economic policy—1981– 2. United States—
Economic conditions—1981– I. Sahu, Anandi Prasad. II. Tracy,
Ronald L.
       HC106.8.E277   1991
       338.973—dc20   90-40952

British Library Cataloguing in Publication Data is available.

Library of Congress Catalog Card Number: 90-40952
ISBN: 0-275-93596-5

First published in 1991

Praeger Publishers, One Madison Avenue, New York, NY 10010
An imprint of Greenwood Publishing Group, Inc.

Printed in the United States of America

∞

The paper used in this book complies with the
Permanent Paper Standard issued by the National
Information Standards Organization (Z39.48-1984).

10 9 8 7 6 5 4 3 2 1

Contents

Tables and Figures

TABLES

FIGURES

Preface

This book examines the economic legacy of the Reagan administration. The importance of economic policy during the Reagan administration cannot be overemphasized. The media-coined term *Reaganomics* has come to represent the economic policies of that era. Although the term is widely used both by the general public and academic economists, there is no consensus among economists on precisely what it means, let alone whether its overall impact was favorable or unfavorable for the U.S. economy. The staunchest supporters of Reaganomics are euphoric about the outcomes—low unemployment, stable prices, economic growth—and view the Reagan era as an unprecedented economic miracle. Critics of the Reagan policies feel that his economic legacy is the chaotic economic environment that President Bush inherited—unprecedented deficits, regulatory chaos, and exchange rate instability—and that the apparent prosperity camouflages an impending economic disaster. While these sentiments represent extreme views, they indicate a lack of consensus and a need to examine the Reagan era.

The purpose of this volume is to provide an analysis of the empirical evidence that comprises the Reagan economic legacy. This book addresses most of the important economic issues that are relevant to this legacy: "supply-side economics," monetary policy, foreign trade, and regulatory environment. Well-known academic economists with diverse institutional affiliations have contributed to this volume. As one would expect, their findings and observations do not always point in the same direction. We as editors have, however, examined their empirical findings and arrived at tentative conclusions.

We recognize that our coverage is not exhaustive. We have concentrated mainly on the first-level economic impacts of the Reagan policies and have not examined the welfare effects of Reagan's economic initiatives. Also, the volume does not contain competing full-length studies on every economic issue. We have therefore included comments on every formal study in order to provide an alternative perspective. Conclusions based on this volume must, however, be considered tentative since the full impact of many Reagan economic policies may not yet have been realized. This volume nevertheless provides further impetus for academic debate on the economic legacy of the Reagan era.

We acknowledge the active cooperation of our colleagues at Oakland University, contributors to the volume, and other friends in the academic community. In particular, we are grateful to Ron Horwitz, Scott Monroe, Kevin Murphy, and Miron Stano for their support. Meticulous assistance was also provided by Helen DeMeritt, Kurt Hanus, and Ravi Somasundaram in preparation of the manuscript. Finally, a grant from Oakland University Research Committee and additional financial support from the Chrysler Corporation Fund greatly contributed to the publication of this volume.

Part I

Introduction

The Economic Legacy
of the Reagan Years:
Euphoria or Chaos?

Anandi P. Sahu and
Ronald L. Tracy

The eight years of the Reagan administration have left an indelible imprint on U.S. economic policy. This impact has often been characterized as the economic legacy of the Reagan era, and epitomized by the media-coined term *Reaganomics*. President Reagan inherited an economy with a relatively low unemployment rate, a modest budget deficit, and a small trade surplus. However, the nation was also saddled with double-digit inflation and interest rates, as well as a general malaise caused by both economic and noneconomic factors. When President Reagan left office at the end of the eight years, the economy had witnessed both the longest peacetime expansion in history (which continued to show strength well into the subsequent Bush administration) and the most severe recession in the postwar period. This economic expansion led to a decreasing unemployment rate that was accompanied by the lowest levels of inflation since the 1960s as well as moderate nominal interest rates. At the same time, the federal budget deficit and the U.S trade deficit reached their highest levels in U.S. history. During the eight years, the national debt increased more than it had during the previous 200 years (which included the fighting of two world wars, a civil war, and numerous other declared and undeclared wars), and the United States changed from being the world's largest creditor to the world's largest debtor. However, instead of malaise about the ability of the United States to compete in the world economic environment of the twenty-first century, there was a renewed optimism about the economy's ability to change, grow, and benefit from world competition. Finally, during the Reagan administration, while the stock market rose an unbelievable 200 percent during the economic expansion phase, it also experienced the greatest one-day fall in stock prices.

Clearly the Reagan economic legacy is one of both major accomplishments

and serious anomalies. On the surface, the eight years of the Reagan administration have been characterized by economic growth, a decline in unemployment, a reduction in inflation, and a generally healthy economy. Is this apparent success due to what George Bush in 1980 referred to as "voodoo economics,"
or to what candidate Reagan called the "miracle of supply-side economics"?
Alternatively, are the record-breaking trade and budget deficits, declining savings ratio, and increasing disparity between the "haves" and "have-nots" an
indication of an economic disaster waiting to happen? Reactions to achieve-
ments of the Reagan years encompass a wide spectrum of views. Some economists and political activists believe that the Reagan era symbolized the miracle
of supply-side policies. These proponents have been euphoric over the success
of Reaganomics. In contrast, the opponents of Reaganomics believe that the
economic policy successes of the Reagan administration were deceptive as they
camouflaged symptoms of impending economic disaster. To these opponents,
Reaganomics led to a chaotic economic environment. The truth may lie some-
where between the two extremes of euphoria and chaos.

In what follows we endeavor to seek this "truth" on the basis of the evidence presented in this volume as well as in other cited literature, and to provide broad conclusions that may aptly characterize the Reagan economic legacy. We address three major policy aspects of this legacy—supply-side economic
policies, monetary policy, and international trade and exchange rate policies.
Clearly this focus ignores certain aspects of the Reagan era such as the social
and economic impact of a potentially widening gap between the "haves" and
"haves-not." These exclusions are unfortunate, but were necessitated by limitations of space. However, the issues that we have addressed form, in our
view, the bases for Reagan's economic legacy.

SUPPLY-SIDE ECONOMIC POLICIES

Perhaps the cornerstone of Reaganomics was the supply-side economic policy that was first emphasized by candidate Reagan. The supply-side economic
policies, in turn, encompassed several major economic policy stands: tax reductions, designed to stimulate the economy through increased incentives to
save, invest, and work; spending cuts, designed to limit the size of the government, to balance the budget, and to keep the economic growth noninflationary;
tax reform, designed to simplify the tax structure; and deregulation, designed
to reduce the negative impact of government on the economy.

The Supply-Side Tax Reduction

Reagan vehemently criticized the malaise caused by high inflation and high
interest rates under the Carter years. He derided these as the evil product of
large government expenditures (financed by large taxes) and the overblown size
of the government. He advocated business and personal income tax cuts to spur

saving, investment, increased labor effort, innovation, and growth. The tax cut constituted an important aspect of the Reagan supply-side policies.

Investment

Several Reagan tax initiatives directly affected the rental price of capital services and thus the incentives to invest. Of course, the effects of the tax policies on business investment were not confined only to the direct effects through changes in the rental price of capital, but also affected investment decisions indirectly via changes in output and interest rates. In what follows we limit the examination of effects of Reagan tax policies to the direct effects on the business investment.

Several major pieces of tax legislation enacted during the Reagan administration directly affected the rental price of capital services. The first major tax legislation was the Economic Recovery Tax Act (ERTA) of 1981. This legislation provided for shorter periods over which equipment and structures could be depreciated, and established Safe-Harbor Leasing. This act was modified by the Equity and Fiscal Responsibility Act (TEFRA) of 1982. This modification effectively repealed Safe-Harbor Leasing. In 1984, further changes in tax laws again affected the rental price of capital. Finally, the Tax Reform Act of 1986 introduced three important changes in the tax laws: The investment tax credit provision was repealed, the maximum federal corporate income tax rate was lowered from 46 to 34 percent, and changes were made in the rules for calculating depreciation for tax purposes. The effects of these changes on investment can be analyzed through their effects on the real rental price of capital services.

Investment is composed of producers' durables (plants and equipment), nonresidential construction, residential construction, and changes in inventories. To examine the effects of tax policies, typically researchers concentrate on business fixed investment in producers' durables and nonresidential construction. Several models of business fixed investment are estimated by Bischoff, Kokkelenberg, and Terregrossa using data over a sample period that included the Reagan years (Chapter 2). Because of a lack of data, they confine their study to business fixed investment in equipment. In order to examine the effects of tax-cut policies on investment, they developed a stable, statistically significant, empirical model for equipment. They used this model to simulate the paths of equipment spending under the assumption that none of the Reagan tax changes took place, and compared these results with those from a simulation that included the actual tax changes introduced during the Reagan period. Their study suggested that the tax changes increased equipment investment by about $10.6 billion between 1981 and 1985, but reduced it by about $6.4 billion between 1986 and 1988. However, in 1989, the effect of the tax changes on the stock of equipment was a decline of only about $1.0 billion. Therefore, the net effect was a small increase in investment due to the tax changes. This result is broadly supported by the findings of Meyer, Prakken, and Varvares (Chapter 4).

The absence of a significantly positive impact of Reagan tax policies on equipment investment is likely due to several offsetting tax changes (for example, the repeal of the investment tax credit was partially offset by a reduction in the corporate tax rate). While the exact figures should not be relied on, Bischoff, Kokkelenberg, and Terregrossa's empirical analysis suggests that the net effect on equipment investment of all Reagan tax policies was at most a modest stimulus.

Household Savings

We have not made a separate effort to examine the impacts of tax changes on household savings. Since the main motivation behind spurring savings was to provide funds for increased investment, we concentrated on this investment effect. Ideally, one could have examined the effect of tax changes on the real after-tax rate of return on savings and then estimated the impact on household savings. However, this is not a very serious omission since previous empirical studies have shown low interest elasticity of consumption and saving (see Dolde 1980 and Penner 1983). Also, a quick look at Table 1.1 reveals that saving rates declined rather than increased during the Reagan years. Thus, in the light of Dolde and Penner studies, it would be highly unlikely that Reagan tax changes led to major increases in savings.

Labor Supply

Augmenting the supply of labor was another important objective of supply-side fiscal policies. Tax cuts were supposed to provide incentives to increase the work effort and entrepreneurship. The Reagan administration implemented two major tax policies designed to increase this work effort. The first involved sharp reductions in marginal and average personal income tax rates. These changes were enacted in 1981 and 1986. The second tax policy involved reforms in public-assistance programs. Although these programs were justified in terms of trying to increase the incentive for public-assistance recipients to work, in fact they were primarily designed to reduce federal spending on these programs (see Burtless, Chapter 3, for details).

Burtless studies the labor-supply effects of Reagan administration reforms by estimating supply functions for the U.S. labor force and comparing their predictions with actual labor market trends. By using two different time trend variables—one covering the entire sample period (1968–88) and one beginning in 1981—for particular demographic groups (men and women, older and younger men, and single mothers) he is able to capture the difference between labor supply trends during the Reagan years and trends that were already well established at the start of the Reagan administration.

Burtless's empirical results suggest that for all males aged 16 and older, the work effort was 3.2 to 5.9 percent higher than it would have been if the previous trends had continued. For women, the work effort was 4.3 to 4.8 percent higher. However, responses among single mothers turned out to be the re-

Table 1.1
Some Key Economic Variables, 1978–88

Year	Real GNP Growth (%)	Unemployment Rate (All Civilians)	Inflation Rate (%) (All Items)	Prime Rate Charged by Banks (%)	Federal Budget Deficit (Billions of $)	Trade Deficit (Billions of 1982 $)	Gross Personal Savings Rate (%)	Per Capita Income (1982 $)	Persons Below Poverty Line (%) (All Races)
1978	5.3	6.1	7.6	9.1	-55	-27	7.1	11436	11.4
1979	2.4	5.8	11.4	12.7	-38	4	6.8	11571	11.7
1980	-0.2	7.1	13.5	15.3	-73	57	7.1	11289	13.0
1981	1.9	7.6	10.3	18.9	-74	49	7.5	11293	14.0
1982	-2.6	9.7	6.1	14.9	-120	26	6.8	10830	15.0
1983	3.6	9.6	3.2	10.8	-208	-20	5.4	11146	15.2
1984	6.8	7.5	4.3	12.0	-186	-84	6.1	11862	14.4
1985	3.4	7.2	3.6	9.9	-222	-104	4.4	12185	14.0
1986	2.7	7.0	1.9	8.3	-238	-130	4.1	12409	13.6
1987	3.7	6.2	3.7	8.2	-169	-116	3.2	12796	13.4
1988	4.4	5.5	4.1	9.3	-194	-75	4.2	13293	13.1

Source: The data in this table are either directly quoted or derived from the information contained in the *Economic Report of the President*, February 1990.

verse—instead of rising, the work effort fell. Burtless's study suggests that there was a break in labor supply trends between 1967–80 and 1981–88. On the whole, we agree with the author's conclusion that "President Reagan's tax policies are probably responsible for a modest increase in the U.S. labor supply. They have not brought the nation a supply-side miracle."

Government Spending and Budget Deficits

One of the main pillars of the supply-side policies was to reduce the size of the government through a reduction in government spending. In fact, the Reagan administration termed it the "leading edge" of its economic program. This policy was motivated by the desire to promote noninflationary economic growth. Meyer, Prakken, and Varvares provide both a theoretical framework and empirical evidence to explain the failure of fiscal policy as a growth-oriented policy, despite the promises of supply-side tax cuts (Chapter 4).

Meyer, Prakken, and Varvares's theoretical analysis suggests that a change in the mix of monetary and fiscal policy, with a tighter fiscal policy being complemented by a looser monetary policy, results in a decline in the real interest rate and an increase in potential output. This would be consistent with a policy that encouraged capital formation. Their theoretical analysis also suggests that pure supply-side policies—tax cuts offset by a spending reduction—unambiguously raise the intermediate-term rate of economic growth. Unfortunately, the economic program of the Reagan administration involved a combination of pro-growth supply-side policies and a growth-retarding mix of monetary and fiscal policies. The net effect of this combination policy is ambiguous and depends on the relative importance of the policy mix and supply-side elements.

These authors show that the failure of Reaganomics to promote growth is due to this combination of pro-growth and growth-retarding policies, as well as the inconsistent way in which the supply-side tax initiatives were implemented. A reduction in government spending was needed to complement the tax reduction in order to achieve a pro-growth impact on the economy. However, as is well known, the Reagan tax cuts were followed by a sharp increase in the budget deficit. The authors therefore argue that since the average tax rate during the Reagan years was virtually identical to that during the Carter years (about 20%), there was a clear failure within the Reagan administration to implement spending restraint.

Meyer, Prakken, and Varvares use simulations from a large econometric model (the Washington University Macro Model) to quantify the "respective influences of policy mix and supply-side tax policies and the relative effect of supply-side incentives operating through the personal and corporate tax codes." Their simulations suggest that Reagan's supply-side policies increased the labor force by 2.4 percent and the capital stock by 1.7 percent. These policies thus made a positive, but small, contribution to productive capacity and economic growth. It may be noted that this finding is broadly consistent with Bischoff, Kokkelenberg, and Terregrossa's investment study (Chapter 2) and Burtless's analysis of labor supply (Chapter 3).

Tax Reform and Economic Efficiency

There are several inflation non-neutralities associated with the tax structure that distort the incentives provided by the market and thus reduce economic efficiency. The initial intention of the Reagan tax reforms was not only to reduce personal and corporate tax rates, but also to eliminate the non-neutralities associated with the tax structure so that taxes are based on real rather than nominal income. A tax reform to accomplish this goal (and nicknamed "Treasury I") was indeed, proposed by the Department of Treasury at the beginning of the Reagan era. However, the tax reform embodied in the Tax Reform Act of 1986 did not implement the Treasury I proposals; the 1986 Act even reversed some of the generous investment incentives of the Economic Recovery Tax Act of 1981. Fullerton and Mackie ask "whether these tax changes reflect any consistency with respect to revenue, economic efficiency, distributional effects, or any of a number of objectives of tax policy" (Chapter 5).

Fullerton and Mackie measure the economic efficiency of capital tax provisions in the Reagan tax initiatives, using a disaggregate general equilibrium model of the U.S. economy and tax system. Their analysis suggests that the 1981 Act, in theory, does not generate welfare gains unless the elasticity of asset substitution is near zero. Their study concludes that the Reagan tax reforms appear inconsistent if one assumes that dividend taxes are relatively unimportant. This hypothesis is also broadly supported by Bischoff et al. (Chapter 2), Burtless (Chapter 3), and Meyer et al. (Chapter 4). Alternatively, if one assumes that dividend taxes do matter, "these reforms may have been part of a coherent plan to achieve greater economic efficiency through incremental tax reform." On the whole, it appears that "recent tax policy decisions were influenced by revenue considerations, distributional effects, and noneconomic objectives" rather than by economic efficiency considerations.

Regulatory Reform and Market Efficiency

Supply-side economists believe that government regulation of industry increases the cost of doing business and imposes impediments on the free market. Deregulation will reduce costs and will consequently shift the aggregate supply curve to the right, increasing the real output. Accordingly, Reagan supply-side policies emphasized regulatory reform to strengthen the forces of the free market. Starting with the crushing of the air traffic controllers' strike, the Reagan administration is said to have put into motion the deregulatory wheel that kept on rolling until the end of the Reagan period.

Free-Market Ideology

Boettke (Chapter 7) examines whether the Reagan regulatory reform constituted any real change or merely represented a new rhetoric. He cites real regulatory expenditure, which increased by more than 21 percent between the 1981 budget and the 1990 budget. Boettke concurs with Niskanen (1988) that ''the Reagan program of regulatory relief promised more than it delivered. The failure to achieve a substantial reduction in, or reform of federal regulations, building on the considerable momentum established during the Carter administration, was the major missed opportunity of the initial Reagan program.'' Boettke argues that the administration failed to implement regulatory reforms as it ''succumbed to political commitments toward those who had supplied votes and campaign contributions, particularly construction, maritime, and trucking unions, among others.'' Those who are now watching the savings & loans crisis and have some idea of the costs that the taxpayers have to bear are likely to disagree with Boettke and Niskanen.

Ken Boyer in his comment on the Boettke paper agrees that the process of deregulation lagged in the Reagan administration, as compared with the Carter years. Boyer, however, points out that ''most of the instances of industries that were not natural monopolies but subject to economic regulation were already deregulated. There simply were not many more industries to deregulate.'' He continues:

Deregulation became confused with the Reagan administration's attempt to narrow the scope of the nonmilitary parts of the federal government. In the latter part of the 1980s, this form of deregulation became discredited. As bank failures have become costly to the national treasury, as the public demand for improved environmental quality has increased, as airline hubs have become more and more concentrated, the discussion has turned to regulation rather than deregulation.

Securities Regulation: Corporate Takeovers and the 1987 Crash

Regulation of the securities industry constitutes an important link in the regulatory superstructure. The Reagan financial market witnessed two important developments: large-scale hostile takeovers and leveraged buyouts, and the stock market crash of 1987. These two developments redirected the focus toward regulation and reforms of the U.S. securities markets. While many blame the two developments in the securities markets on the lenient enforcement of existing regulations, Davis and Lehn argue that ''the administration's laissez-faire policies reflect sound economic thinking and an appreciation of the academic literature on corporate takeovers and the microstructure of securities markets'' (Chapter 8).

Davis and Lehn argue that the evidence from the academic literature on corporate takeovers strongly suggests that takeover transactions promote economic efficiency. In particular, according to one estimate, shareholders are said to have received approximately $346 billion in wealth gains due to takeovers and restructurings in the 1980s. Davis and Lehn also point out that the "stock market crash of October 1987 provided a very strong test of the Reagan administration's attitude toward the regulation of securities markets." The administration's response was to establish a Presidential Task Force on Market Mechanisms, also known as the Brady Commission. When the Commission submitted its report the Reagan White House, instead of acting on its recommendations, created a new group, the Presidential Working Group on Financial Markets, to further study means of improving market mechanisms. In the final analysis, the administration "resisted demands for sweeping changes in market mechanisms, and instead opted for a minimal regulatory response."

On close examination of the evidence presented in this volume and elsewhere, we feel that the pro-market laissez-faire bias of the Reagan administration is justified on the grounds of economic efficiency. However, there has been a laxity in the enforcement of existing regulatory laws that has led to numerous current problems—the S&L crisis, the Boesky affair, and near-monopolization in some airline markets. Fortunately, the current *reregulation* discussions have centered around changing particular rules for individual industries to enhance their performance, rather than the imposition of the old form of economic regulation in industries with competitive structures.

Overall Conduct of Supply-Side Policies: A Policymaker's View

Thomas Moore, a member of the Reagan council of economic advisers, provides an evaluation of the overall performance of Reagan supply-side policies (Chapter 6). He contends that the reduction in marginal tax rates succeeded in encouraging investment, savings, and work effort. Consequently, he argues that the "U.S. economy grew vigorously, while European economies largely stagnated." However, he admits that Reagan proposals to reduce government spending were less successful. While federal spending kept growing throughout his term, spending as a percentage of GNP reached a peak in 1983. Moore thus infers that Reagan can claim some success in reducing the rate of spending. This argument appears quite farfetched. A decline, even in the rate of spending, should be measured not from the peak of the Reagan term but from the level at the time Reagan assumed office.

Moore does show disappointment with the Reagan administration's inability to reduce regulation even more. In his view, many more industries should have been deregulated. Government did reduce regulation of the financial markets, but that deregulation too did not go far enough.

Overall, Moore feels very positive about the performance of economic policies under the Reagan administration. He does not consider even the budget deficit a problem. He concludes, "Except for trade policy, I find it difficult to think of how to improve on" the Reagan economic performance.

MONETARY POLICY DURING THE REAGAN YEARS

Technically, the conduct of monetary policy is under the jurisdiction of the Federal Reserve, which is presumed to be independent. In reality, however, the Fed rarely goes against the expressed wishes of the White House and/or Congress. It is in this light that we can talk of the Reagan monetary policy. One of the stipulated goals of the Reagan administration was to reduce inflation. Monetary policy was expected to play an important role in achieving this goal. Accordingly, a reduction in nominal interest rates would also be achieved. Three chapters in this volume—those by Hendershott and Peek, Rasche, and Seger—evaluate the success of the monetary policy during the Reagan years in achieving the stated goals.

Nominal/Real Interest Rates

Hendershott and Peek examine the roles played by monetary policy as well as other factors in determining the behavior of nominal/real rates during the Reagan administration (Chapter 9). In explaining the decline in nominal rates, they consider the following specific factors: the reduced inflation rate, the tight money supply, the switch from interest rate to money supply targets, increased structural deficits, reduced personal and corporate tax rates, and the deregulation of the thrift industry.

While the nominal interest rate was successfully lowered, real rates rose sharply in the early 1980s. Hendershott and Peek's study suggests that the tight monetary policy, needed to lower inflation, put an upward pressure on the real interest rate. Similarly, the increased volatility of interest rates, caused by the switch in the Fed's operating procedure, also raised the real rates somewhat. They do not believe that fiscal policy had much impact on real rates since "decreasing marginal tax rates more than [offset] the increase in structural deficits." Meyer, Prakken, and Varvares (Chapter 4) come to a different conclusion regarding this matter. Contrary to popular belief, Hendershott and Peek contend that "the emphasis on the high real interest rates in the early 1980s has been overdone." In their view, it is in comparison with the low real rates of the 1970s that the rates in the 1980s appear high. Notwithstanding the real rate puzzle, it is obvious that the Reagan monetary policy was successful in reducing inflation and, consequently, nominal interest rates.

Price Stability

Robert Rasche (Chapter 10) examines the success of the Reagan monetary policy in terms of the ability of the Fed to restore price stability by the end of the administration. Price stability was defined as achieving a zero average rate of inflation.

Even though the Reagan monetary policy was successful in substantially reducing the inflation rate from about 12 percent to about 5 percent, Rasche
argues that the administration failed to achieve the price stability objective.
Rasche then examines alternative hypotheses designed to explain the failure of
the Reagan monetary policy in achieving this objective.

This failure of monetary policy is due to defining price stability as achieving
a goal of a zero average inflation rate. However, this may be a harsh judgment
of the Reagan administration's performance on the inflation front. As Rasche
himself has pointed out, "On a December to December basis, the CPI excluding food and energy only fluctuated in the range of 3.8 to 4.8 percent during
the 1982–87 period." This performance on the price front should be compared
with the backdrop that from December 1976 through December 1980 the rise
in the consumer price index (CPI), excluding food and energy, ranged from
about 6 percent to about 12 percent. Clearly, the reduction in inflation was
impressive although not as dramatic as the administration had hoped.

Rasche is probably right in pointing out that "price stability was not achieved
during the 1980s because monetary policy was utilized for other objectives, in
particular attempts in the short run to influence real economic growth and the
exchange rate." However, while the inflation rate is still somewhat high, the
Reagan monetary policy can take credit for bringing it down.

Overall Conduct of the Monetary Policy:
A Policymaker's View

Martha Seger (Chapter 11) argues that the monetary policy was a key element of the major reorientation in economic policies at the outset of the Reagan
administration that led to unprecedented economic expansion. Like Rasche, she
points out that the paramount objective of Reagan monetary policy was a noninflationary environment, which "was seen as the path to sustainable and stable
economic growth."

Stringent control of the rate of growth of the money supply became imperative to containing inflation. At the expense of interest rate stability, the Fed
pursued a money-supply path consistent with low inflation. The Reagan administration provided unqualified support to the Fed in combating inflation. The
bitter medicine of this tight monetary policy required "strong political will and
support." The result was the worst postwar recession (1981–82). The Reagan
administration was able to withstand the political costs of the recession due to
the President's popularity and persuasiveness. In sum, we agree with Governor
Seger that "while Reagan's advisers may have preferred to pursue a more gradual and smoother transition to lower inflation, their support for the Fed's stringent policy in the early 1980s was essential to the success of monetary policy
in bringing down inflation."

INTERNATIONAL TRADE AND POLICY

The world economy has become increasingly interdependent. Even for a large economy like the United States, international trade influences the domestic economy in important ways: it affects domestic unemployment, inflation, and growth, among other factors. Three studies in this volume—those by Deardorff, Husted, and Hakkio—deal with different facets of the foreign trade component of the Reagan economic policies.

The Reagan Trade Policy

Alan Deardorff (Chapter 12) reviews the record of the Reagan years as it relates to trade policy, to examine whether the Reagan administration was inclined toward free trade or protectionism. He argues that, "given the free-market orientation of the administration's ideology, one might have expected to witness a marked movement in the direction of freer trade." After examining the major trade agreements and major trade barriers—such as tariffs, voluntary export restraints (VERs), administered protection, and fear of trade intervention—Deardorff fails to find a clear-cut conclusion.

While trade barriers in the form of tariffs declined over the period, filings under the various sections of the U.S. trade acts increased substantially after 1980. Similarly, while the administration undertook new rounds of trade negotiations in order to "expand the province of liberal trade," it often gave in to pressures for protection in particular sectors. Deardorff thus concludes: "As an enthusiastic advocate of free trade myself, I would certainly not say that the record of the Reagan years was the answer to my prayers. But on the other hand I find it difficult to see the basis for the view . . . that Reagan was the most protectionist President since Hoover." Deardorff's conclusion aptly describes our own views.

The Trade Deficit of the Reagan Years

Trade policy and the trade deficit are naturally interlinked, and they inevitably influence each other. As a result, some of the Reagan administration's trade policy responses originated from the trade deficit problems. At the time President Reagan assumed office, the United States had a moderate trade surplus of $57 billion (see Table 1.1). However, the trade deficit had risen to a high of $130 billion by 1986. Sachs (1988), Hooper (1989a, 1989b), and Helkie and Hooper (1989) have provided empirical evidence to support the hypothesis that the overall trade deficit can be attributed to Reagan economic policies—the supply-side tax cuts, the large budget deficits, and the tight monetary policy of the early 1980s.

We find these arguments persuasive. Steven Husted (Chapter 13), while not disagreeing with these researchers, would add that the rapid rise in the U.S trade deficits in the 1980s was in part due to rapid expansion in real U.S. domestic demand, as well as the strong U.S. dollar, which acted to further encourage U.S. imports and to discourage exports. He reached this conclusion by analyzing the overall trade performance of the Reagan era by "studying each of the major U.S. bilateral trading relations." Based on this study, he does not find any evidence that the bilateral trade deficits are due to unfair trade policies of foreign governments.

The Dollar Exchange Rate in the 1980s

The behavior of the dollar exchange rate displayed an unusual pattern during the Reagan years: First, it rose dramatically by 48 percent between 1980–85, and then it fell sharply by 48 percent by the close of the Reagan administration. As Husted points out, the dollar exchange rate had an important influence on the U.S. trade deficits.

The anti-inflationary Reagan monetary policy and the increase in federal budget deficits are often considered as reasons for the rise and fall in the dollar exchange rate. Craig Hakkio (Chapter 14) addresses the question of whether the exchange rate behavior during the Reagan administration was unusual. After considering the evidence from the Reagan years, he concludes that "the dollar exchange rate in the 1980s was not unusual, given that we were in a flexible exchange rate regime; the dollar exchange rate was unusual [only] when compared to fixed exchange rate regimes." His chapter also suggests that it is the long swings in the dollar—not the short-run volatility—that were unusual, and that all foreign exchange rates (dollar and non-dollar) exhibited large swings in the 1980s.

Hence, it appears that the exchange rate changes and volatility probably cannot be blamed on the Reagan trade and economic policies. Using Hakkio's logic some part of the trade deficit problem was probably beyond the control of the administration. However, in general, we agree with the findings of Sachs, Hooper, and Helkie and Hooper that an important part of the deficit is due to Reagan economic policies.

THE REAGAN ECONOMIC LEGACY: EUPHORIA OR CHAOS?

The analysis of the economic legacy of the Reagan era has been dealt with by the academic economists in many diverse ways. Some have even looked at the Reagan legacy as a result of the optimistic expectations (of better future opportunities) that were so prevalent during the Reagan period (see Kormendi, Chapter 15), rather than the malaise that was prevalent during the Carter years. Others subscribe to the "crowding out" theory that large Reagan budget deficits crowded out private sector investment. We, however, have attempted to look at a wide range of Reagan economic policies and their consequences in evaluating the Reagan economic legacy. Table 1.1 summarizes some of these key economic statistics.

We discussed five important components of the Reagan supply-side policies: (1) effects of the tax cut on investment/savings; (2) effects of Reagan tax/welfare policies on the U.S. labor supply; (3) effects of budget deficits and lack of spending restraints on economic growth; (4) effects of Reagan tax reforms on economic efficiency; and (5) effects of deregulatory efforts on the working of the free market. In addition to discussing supply-side economic policies, we also discussed the conduct of the monetary policy in promoting economic stability, and the role of international trade and exchange rate policies in generating the trade deficit.

Evidence suggests that the supply-side tax cuts and other Reagan tax legislations had only a slight positive impact on investment, and a modest positive effect on the labor supply. With respect to reduction in the budget deficits and restraints on federal spending, the Reagan administration seems definitely to have failed. In fact, the failure to implement spending restraints contributed to the failure of the Reagan tax cuts to promote economic growth. Similarly, various tax initiatives and reforms resulted in inconsistent tax changes, and thus failed to deliver on the administration's promise of improved economic efficiency. Finally, the pro-market laissez-faire bias of the Reagan administration was justified. It is true that the process of deregulation lagged in the Reagan administration as compared with the Carter years. But this was simply because there were no non-natural monopolies left to deregulate. Many current problems, such as the S&L mess, that had their beginnings during the Reagan years are due to lenient enforcement of regulatory laws. Overall, the supply-side promises that candidate Reagan made were at best only partially fulfilled.

The performance of monetary policy during the Reagan years was commendable. The Federal Reserve was successful in bringing both inflation and nominal interest rates down from their high levels in 1980, although perhaps not by as much as the administration had hoped. The real interest rate did rise during the early 1980s; however, this may have been due to fiscal policy. Whatever the reasons for the rise in real rates, it affected economic growth adversely.

On the international trade front, there is no way to deny that a trade surplus turned into a large deficit. This could not be blamed on either the free trade ideology of the administration or the unfair trade practices of foreign governments. The large trade deficits were most likely the result of the Reagan economic policies—the supply-side tax cuts, the budget deficits, and the tight monetary policy.

Perhaps President Reagan's greatest legacy will be the change in the mood of the nation that accompanied his inauguration. In contrast to the malaise that characterized the Carter years, there was an almost immediate and long-lasting optimism during the Reagan era. Even the increasing budget and trade deficits, and the growing U.S. indebtedness, did not seem to alter this mood.

Overall, the supply-side policies do not seem to have spurred the robust economic growth that was expected. While the U.S. economy has witnessed an unprecedented economic expansion in terms of the length of the expansion phase, as Meyer, Prakken, and Varvares have pointed out, "the rate of growth of potential output during the Reagan years was about 2.5 percent per year, about the same as recorded in the Carter years." The administration can, in fact, take credit for bringing down inflation and nominal interest rates. Several economic problems, such as the budget and trade deficits and the consequences of lenient regulatory enforcement, remain. Thus the Reagan economic legacy is truly mixed: It is neither rosy enough to generate euphoria nor gloomy enough to foreshadow economic chaos!

Part II

Supply-Side Fiscal Policies

2

Tax Policy and Business Fixed Investment during the Reagan Era

Charles W. Bischoff,
Edward C. Kokkelenberg,
and Ralph A. Terregrossa

The Reagan administration carried out a series of major legislative changes in tax incentives affecting business fixed investment that has been perceived by casual observers as both favorable and unfavorable to U.S. businesses.[1] The question of the overall quantitative impact on investment naturally arises. If this question is to be answered, the first requirement is agreement on the best model relating the decisions of businesses to make capital investments to the presumed determinants. This chapter examines contending models, and then essays an answer to the quantitative issue.

A number of studies have compared investment equations developed in the 1960s and 1970s.[2] These studies show that equations purporting to explain postwar investment spending are notable for their parameter instability and/or their inability to provide accurate ex-post forecasts beyond the sample period.

In this chapter we focus on one plausible explanation for this instability, the one suggested by Lucas (1976), in what has become known as the Lucas Critique. Lucas noted that endogenous economic time series often depend on the decisions of policymakers or on other forces which may be modeled as exogenous. A regime change occurs when the policymaking process changes or when the exogenous forces change. If an economic decision-maker must forecast the dependent series in order to make his decision, he will have to use different forecasting equations before and after the change, if his forecasts are to be rational. This implies that model builders should expect the parameters of their lag functions to vary when regimes change.

In what follows, we first outline the manner in which taxes are introduced into the various models, then review the Reagan tax initiatives with this in mind. Next we discuss several models and report the results of estimation using quarterly data through 1988. We then posit a new model recognizing the influ-

ence of regime changes and fit the model to the same data. We next evaluate
the quantitative impact of the tax initiatives of President Reagan's tenure, and
finally draw conclusions.

THE RENTAL PRICE OF CAPITAL SERVICES

The centerpiece of the neoclassical theory of investment behavior is the rental
price of capital services denoted by the letter c, which represents the rental
price capital goods could command in a perfect market. In the presence of
taxes, the rental price may be written as:

$$c = q\,(\delta + r)\,(1 - uz - k)/(1 - u) \tag{2.1}$$

Here, q denotes the price of new capital goods, δ the rate of economic decay
of capital, r the after-tax real interest rate, u the rate of taxation of business
income, z the present discounted value of the stream of depreciation deductions
from a dollar's worth of capital goods,[3] and k the rate of investment tax credit.

In this chapter, we will frequently specify equations as if the desired ratio of
capital to output is proportional to the ratio p/c, where p is the price of output.
This ratio is the inverse of the real rental price of capital. This specification
may be derived theoretically from the assumption of a Cobb-Douglas production function. However, even if the desired capital/output ratio is specified proportional to p/c, this does not guarantee that the estimated price elasticity of
the investment or capital stock with respect to the inverse of the real rental will
be unity. If the equation contains an intercept, and also if the actual capital
stock appears in a gross investment equation with a free coefficient, almost any
estimated price elasticity may result.

In this chapter, investment is disaggregated into two major asset groups:
producers' durable equipment, denoted E, and nonresidential structures, denoted S. The estimates of δ, k, and z are weighted averages of these variables
for 20 different types of equipment and 14 types of structures.[4] The real discount rate for equipment r_ϵ, is given as:

$$r_\epsilon = ((2RB - p^e) + RD)\,(1 - hu) \tag{2.2}$$

Here RB is Moody's Industrial bond yield, RD is a splicing of Moody's and
Standard and Poor's Industrial dividend price ratios, p^e is the expected rate of
price change derived in Ando et al. (1974), u is the combined rate of corporate
tax by federal, state, and local governments, and h is the proportion of debt in
the corporate capital structure. The formula[5] for r_s, the real discount rate for
structures, is given as:

$$r_s = 2RD(1 - hu) \tag{2.3}$$

PRESIDENT REAGAN'S INVESTMENT TAX POLICIES

Five major pieces of tax legislation that directly affected the rental price of capital services were passed during President Reagan's two administrations. Of course, the impact of Reagan's tax policies on business investment was not limited to direct effects through the rental price of capital. Other major tax and non-tax policies clearly affected demand and output, and had effects on investment via these channels. Also, Reagan's fiscal policies affected interest rates, which indirectly affected the rental price. These effects, however, are beyond the scope of this chapter.

The first piece of Reagan tax legislation was the Economic Recovery Tax Act (ERTA) of 1981, which shortened the lifetimes to be used to depreciate equipment and structures for tax purposes. We model this shortening of lives by decreasing the weighted average lifetime for equipment, which we calculate to move from 7.947 years to 4.858 years, and the weighted average lifetime for structures, which we calculate to move from 20.303 years to 12.021 years.[6] ERTA also changed the patterns by which these assets could be depreciated. We model these changes by assuming that before ERTA, 14 percent of equipment investment was depreciated by straight-line methods, 43 percent by double-declining-balance with switch to straight-line, and 43 percent by sum-of-the-years' digits. After ERTA, all equipment investment was depreciated by 150 percent declining-balance with switch to straight-line. Similarly, before ERTA it is assumed that 14 percent of structures investment was depreciated by straight-line methods and 86 percent by 150 percent declining-balance with switch to straight-line, whereas after ERTA all structures investment was depreciated by 175 percent declining-balance with switch to straight-line. ERTA increased the tax credit for autos, trucks, buses, and trailers. ERTA also instituted the Safe Harbor Leasing method, by which unused investment tax credits could be shifted between firms. We model these two provisions by changing the effective rate tax credit for equipment from 8.50 percent in 1980 to 9.80 percent in 1981. Of this rise, 0.32 percent is due to the increase for vehicles. Similarly, the effective rate of tax credit on structures is increased from 2.52 percent to 2.80 percent.

The Tax Equity and Fiscal Responsibility Act (TEFRA) of 1982 changed several of these provisions. The basis for depreciation of both equipment and structures is modeled as reduced by 50 percent of the effective rate of tax credit. Safe Harbor Leasing was effectively repealed. This is modeled as reducing the effective investment tax credit rate to 8.82 percent for equipment and 2.52 percent for structures.

Further tax changes in the first quarter of 1984 increased our measure of the weighted average depreciation lifetime for structures from 12.021 years to 13.087 years; another increase during the second quarter of 1985 increased it to 13.401 years.

Finally, the Tax Reform Act of 1986 made three major changes. The investment tax credit was repealed. The maximum federal tax rate on corporate income was lowered from 46 percent to 34 percent. Depreciation changes also were made. After the tax reform act, we model all equipment investment depreciation as double-declining-balance with switch to straight-line; and 61.016 percent of structures investment depreciation as straight-line, 22.877 percent as 150 percent declining-balance, and 16.107 percent as double-declining-balance. The weighted average depreciation lifetime for equipment investment is increased from 4.858 to 6.545 years, while for structures investment the increase is from 13.401 to 17.434.

Between the fourth quarter of 1980, or 1980:4, and 1988:4, we find the real rental price of capital service, c/p, fell from 0.329 for equipment and 0.182 for structures to 0.283 for equipment and 0.112 for structures. The drop for structures occurred because the discount rate for structures is based heavily on the stock market. The present value of the depreciation deduction for equipment rose from 0.601 to 0.689; for structures the rise was from 0.314 to 0.532. The repeal of the investment tax credit counteracts these increases.

Turning to individual pieces of legislation, the changes from ERTA in 1981 directly reduced our calculated rental price (rent) for equipment by 7.25 percent, and for structures by 11.34 percent. TEFRA, in 1982 raised equipment rent by 3.96 percent and structures rent by 0.82 percent. The 1984 and 1985 laws increased structures rental by 1.66 percent and 0.46 percent respectively. The Tax Reform Act of 1986 pushed up equipment rent by 15.51 percent by repealing the investment tax credit and by 0.68 percent by depreciation changes. The same two shifts increased structures rentals by 3.92 percent and 7.56 percent respectively. The cut in corporate tax rates reduced equipment rent by 6.66 percent and structures rent by 8.80 percent. Computing the real rental price of capital services for 1988:4, but using all of the 1980:4 tax parameters, we calculate that the Reagan changes raised the rental price for equipment by 2.71 percent but lowered the rental price for structures by 8.43 percent. The rest of the changes in real rentals noted in the last paragraph were due to changes in relative prices, in real discount rates, and in nominal discount rates.

TRADITIONAL MODELS OF INVESTMENT EXPENDITURE

Three popular models of business fixed investment are analyzed in this section. Two are versions of the neoclassical model; the third, the accelerator model, is one in which tax policy plays no direct role through a rental price of capital term. Each of the three models is applied to data on two components of real nonresidential fixed investment: producers' durable equipment and nonresidential structures.[7]

The Generalized Accelerator Model

As first formulated by J. M. Clark (1917), the accelerator model postulated a proportional relationship between net investment and the change in output.

Later, flexible accelerator models allowed for partial adjustment of capital stock by making net investment a linear function of the deviation between current output and existing capital stock. In some variants, current output was replaced by expected output. We allow for both the formation of expectations and partial adjustment by estimating the parameters of two long-lag distributions on levels and on changes in output.

Our accelerator equations are given as:

$$X_t = A_1 + \sum_{i=1}^{21} M_{1i} Q_{t-i} + D_1 K_t + U_{1t} \tag{2.4}$$

and

$$X_t = A_2 + \sum_{i=1}^{21} M_{2i} \Delta Q_{t-i} + D_2 K_t + U_{2t} \tag{2.5}$$

Here, $X' = [E\ S]$ where E represents quarterly seasonally adjusted expenditures on producers' durable equipment in billions of 1982 dollars, S represents quarterly seasonally adjusted expenditures on nonresidential structures in billions of 1982 dollars, and Q denotes quarterly seasonally adjusted business gross national product in billions of 1982 dollars. ΔQ_{t-i} represents the change in Q, $Q_{t-i} - Q_{t-i-1}$. The vector $K' = [KE\ KS]$ denotes the stocks of equipment and structures at the beginning of period t, computed using the geometric mortality distribution and data from the U.S. Department of Commerce (1987) extending back to 1832 for structures and 1877 for equipment.[8] The terms A and D and the 21 terms in M are vectors of parameters and the U's are vectors of error terms.[9]

The parameters were estimated using Almon (1965) polynomial distributed lags. The 21 quarter lags were chosen to approximate five-year lags used by Clark (1979). However, unlike Clark, we used no current right-hand variables in any equation in this chapter. In all cases, third-degree polynomials with no zero restriction are used. Thus, both equations (2.4) and (2.5) had seven parameters to be estimated: the intercept, four parameters for the lag distributions, the coefficient of capital stock, and the autoregressive parameter.

The Standard Neoclassical Models

Jorgenson's (1965) standard neoclassical model is also fitted in levels and first differences versions given as:

$$X_t = A_3 + \sum_{i=1}^{21} M_{3i}[(p/c)_{t-i}\ Q_{t-i}] + D_3 K_t + U_{3t} \tag{2.6}$$

and

$$X_t = A_4 + \sum_{i=1}^{21} M_{4i}[\Delta[(p/c)_{t-i}\ Q_{t-i}]] + D_4 K_t + U_{4t} \tag{2.7}$$

The variables and parameters are as defined above.

The Modified Neoclassical Models

The modified neoclassical equations that are based on the putty-clay model are a bit different. The idea behind these equations is that changes in capital intensity can take place only when gross additions to capacity are already occurring.[10] Thus, in the quasi-difference version of this equation each lagged term is $(Q_{t-i} - (1 - \delta)Q_{t-i-1})$ $(p/c)_{t-i-1}$. For comparison to the other equations we fitted a levels equation for equipment given as:

$$E_t = A_5 + \sum_{i=1}^{21} M_{5i} [(p/c)_{t-i-1} Q_{t-i}]$$
$$+ \sum_{i=1}^{21} N_{5i} [(p/c)_{t-i-1} Q_{t-i-1}] + D_5 K_t + U_{5t} \qquad (2.8)$$

We also fitted a differences version:

$$E_t = A_6 + \sum_{i=1}^{21} M_{6i} [(p/c)_{t-i-1} \Delta Q_{t-i}] + D_6 K_t + U_{6t} \qquad (2.9)$$

Finally, we fitted a quasi-differences version:

$$E_t = A_7 + \sum_{i=1}^{21} M_{7i}[(p/c)_{t-i-1} \{Q_{t-i} - (1 - \delta)Q_{t-i-1}\}]$$
$$+ D_7 K_t + U_{7t} \qquad (2.10)$$

The putty-clay paradigm seems less applicable to structures, and empirical results bear this out. The modified neoclassical structures equation is simply a standard neoclassical equation with p/c raised to the power 0.5.[11]

Estimation Results of Contending Models

Summary statistics for equations 2.4 through 2.10 are contained in Table 2.1, and parameter stability tests results are given in Table 2.2. The sample period for all equations in Table 2.1 is from 1953:1 through 1988:4. The modified neoclassical levels equation appears the best of the equipment equations shown in Table 2.1. All of the other equations have only seven parameters, while this one has eleven, but the statistics s_e and s_v are adjusted for degrees of freedom.

The variation between the best and worst s_e statistics for equipment is less than 12 percent. Two of the three versions of the modified neoclassical equation fit best by this statistic and the standard neoclassical equations are worst. For s_v, the variation is greater but the ordering is the same. There is substantial serial correlation of residuals in all equations, as evidenced by the value of rho.

The picture for structures is different, as all equations are the same in terms of s_e, and the range in s_v is less than 16 percent. The accelerator equations are best by the second measure. The serial correlation is worse, and the Durbin-

Table 2.1
Summary Statistics, Traditional Equations

Equation	$S_e{}^a$	$S_v{}^b$	$\bar{R}^2$	Log of Likelihood Function	DW	Rho^c
Equipment						
Accelerator						
Levels	.17	.35	.98	914	1.92	.87
Differences	.17	.37	.98	912	2.06	.88
Standard Neoclassical						
Levels	.19	.47	.97	902	1.68	.92
Differences	.19	.51	.97	900	1.56	.93
Modified Neoclassical						
Levels	.16	.24	.98	923	1.92	.74
Differences	.17	.26	.98	917	1.99	.77
Quasi-differences	.18	.38	.98	912	1.94	.89
Structures						
Accelerator						
Levels	.11	.46	.96	977	1.67	.97
Differences	.11	.43	.95	972	1.58	.96
Standard Neoclassical						
Levels	.11	.49	.96	976	1.58	.97
Differences	.11	.49	.96	979	1.62	.97
Modified Neoclassical						
Levels	.11	.49	.96	978	1.61	.97
Differences	.11	.50	.96	979	1.65	.98

^{a}Estimate of standard deviation of white noise error e, measured in fractions of one percent of "natural" real GNP.

^{b}Estimate of standard deviation of autocorrelated error v, measured in fractions of one percent of "natural" real GNP.

^{c}Estimated autocorrelation coefficient of errors v.

Watson statistics indicate that a first-order autoregressive process may not be general enough.

The likelihood ratio tests of stability in Table 2.2 confirm our earlier doubts about the stability of time-series investment equations. The null hypothesis for each of the tests reported in Table 2.2 is that all parameters, and the variance of the error e, are constant across all subperiods. If the null hypothesis is true, the test statistic asymptotically will be distributed as a chi-square variate with λ degrees of freedom. For all equations except the modified neoclassical equation in levels, the parameter λ is equal to 8, except for the test in the third column, where λ is 16. For the modified neoclassical equation in levels, λ is equal to 12, except for the third test where it is 24.

The best-fitting equipment equation, the modified neoclassical equation in levels, fails every stability test, at least at the 0.01 significance level. But the performance of the other equations is not much better. Only the standard neoclassical equipment equation, in differences form, with the worst s_e and s_v,

Table 2.2
Tests of Stability, Traditional Equations, Calculated Chi-Square Values

Equation	Period 1[a]				Period 6	Period 5
	vs 2 & 3	vs 4 & 5	vs 4,7 & 8	vs 6 & 8	vs 4 & 7	vs 7 & 8
Equipment						
Accelerator						
Levels	23.1	19.0	52.5	31.6	20.9	33.4
Differences	13.1[b]	11.5[b]	41.9	18.2	23.7	30.4
Standard Neoclassical						
Levels	25.3	30.8	36.8	10.5[b]	26.3	6.0[b]
Differences	5.9[b]	9.0[b]	15.2[b]	3.5[b]	11.7[b]	6.2[b]
Modified Neoclassical						
Levels	27.7	31.7	65.9	25.0	40.9	40.1
Differences	6.6[b]	5.6[b]	38.4	18.3	20.1	32.8
Quasi-Differences	22.6	22.9	42.9	22.8	20.2	20.0
Structures						
Accelerator						
Levels	11.1[b]	12.6[b]	54.6	34.0	20.6	42.0
Differences	9.1[b]	11.9[b]	25.0[b]	22.4	2.6[b]	13.0[b]
Standard Neoclassical						
Levels	16.8	23.4	50.9	36.3	14.6[b]	27.5
Differences	15.1[b]	16.8	70.8	52.4	18.5	54.0
Modified Neoclassical						
Levels	17.4	24.6	49.2	36.8	12.4[b]	24.6
Differences	14.2[b]	16.5	50.4	38.2	12.2[b]	33.9

[a] Period 1 - 1953:1 through 1988:4; Period 4 - 1953:1 through 1973:3; Period 7 - 1973:4 through 1980:4;
Period 2 - 1953:1 through 1970:4; Period 5 - 1973:4 through 1988:4; Period 8 - 1981:1 through 1988:4.
Period 3 - 1971:1 through 1988:4; Period 6 - 1953:1 through 1980:4.

[b] The null hypothesis (parameter stability) is not rejected at the 0.05 level.

emerges unscathed. Every other equation rejects the null hypothesis for at least three of the tests. Of course, these tests are not independent of one another, but the impression of instability is strong. Things are no better for structures: For every equation except one, the null hypothesis is rejected for at least three divisions of the sample. For that one equation, the null hypothesis is rejected when the sample is split at the end of 1980.

We are left with a situation in which we must project the effects of the Reagan tax policies either with an equation that fits very badly and can be rejected on the basis of comparative fit, or with an equation that exhibits parameter instability, especially around the Reagan inauguration.[12] Alternatively, we can try to find a different equation that is stable.

A NEW MODEL OF EXPECTATIONS AND INVESTMENT

Expectations may enter the investment process if there is a lag between the placement of orders and deliveries of capital goods. Even if adjustment costs are zero, so that investment decisions do not lock producers in beyond the delivery lag, expectations over this period are important. Between the different policy regimes, measured variables may have differing relationships to expected variables. In the putty-clay model the commitment by firms is considerably longer as factor proportions are fixed for as long as the equipment is in place. In both cases, the Lucas Critique clearly is relevant. We developed models that deal with these concerns.

Consider a simple accelerator model with zero adjustment cost but with a finite, distributed, time-to-build lag between the time orders are placed for investment goods and the time the goods become productive. Suppose that each industry uses a different kind of capital good, for which the lag is discrete, and that the output of each industry is a fixed fraction of aggregate output. Assume that all industries have the same technologically fixed capital-output ratio and that an efficient market for second-hand assets exists.

Under these conditions, the decision on how much output the jth firm wishes to produce in period t completely determines the firm's orders for capital goods in period $t - L_j$ where L_j denotes the time-to-build lag for the jth firm. At the time $t - L_j$ we assume that the firm makes a rational forecast of its output, then orders enough investment goods so that, given necessary replacement and previous orders, it will later have enough capital stock to produce that expected output. Formally, let V be the capital-output ratio for all firms.[13] Then new orders, NO, for expansion investment by firm j are given by:

$$NO_{j,t} = V\{(Q^e_{j,t+L_j} \mid \Omega_{t-1}) - (Q^e_{j,t+L_j-1} \mid \Omega_{t-2})\} \tag{2.11}$$

where Ω_t is the information set at time t and where we assume a one-quarter information lag. The superscript e denotes expectations.

If the proportion of investment carried out by firms with lead time L is W_L, then the proportion of output produced by those firms also is W_L. Let the maximum lead time be m. Aggregate net investment, NI, may then be written as:

$$NI_t = \sum_{L=0}^{m} W_L V\{(Q^e_t \mid \Omega_{t-L-1}) - (Q^e_{t-1} \mid \Omega_{t-L-2})\} \tag{2.12}$$

Now suppose that between period t and period $t+1$ there is a change in the process of generating Q^e. All orders placed in periods up to t would be based on forecasts generated under the old process. All orders placed in $t+1$ and afterwards would be based on the new process, assuming knowledge of the new process is disseminated immediately. For a few periods there is an ambiguity about what initial conditions should be used to start up the new forecasts. We assume that actual output under the old process is used here. Let $(Q^{e\,old}_{t+i} \mid \Omega_t)$, $i=0, \ldots m$, be the forecasts of output under the old process. Then if W_L, $L=0, \ldots m$, are known, we define Z_t as:

$$Z_t = \sum_{L=0}^{m} W_L V(Q^{e\ old}_t \mid \Omega_{t-L-1}), \quad t=1, \ldots T \tag{2.13}$$

For periods after $T+m$, Z_t is defined by

$$Z_t = \sum_{L=0}^{m} W_L V(Q_t^{\text{new}} \mid \Omega_{t-L-1}), \quad t = T+m+1, \ldots \tag{2.14}$$

For time periods starting in $T+1$ and including $T+m$, Z_t is a mixture of forecasts based on the old and new processes:

$$Z_{T+i} = \sum_{L=0}^{i-1} W_L V(Q_t^{e \text{ new}} \mid \Omega_{t-L-1}) + \sum_{L=i}^{m}$$
$$W_L V(Q_t^{e \text{ old}} \mid \Omega_{t-L-1}), \quad i = 1, \ldots m \tag{2.15}$$

If this model of expectational change has explanatory power, a regression of the form

$$NI_t = \beta_0 + \beta_1 (Z_t - Z_{t-1}) + \text{error} \tag{2.16}$$

should provide an explanation superior to one in which the Z's are based on the same expectational form throughout the sample. To allow for the presence of decision and other lags, we estimate

$$E_t = A_8 + \sum_{k=0}^{3} M_{8i} Z_{t-k} + D_8 K_t + U_{8t} \tag{2.17}$$

and

$$E_t = A_9 + \sum_{k=0}^{3} M_{9i} \Delta Z_{t-k} + D_8 K_t + U_{9t} \tag{2.18}$$

which are the analogs to our equations (2.4) and (2.5). Only the equations for equipment were estimated because of the lack of data on new structures orders.

In order to construct the variable Z_t we need equations for the laws of motion of output. There is a good deal of controversy today over whether output is a random walk or whether it reverts to a trend. Since the controversy has not yet been resolved, we use a simple form to represent output. An ARI (1,1) process was fitted for the period from 1947:1 to 1988:4, and then for the three subperiods 1947:1 to 1973:3, 1973:4 to 1980:4, and 1981:1 to 1988:4.[14] The process was found to differ significantly over these subperiods. The estimated equations are:

1947:1–1988:4	$(Q_t - Q_{t-1}) = 10.579 + .3254 \, (Q_{t-1} - Q_{t-2})$
1947:1–1973:3	$(Q_t - Q_{t-1}) = 10.062 + .2490 \, (Q_{t-1} - Q_{t-2})$
1973:4–1980:4	$(Q_t - Q_{t-1}) = 10.720 + .1997 \, (Q_{t-1} - Q_{t-2})$
1981:1–1988:4	$(Q_t - Q_{t-1}) = 9.430 + .5761 \, (Q_{t-1} - Q_{t-2})$

The overall equation implies that output reverts to trend growth of $15.7 billion (1982 dollars) per year, while the three equations for the subperiods imply trend growth of \$13.4 billion, \$13.4 billion, and \$22.2 billion respectively.

To compute the variable Z, we also need a set of estimated weights, W_L. We used the Department of Commerce's series on orders and shipments of producer capital goods. We estimated a fixed weight lag, and found the best results in terms of a minimum standard error were obtained with a polynomial distributed lag ranging up to 14 quarters. Thus, in equations (2.13) through (2.15), m equals 14. Half of the weight is on the current quarter and the first two lags, and three-quarters of the orders are filled within five quarters. The mean lag is 3.47 quarters. Using equations (2.13) through (2.15) two versions of Z_t were derived, one assuming a single regime for output and one assuming three regimes.

The real rental price of capital services in the neoclassical model may be forecasted in a similar fashion. Instead of equations such as (2.13) through (2.15) in which the capital ratio is fixed, it can be made a function of expected c/p. We construct a term ZJ and define it as:

$$ZJ_t = \sum_{L=0}^{14} W_L (Q_t^e \mid \Omega_{t-L-1}) / ((c/p)_t^e \mid \Omega_{t-L-1}) \qquad (2.19)$$

As in the case of output, we estimated autoregressive equations for the whole period and for three subperiods for c/p for equipment. The chosen specification was AR(2) and the estimated equations were:

1947:1–1988:4	$(c/p)_t = 0.01554 + 1.1531(c/p)_{t-1} - 0.1998(c/p)_{t-2}$
1947:1–1973:3	$(c/p)_t = 0.01105 + 1.2154(c/p)_{t-1} - 0.2483(c/p)_{t-2}$
1973:4–1980:4	$(c/p)_t = 0.02614 + 1.1245(c/p)_{t-1} - 0.2148(c/p)_{t-2}$
1981:1–1988:4	$(c/p)_t = 0.03923 + 1.0734(c/p)_{t-1} - 0.1880(c/p)_{t-2}$

The parameters for the subperiods differ significantly by a likelihood ratio test. The equations imply that the equilibrium real rent for the whole period was about 33.3 cents per year per dollar's worth of equipment, while for the subperiods it was 33.5 cents, 29.0 cents and 34.2 cents respectively.

The equations estimated using ZJ are similar to (2.17) and (2.18), except that ZJ is substituted for Z, and we estimated the parameters A_{10}, A_{11}, M_{10}, M_{11}, D_{10}, and D_{11}.[15]

Turning to the choice of factor proportions in a putty-clay model, the situation seems much different. However, it may be shown that if certain conditions hold, then the optimal amount of capital per unit of output capacity for equipment installed at time t should be proportional to p/c at the time of installation. These conditions are that the firm is assumed to minimize the present value of total costs per unit of equipment, over the economic lifetime of that equipment, and to set the price of output as a markup on the present discounted value of average cost on the marginal vintage. We define:

$$ZB_{1t} = \sum_{L=0}^{14} W_L \ [Q_t^e \mid \Omega_{t-L-1}]/[(c/p)_{t-1}^e \mid \Omega_{t-L-2}] \qquad (2.20)$$

$$ZB_{2t} = \sum_{L=0}^{14} W_L \ [Q_{t-1}^e \mid \Omega_{t-L-2}]/[(c/p)_{t-1}^e \mid \Omega_{t-L-2}] \qquad (2.21)$$

$$ZB_{3t} = \sum_{L=0}^{14} W_L \ \{[Q_t^e \mid \Omega_{t-L-1}] - [Q_{t-1}^e \mid \Omega_{t-L-2}]\}$$
$$/[(c/p)_{t-1}^e \mid \Omega_{t-L-2}] \qquad (2.22)$$

Analogs to (2.17) using ZB_1 and ZB_2, and to (2.18) using ZB_3, were developed. These in turn were estimated yielding the estimators A_{12}, A_{13}, M_{12}, N_{12}, M_{13}, D_{12}, and D_{13}. In addition, a quasi-differences version was estimated which is given as:

$$E_t = A_{14} + \sum_{k=0}^{3} M_{14k} \ [ZB_{1t-k} - (1-\delta) \ ZB_{2t-k}] + D_{14}K_t + U_{14t} \qquad (2.23)$$

The modified neoclassical equations were estimated using the same expectational scheme used throughout the sample (the one-regime equations) and also with three sets of expectational schemes (the three-regime equations).

The results are given in Tables 2.3 and 2.4. As compared with Table 2.1, the fits in Table 2.3 are slightly worse. Judging by the statistic s_v, the modified neoclassical equations once again seem best among the expectational equations, although the differenced accelerators are close. The three-regime equations fit no better than the one-regime equations except in the case of the modified neoclassical equations, when judged by s_v. However, regardless of the number of regimes, the differences and quasi-differences equations reported in Table 2.4 are all stable, while the levels equations all fail at least four tests. We are not certain what accounts for this stability, but it is possible that the Almon polynomial technique does not sufficiently constrain the lag distributions and that they shift about randomly from period to period. However, our combination of the orders-shipment lag plus the expectational lag apparently puts on sufficient constraints.

The reasons that the levels versions of these equations failed the stability tests are not clear. One possibility is Hall's (1977) observation that investment equations estimated in level form may really be savings equations and suffer from simultaneous equations bias.

LAG DISTRIBUTION AND ELASTICITIES

In this section we report the results of several dynamic simulations of equations we have fitted above. We simulate the effects of various permanent shocks on the path of the predicted values in each equation.

In the case of the expectational equations, in order to be consistent in our treatment of expectations and to avoid the critique of Lucas, when simulating a permanent shock we should adjust the expectational equation to reflect the assumed path of the shocked variable. At this point, we avoid the necessity for

Table 2.3
Summary Statistics, Expectational Equations, Equipment

Equation	S_e^a	S_v^b	$\bar{R}^2$	Log of Likelihood Function	DW	Rho^c
Accelerator						
Levels						
1 Regime	.18	.81	.98	908	1.94	.98
3 Regimes	.18	.83	.98	910	1.96	.98
Differences						
1 Regime	.18	.42	.98	905	1.83	.90
3 Regimes	.18	.42	.98	906	1.83	.90
Standard Neoclassical						
Levels						
1 Regime	.20	.59	.97	894	1.39	.94
3 Regimes	.20	.60	.97	894	1.39	.94
Differences						
1 Regime	.20	.53	.97	892	1.32	.92
3 Regimes	.20	.52	.97	892	1.33	.92
Modified Neoclassical						
Levels						
1 Regime	.18	.38	.98	913	1.74	.88
3 Regimes	.17	.37	.98	915	1.76	.88
Differences						
1 Regime	.18	.41	.98	904	1.79	.89
3 Regimes	.18	.40	.98	906	1.81	.89
Quasi-Differences						
1 Regime	.18	.41	.98	906	1.80	.90
3 Regimes	.18	.41	.98	908	1.83	.90

See Table 2.1 for definition of notes.

doing so by simulating a small shock so that the change in the expectational equation is negligible.

We report simulations only for the traditional standard neoclassical equation for equipment and two versions of the expectational modified neoclassical equipment equation. According to the traditional standard neoclassical equipment equation in differences form, when simulated with a permanent change in real rental price starting in the first quarter of 1981, the maximum (in absolute terms) elasticity of investment is −0.40. This occurs in the sixth quarter after the shock (see the left-most column of Table 2.5). The response overshoots and by the seventeenth quarter, the elasticity is positive. It remains positive for four quarters, then settles down in the neighborhood of −0.15, which is the elasticity after eight years. The eight-year elasticity of the capital stock with respect to the rental price is about −0.12. The elasticities for a change in output are of the same magnitude but of opposite signs.

The modified neoclassical three-regime equation in differences form is the best-fitting stable expectational equation. The responses in this equation to shocks

Table 2.4
Tests of Stability, Expectational Equations, Equipment, Calculated Chi-Square Values

Equation	Period 1[a]				Period 6	Period 5
	vs 2 & 3	vs 4 & 5	vs 4,7 & 8	vs 6 & 8	vs 4 & 7	vs 7 & 8
Accelerator						
Levels						
1 Regime	25.5	20.2	29.1	12.3[b]	16.8	8.8[b]
3 Regimes	23.4	19.5	50.6	9.1[b]	41.5	31.1
Differences						
1 Regime	5.8[b]	5.4[b]	11.9[b]	5.1[b]	6.8[b]	6.5[b]
3 Regimes	5.0[b]	4.6[b]	9.0[b]	2.2[b]	6.8[b]	4.4[b]
Standard Neoclassical						
Levels						
1 Regime	22.4	28.5	32.3	6.2[b]	26.2	3.9[b]
3 Regimes	21.8	28.2	42.6	7.3[b]	25.3	4.5[b]
Differences						
1 Regime	4.6[b]	1.9[b]	3.4[b]	1.5[b]	1.9[b]	1.5[b]
3 Regimes	3.8[b]	1.6[b]	3.4[b]	2.0[b]	1.5[b]	1.8[b]
Modified Neoclassical						
Levels						
1 Regime	27.7	31.0	44.8	11.1[b]	33.1	13.8[b]
3 Regimes	26.9	20.4	39.8	7.0[b]	32.9	9.4[b]
Differences						
1 Regime	5.8[b]	6.4[b]	17.0[b]	7.7[b]	9.4[b]	10.6[b]
3 Regimes	5.3[b]	5.8[b]	12.3[b]	3.6[b]	8.7[b]	6.5[b]
Quasi-Differences						
1 Regime	9.8[b]	12.9[b]	23.2[b]	8.8[b]	14.4[b]	10.3[b]
3 Regimes	9.8[b]	13.0[b]	20.9[b]	7.3[b]	13.6[b]	7.9[b]

See Table 2.2 for definition of notes

were computed but are not shown. Using this model, the output elasticity of investment rises to 1.59 after four quarters and settles down to about 0.49 after eight years. However, the rental price elasticity is positive for the first eight quarters of non-zero response, and even when it becomes negative it never rises above 0.08 in absolute value during the first eight years. After eight years the stock of equipment is only 0.04 percent higher for each 1 percent drop in the real rental price. The response in the first eight quarters may be explained by noting that all relative price effects are forced to act multiplicatively with the change in output. With several negative output changes in the 1981–82 recession, the equation is forced to predict that a fall in the rental price of capital services will increase the capital intensity of disinvestment, which means lower, not higher, investment. But this is a defect of that specific model and not a reflection of the real world. A more attractive specification is the modified neoclassical quasi-differences version.

Table 2.5
Simulation Results

Period	Simulation Elasticities			Simulated Effects of Reagan Tax Policies* Quarterly Flow, Billions of 1982 Dollars at Annual Rates		
	I	II	III	IV	V	VI
1981:1	-.00	.00	-.00	0.0	0.0	0.0
1982:1	-.38	1.37	-.06	6.7	1.1	1.4
1983:1	-.36	.62	-.12	3.3	1.4	2.4
1984:1	-.17	.78	-.22	-0.4	2.2	2.2
1985:1	.005	.67	-.24	-2.3	2.6	3.6
1986:1	-.08	.65	-.26	1.1	2.8	2.9
1987:1	-.14	.68	-.27	-11.5	0.0	-1.0
1988:1	-.15	.71	-.31	-11.6	-4.0	-5.9
1988:4	-.15	.73	-.32	-1.9	-2.2	-4.0

I. Simulation results of a permanent equipment rental price shock on producers' durable equipment, traditional equation, standard neoclassical model, differences. Elasticity with respect to output shocks is the same with opposite sign.

II. Simulation results of a permanent output shock on producers' durable equipment, modified neoclassical expectational equation, three regimes, quasi-differences.

III. Simulation results of a permanent equipment rental price shock on producers' durable equipment, modified neoclassical expectational model, three regimes, quasi-differences.

IV. Differences between a simulation with Reagan tax parameters and a simulation with all tax parameters held at 1980:4 levels on producers' durable equipment, traditional equation, standard neoclassical model, differences.

V. Differences between a simulation with Reagan tax parameters and a simulation with all tax parameters held at 1980:4 levels on producers' durable equipment, expectational equation, modified neoclassical model, three regimes, quasi-differences (constant tax simulation based on inconsistent expectations).

VI. Differences between a simulation with Reagan tax parameters and a simulation with all tax parameters held at 1980:4 levels on producers' durable equipment, expectational equation, modified neoclassical model three regimes, quasi-differences (constant tax simulation based on consistent expectations).

* Positive sign indicates Reagan simulation higher.

The second and third columns of Table 2.5 report on the simulation of the expectational modified neoclassical three-regime equipment equation in quasi-differences form. The output elasticity peaks at 1.50 in the fourth quarter, and settles down near 0.73 after eight years. The real rental price elasticity is always negative and builds gradually to -0.32 after eight years. Eight years after a negative shock of 1 percent in the real rental price, the stock of equipment has risen by 0.21 percent.

An elasticity of -0.32 is much smaller in absolute terms than the theoretical elasticity in the Cobb-Douglas model of -1.0. Our results are in fact much smaller than some earlier results, but higher than others. Hall and Jorgenson (1971) and Bischoff (1971a) simulated equipment spending under the assumption that the investment tax credit had never been adopted. Hall and Jorgenson found that in this case equipment spending would have been 10.0 percent lower in 1966, while Bischoff found it would have been 8.8 percent lower in 1966:4. Our simulation found spending would have been 4.2 percent lower for all of

1966, and 4.3 percent lower in the fourth quarter. All of these simulations involved single equations only.

Chirinko and Eisner (1983) used six leading large-scale macroeconometric models to simulate a doubling of the investment tax credit for equipment to 14 percent in 1973 and 20 percent in 1975 and thereafter. They carried out both single-equation and full-model simulations. Because we do not have a full model, we compare only single equation simulations. Using the original models, the simulated results ranged from an increase in investment in 1977:4 of 1.5 percent (Michigan) to 14.2 percent for DRI and 15.1 percent for MPS, with an average of 8.4 percent. After Chirinko and Eisner made various adjustments that seemed reasonable to them, the results were dramatically lower, with the responses ranging from 1.7 to 8.6 percent, and a mean response of 3.7 percent. The authors emphasized that there was now a consensus: Chase, DRI, MPS, and Wharton all predicted between 2.8 and 3.1 percent.

Our results show an increase of 6.8 percent, more than double the revised Chirinko-Eisner consensus, and below three of their six original models but above their remaining three.

POLICY ANALYSIS

Traditionally, policy analysis has been carried out by computing a baseline simulation and then a second simulation with one or more policy parameters changed. The difference in results is attributed to a policy change. Policy analysis of this sort is criticized by Lucas (1976). In one of our simulations below, we attempt to respond this point. We also report traditional simulations.

Using the traditional standard neoclassical equipment equation in differences form, we compare a simulation of the path of equipment spending under the assumption that none of the Reagan tax changes took place, with a simulation with all the actual changes (see the fourth column in Table 2.5).

We also compare two similar simulations using the expectational modified neoclassical three-regime equipment equation in the quasi-differences form (see the fifth column, Table 2.5). In this case, the expectational parameters for the counterfactual case are held at their values computed using the actual policies. Since the tax parameter changes are large in this simulation, the counterfactual case is based on inconsistent expectations.

In the sixth column of Table 2.5, we report the use of the same equation but with a change in the expectational equation for the real rental prices to the counterfactual case. The equation we use, fitted to counterfactual data for 1981:1 to 1988:4, is:

$$(c/p)_t = 0.02365 + 1.3525(c/p)_{t-1} - 0.4223(c/p)_{t-2}$$

According to the standard neoclassical equipment equation in differences form, we calculate that between 1981 and 1985, the tax changes led to an increase in investment totalling about $7.3 billion (1982 dollars). In the three subsequent years, this equation indicates that equipment investment was reduced by $23.5 billion. The net effect is to reduce the stock of equipment at the beginning of 1989 by $17.6 billion, or about one percent. Because this equation indicates a tendency to overshoot, investment is predicted to be lower between 1984:1 and 1985:4 than it would have been in the absence of the policy. Also, the response between 1986:3 and 1988:2 to the repeal of the investment tax credit and the depreciation change was large and rapid.

The modified neoclassical expectational three-regime equipment equation in quasi-differences form presents a more gradual response to the tax policy changes. This is so whether it is simulated with inconsistent or consistent expectations. In the latter version, the response between 1981 and 1985 is about $10.6 billion (1982 dollars). The reduction between 1986 and 1988 is only $6.4 billion. The effect on the stock of equipment in 1989 is only − $1.0 billion, or less than one-tenth of 1 percent.

Because the absolute value of the long-run rental price elasticity for the modified neoclassical equation simulated here appears to be higher than the similar elasticity for the standard neoclassical equation, the long-run negative response of investment and of capital stock from all of the Reagan tax policies together should be projected to be larger under the modified neoclassical equation. Since the real rental price is calculated to have increased by about 3 percent as a result of these policies, the eight-year elasticities suggest an effect on investment and capital stock of less than 1 percent.

The results using consistent expectations are not very different from the results using the same equation with inconsistent expectations. This is not surprising, since the coefficients of the two fitted regressions for the real rental price for the period 1981 to 1988 do not differ significantly by conventional statistical standards.

CONCLUSIONS

In this chapter we have presented evidence supporting the proposition that traditional models of business investment in equipment and structures suffer from parameter instability, as predicted by the Lucas Critique. We have also developed new expectational models of equipment spending that, in differences form, appear to have stable parameters.

Thus our new model of expectations and investment, in the differences and quasi-differences forms, seems to be promising for future research. The expectational version of the modified neoclassical equipment equation, in quasi-differences form, seems slightly superior to the corresponding accelerator equation. The expectational modified neoclassical equation appears useful for future research into tax policy effects on investment.

As for the direct effects of the Reagan tax policies on equipment investment, the net effects are calculated to be small because the policies cancelled each other out. Nevertheless, the stable equations simulated indicate that a sustained tax policy can have substantial effect, either positive or negative, on equipment investment.

NOTES

The authors would like to thank: Robert Basmann, Robert S. Chirinko, Peter K. Clark, Augustin Fosu, and Kevin Murphy for suggestions; Albert Ando, Don Fullerton, Dale W. Jorgenson, and Emil Sunley for help in compiling the data; Tao Bo, Hong-Yih Chu, Young Youl Koh, Bai-Yang Liu, and Lu Xu for computational assistance; Rhonda Blaine, Bernie Bobal, and Sandy Hine for patiently typing the manuscript; and Babs Putzel for editorial assistance. The remaining errors are, of course, ours.

1. Throughout this chapter we will refer to the Reagan tax program as if President Reagan alone had shaped it. Congress, of course, also had a role in the legislation.

2. See Bischoff (1971b), Clark (1979), Kopcke, (1977, 1982, 1985), and Bernanke et al. (1988).

3. With the basis adjusted for any deduction of part or all of the investment tax credit.

4. The disaggregated details for these estimates come from Hulten and Wykoff (1981), Jorgenson and Sullivan (1981), Fullerton and Henderson (1984), Fullerton, Gillette, and Mackie (1987), and Fullerton, Henderson, and Mackie (1987).

5. Bischoff (1971b) used both of these formulas.

6. These and the other underlying calculations in this section were done by applying the tax changes to specific asset classes as appropriate, and by aggregating the classes to obtain an overall effect for equipment and structures.

7. Tobin's "Q" model, based on the ratio of market value to the replacement cost of capital, was excluded because of the absence of an accepted theory relating tax changes to equity and bond prices.

8. All variables, including the intercept, are divided by Gordon's (1987) version of natural real gross national product (GNP), following Clark (1979), as a heteroskedasticity correction.

9. Each vector U has elements, which we denote by v's. Each v is assumed to be a first-order autoregressive processes with $v_t = \rho v_{t-1} + e_t$. We used the Beach-MacKinnon (1978) maximum-likelihood algorithm to estimate the equations. Below, we will refer to s_v, which is an estimate of the square root of the variance of v, and s_e, which is an estimate of the square root of the variance of e. Note that the structures and equipment equations were estimated separately.

10. See Bischoff (1971a).

11. See Bischoff (1970).

12. Chirinko (1988) studied the effect of the "Reagan revolution" on the forecasts of four models explaining business fixed investment. He found that "these investment equations considered as a whole do not show any signs of important structural instability" (p. 209). Chirinko's methods for testing for stability differ considerably from ours, and we have not attempted to reconcile our results with his.

13. The assumption that all industries have the same capital/output ratio may be relaxed with no change in the results.

14. These divisions of the sample period represent possible structural breaks or re-

gime changes. They occur at the time of the OPEC boycott and at the Reagan inauguration.

15. As earlier, all equations are estimated as first-order autoregressive processes and are adjusted for heteroskedasticity. As with the accelerator equations, for each version of the standard neoclassical model there is one equation that is fitted with one expectational regime, and one equation fitted with three expectational regimes. This also applies to the modified neoclassical equations below.

"Tax Policy and Business Fixed Investment during the Reagan Era": *Comment*

Kevin J. Murphy

The central plank in the platform of supply-side economics as proffered by its proponents in the late 1970s and early 1980s was the notion that appropriate cuts in marginal tax rates on factors of production would raise the net return to such factors, thereby spurring increases in their supply. This, in turn, would lead to an increase in the natural level of output and would relieve, if not eliminate, inflationary pressures in the economy. A tantalizing side plank of the platform suggested that the subsequent increase in productive activity would increase incomes to such a significant degree that the rise in taxable income would swamp the reduction in the average tax rate and, as a consequence, tax revenues would actually rise. Few economists took this latter suggestion seriously. Output, while it might respond to a cut in tax rates, could not possibly respond by the degree necessary to compensate for the reduction in the rate itself. The large government budget deficits of the 1980s serve as stark confirmation of this skepticism.

But the central proposition of the supply-siders was a different matter. There is nothing in it contrary in principle to received economic theory. What really matters in this regard is the elasticity of the relevant factor supply curves. While most of us at the inception of the Reagan presidency had preconceived opinions regarding the size of factor supply elasticities (based on the existing empirical literature), substantial curiosity nevertheless existed in the profession as to whether or not our priors would be confirmed or rejected by the Reagan experiment.

Now that the Reagan era has ended and we are well into the Bush presidency, we can stand back and objectively evaluate what impact Reagan's tax reform had on the aggregate supply of labor and capital. This issue has not, to date, been adequately resolved. With the chapter addressing the impact of Reagan tax reform on investment by Charles Bischoff, Ed Kokkelenberg, and Ralph Terregrossa, and with the chapter on the labor market by Gary Burtless, I believe we have progressed significantly down the road to an understanding of the Reagan legacy on the supply-side of the economy. In brief, the two chapters tell us respectively, though for different reasons, that the impact of Reagan tax reform on capital accumulation and on labor force growth has been marginal.

I shall focus my comments on the Bischoff, Kokkelenberg, and Terregrossa contribution. This chapter assesses the impact of Reagan's tax policy on investment and capital accumulation. Its opening sections examine the appropriate specification of the cost of capital and what happened to this variable during Reagan's time in office. What one learns here is that while the provisions of the initial piece of tax reform—the Economic Recovery Tax Act (1981)—succeeded in substantially reducing the cost of capital, many of the tax changes enacted throughout the remainder of the 1980s actually raised the cost of capital. The authors conclude, using two different measures of the cost of capital, that Reagan tax policy, on net, raised the cost of equipment, and possibly, the cost of structures. Thus Reagan was not much of a supply-sider, all pretenses in that direction aside, with regard to capital during the course of his presidency.

The remainder of the chapter asks (though not explicitly): Supposing that Reagan had been a supply-sider, would supply-side–type policies designed to spur capital accumulation have had much of an impact? In order to answer this question properly, the authors go to great lengths to show that traditional investment models such as the accelerator model and the neoclassical investment model will likely give the wrong answer because such models fail to account for the fact that investment determinants are endogenous. Bischoff et al., using a variety of specifications, show that traditional investment models yield unstable parameter estimates over time, but more importantly, because of the failure of such models to incorporate rational expectations, they show that traditional investment models overestimate the efficacy of a dose of supply-side fiscal policy on investment behavior.

The authors then go on to estimate several models that do incorporate rational expectations. These specifications generally result in stable parameter estimates. The models incorporating rational expectations, however, also suggest that the elasticities of investment with respect to both output and to the real cost of capital are relatively small, the latter particularly so. The bottom-line conclusion to this chapter, then, is that even if Reagan had attempted to stimulate growth in the capital stock via tax policy, which he did not, the results would have been very minor indeed.

To conclude, both the chapters by Bischoff et al., and by Burtless help put into perspective Reagan's accomplishments with respect to tax policy and help shed some light on the verity of the supply-side propositions. Reagan was not really a supply-sider with respect to capital. Even if he had been, Bischoff et al. suggest the impact would not have been very significant. Reagan was a supply-sider in the labor market, but for the most part only in his second term in office. The Burtless chapter shows us that in spite of relatively large cuts in marginal tax rates, the impact on labor force trends typically was not sizable and in some cases was even contrary to what one would expect.

3

The Supply-Side Legacy of the Reagan Years: Effects on Labor Supply

Gary Burtless

One of the early hopes of the Reagan administration was that dramatic changes in U.S. tax and transfer policy could spur equally dramatic improvements in national saving, investment, work effort, and entrepreneurship. President Reagan proposed two major policy reforms that offered incentives for workers to raise their labor supply, either through increases in their weekly work effort or through reductions in the amount of time spent out of the labor force. The first was a sharp reduction in marginal (and average) income tax rates, enacted in 1981 and phased in over four years. Subsequent tax reform legislation passed in 1986 provided further reductions in marginal rates, especially at the top of the earnings distribution.

A second Reagan administration initiative was targeted at low-income breadwinners and potential breadwinners dependent on some form of public assistance. Although the President was unsuccessful in his early efforts to turn responsibility for some assistance programs over to the states, he succeeded in restraining public spending on means-tested transfers. In addition, he was at least partly successful in reforming several major assistance programs, including Aid to Families with Dependent Children (AFDC), food stamps, and housing assistance. Many of the administration's specific reform proposals were aimed at reducing outlays on means-tested transfers, rather than in enhancing labor-supply incentives. But several of the reforms were justified in terms of their supposed incentives for extra work on the part of low-wage earners.

The purpose of this chapter is to examine the impact of Reagan administration policies on U.S. labor supply. The first part of the chapter will explain why an effect on labor supply could have been anticipated, and the second will attempt to determine whether that effect has materialized and, if so, how large it has been. In the initial section I will discuss the reforms proposed by the

President and enacted by Congress and describe how these reforms might, in theory, affect individual labor-supply incentives.

The empirical section of the chapter will attempt to show how aggregate trends in labor supply during the 1980s have responded to tax and transfer reforms. This analysis is based on labor supply data obtained in the Census Bureau's March Current Population Survey (CPS). Using simple analytical techniques, population trends in employment, hours, and earnings will be examined to see whether the Reagan policy reforms during the 1980s led to a noticeable break in previous labor market patterns.

SIGNIFICANT REAGAN-ERA REFORMS

Income Tax Changes

The Reagan administration entered office with the firm hope of reducing the size and scope of federal government activity. This goal was achieved by sharply reducing federal income tax rates, thus limiting the rate of increase in general government revenues, and by obtaining cuts in appropriations for a wide variety of federally supported programs. The tax rate cuts were justified in large measure by their supposed beneficial effects on private economic activity. Although apologists for the Reagan administration sometimes claim otherwise, there is good evidence that some administration advisers and officials, including President Reagan himself, believed the positive effects on private activity would loom so large that tax revenues would swell rather than shrink as a result of the tax rate reductions. (See Laffer 1981 and Reagan 1982: 605, 710, and 719).

The potential effects of a tax reduction on private economic activity are numerous, but for most taxpayers a major positive economic response can occur mainly in the form of labor supply increases. This is the case because few Americans are entrepreneurs, and even fewer make substantial economic contributions through their capital investments. About three-quarters of national income represents factor income to labor, and labor is the only factor of production over which most Americans exercise much control.[1]

The President proposed, and Congress enacted, two pieces of major tax legislation during the 1980s: the Economic Recovery Tax Act of 1981 and the Tax Reform Act of 1986. The 1981 Act reduced marginal tax rates by 23 percent within all tax brackets, with the rate reduction phased in over the four years ending in 1984. It reduced the top marginal tax rate from 70 percent in 1980 to 50 percent in 1982. To prevent bracket creep because of inflation, the act also indexed personal exemptions, the standard deduction, and income thresholds on all tax brackets beginning in 1985. Finally, one provision in the act offered a special deduction for married couples to reduce the tax penalty when both spouses had earnings. Under a progressive tax system with joint husband-wife filing, the secondary family earner faces very high marginal tax rates on initial earnings if he or she should decide to work. To reduce this penalty and encourage the labor force participation of both spouses, the 1981 Act provided a deduction for two-earner couples equal to 10 percent of the earnings of the spouse with lower wages, up to annual earnings of $30,000.

The Tax Reform Act of 1986 represents the most important structural overhaul of the income tax system since World War II. The act significantly broadened the tax base, increased personal exemptions and standard deductions, eliminated most tax brackets, and reduced marginal tax rates for many wage earners. In 1984–86 there were 14 income tax brackets, with associated marginal tax rates ranging from 11 to 50 percent. The 1986 Act reduced the number of brackets to four, with associated marginal tax rates equal to 15 percent, 28 percent, 33 percent, and 28 percent respectively.[2] With the reduction in marginal rates and the number of tax brackets, Congress decided to eliminate the 10-percent-of-earnings tax deduction for dual-earner couples. Such couples once again face a marriage penalty, but the penalty is smaller than it was before 1982, when the tax rate schedule was more progressive.

To understand the potential effects of these tax revisions on labor supply, it is first necessary to understand how the main provisions affected workers at the top, middle, and bottom of the earnings distribution. Earners at the top were subject to special tax provisions, even before 1981, that limited the marginal tax rate they faced on earned income. A provision in the 1969 Tax Reform Act, known as the Maximum Tax on Personal Service Income, effectively reduced the marginal tax on earned income for taxpayers with substantial earnings who would otherwise have faced marginal rates in excess of 50 percent. Although this provision did not, as is popularly assumed, limit the maximum rate on earnings to 50 percent, it reduced the rate below the one applicable on unearned income for taxpayers in brackets in which the nominal tax rate was over 50 percent. For these top earners, the 1981 tax act resulted in an immediate reduction in the effective marginal tax rate to 50 percent. The 1986 reform act yielded a further reduction in marginal rates to either 33 or 28 percent. For some top earners, marginal rates have been cut in half in the past decade. For all top earners, rates have been slashed no less than a third. At the same time, average tax burdens have been substantially reduced; thus after-tax incomes in this group would have risen, even if there had been no behavioral response to the reform.

At the other end of the income scale, the effects of tax reform have been a bit more mixed. Before 1975, the major provisions used to shelter low-wage workers against paying substantial income taxes were the standard deduction and the personal exemption. These were raised through the 1970s, exempting most families with poverty-level incomes from paying positive taxes. In 1975 Congress enacted the Earned Income Tax Credit (EITC) as a method of providing tax relief to working low-income breadwinners with children. The EITC is a refundable credit, implying that wage earners can receive an earnings subsidy under the program even if they do not owe positive taxes.

The 1981 tax act reduced marginal tax rates but did not adjust nominal income thresholds in the tax formula until 1985, when the thresholds began to be indexed. Consequently, inflation reduced the real income level at which poor families became liable for taxes and lowered the real value of the Earned Income Tax Credit, raising tax burdens on low-income wage earners. In 1979, the federal income tax threshold was 3 percent above the poverty level for a family of four; by 1984 it had fallen 17 percent below the poverty line. Families with a poverty-line income owed no federal income taxes in 1979; by 1984 their income tax liabilities were 3.5 percent of income (U.S. Congress, Committee on Ways and Means 1989: 874–75). The 1986 Tax Reform Act reduced or eliminated federal income tax burdens on the poor and provided a moderate liberalization of the EITC. The positive income tax liability of poor wage earners has been reduced to its level in the late 1970s, while the liberalization in the EITC has approximately offset the rise in Social Security payroll tax rates that has occurred over the 1980s. Average and marginal tax burdens on the poor are now about the same as they were in 1978. On balance, there seems little reason to believe that changes in the tax system should have dramatically affected labor supply of low-wage earners.

Trends in marginal tax rates nearer the middle of the income distribution are shown in Table 3.1. Columns 2, 4, and 6 in the table show the marginal federal income tax rate for four-person families earning 50 percent, 100 percent, and 200 percent of median income respectively. (The exact income level at the median is shown in column 1.) The marginal income tax rate of a family with median income rose from 17 percent in 1965 to 24 percent in 1980. For families with twice the median earnings, the increase was even sharper—from 22 percent in 1965 to 43 percent in 1980. The effects of the 1981 legislation are apparent in the reduction in marginal rates between 1980 and 1985. The drop in rates is more modest than the 23 percent reduction advertised by Congress and the President because nominal income growth continued to push wage earners into higher tax brackets through the early 1980s. The effects of the 1986 Tax Reform Act on marginal rates are even more striking, especially for families earning median or twice-median incomes.

In order to calculate the total marginal tax rate faced by typical earners, it is necessary to account for income taxes paid to state and local governments and payroll taxes paid for social insurance. State and local taxes will be ignored here. Economists do not agree on how social insurance taxes should be included in the analysis. Most applied public finance economists appear to believe that payroll taxes are viewed by workers as indistinguishable from income taxes. Under this interpretation, the FICA tax paid by workers should be added to the income tax rate in calculating total effective tax rates. The combined marginal income and payroll tax rate is shown in columns 3, 5, and 7 of Table 3.1 for the three categories of families discussed earlier. In order to make the calculations, it is assumed that each family contains only a single earner and that all taxable income consists of wage earnings.

Table 3.1
Marginal Federal and Payroll Tax Rates at Alternative Levels of Family Income, 1955–88 [a]

		Marginal tax rate (in percent) at:					
		One-half Median income		Median income		Twice Median income	
	Median income (dollars)	Federal	Combined[b]	Federal	Combined[b]	Federal	Combined[b]
Year	(1)	(2)	(3)	(4)	(5)	(6)	(7)
1955	4,847	0	2.0	20	20.0	22	22
1965	7,800	14	17.625	17	17.0	22	22
1975	15,848	17	16.85	22	22.0	32	32
1980	24,332	18	24.13	24	30.13	43	43
1985	32,684	14	21.05	22	29.05	38	38
1987	36,805	15	22.15	15	22.15	35	35
1988	39,000[c]	15	22.51	15	22.51	28	28

Source: Bosworth (1984), p. 133, and U.S. Bureau of the Census (1988).

a. Tax rates for a four-person family with a single earner.

b. Combined marginal tax rate, including federal income tax and FICA payroll tax (employee contribution only).

c. Estimate.

Since the beginning of the 1980s, combined marginal tax rates have fallen 7 percent for an earner receiving half the median income, 25 percent for an earner receiving the median income, and 35 percent for an earner receiving twice the median income. For purposes of comparison, the average tax rate for earners in the lowest income group has risen 3 percent, while average rates for earners in the middle and top groups have fallen 12 percent and 20 percent respectively. If the net labor supply effect of a tax rate change is proportional to its relative magnitude, it seems plausible to expect that the larger responses will be observed at the top end of the earnings distribution. Workers at the lower end of the distribution have not been affected by the reforms to the same degree as workers who have high earnings.

Transfer Programs for the Able-Bodied Poor

In addition to reforming the income tax system, the Reagan administration vigorously pressed Congress to reform the nation's income transfer system.

Two of its most significant reform proposals were dismissed out of hand. In 1981 Congress overwhelmingly rejected the President's proposal to scale back Social Security benefits. It ignored the administration's subsequent proposal to turn responsibility for the AFDC and food stamp programs over to the states. While the President was unsuccessful in his efforts for thoroughgoing reform in the transfer system, he achieved some initial success in his attempts at scaling back the growth in income transfer programs, particularly those programs offering benefits to able-bodied adults. He also succeeded in introducing modest work programs in welfare, so that some transfer recipients are now expected to work or accept training as a condition for receiving benefits.

The transfer program reforms achieved by the Reagan administration were primarily accomplished during its first two years in office. Since the President did not achieve the drastic overhaul he initially sought, he was forced to settle for more modest reforms in dozens of individual programs. Many of the reforms were quite petty and were frankly aimed at reducing outlays. For example, in some programs the President proposed rounding down benefit levels to the next lower dollar rather than rounding up.

Other reform proposals were more fundamental and apparently arose from a consistent philosophy toward aiding the needy. In several programs, including AFDC, food stamps, and housing assistance, the administration proposed increases in the benefit reduction rate to be applied against earnings and/or sharp limitations on the incomes that people could earn while retaining their eligibility for benefits.[3] This set of reform proposals reflected the President's deeply held view that transfer benefits should be reserved for those who are unquestionably indigent. Liberals and even a few conservatives attacked these proposals as inconsistent with the President's basic supply-side message. The nation had just reduced tax rates on upper- and middle-income taxpayers. Why should the President seek to impose higher marginal rates on the poor? While work incentives were being improved for the affluent, they were being eliminated for the indigent.

In fact, it is not clear that this criticism of the President has much merit. By scaling back the generosity of benefits available to the poor, the administration was probably raising—not reducing—aggregate work incentives. Many specific proposals reduced basic support levels available to families that had no earnings. This type of reform clearly provides a work incentive, since it gives rise to a positive income effect on hours. Other reforms raised the marginal tax on earnings received by working transfer recipients. For example, in 1981 the President succeeded in raising the benefit reduction rate in AFDC from 67 percent to 100 percent. This reform reduced the marginal reward from working among transfer recipients who remained eligible for benefits. However, it also reduced the number of earners who were eligible to receive benefits.

We should distinguish the effects of the reform on two groups of initial welfare recipients. Those recipients who originally earned less than a very low level of earnings remained eligible for benefits. However, since they now faced a 100 percent tax rate on earnings, these earners had little reason to remain at work. On the whole, we might expect these initial recipients to reduce their work effort, although some might choose instead to seek a better job since their disposable income had been cut. The second group of initial recipients consisted of workers who earned more than the new and lower eligibility limit, but less than the old income eligibility limit. As a result of the reform, these workers were no longer eligible for benefits. Their incomes were reduced, giving rise to a positive income effect. In addition, their marginal tax rate fell, giving rise to a positive substitution effect.

To see whether the tax rate hike was a work disincentive in the aggregate, it is necessary to compare the average reduction in hours among the first group of initial recipients with the average gain in hours among the second. The overall effect of the reform clearly depends on the size of the average response in each group and the relative size of the two groups. The increase in the AFDC tax rate from 67 percent to 100 percent might either have increased or decreased labor supply among initial recipients. Unfortunately, the econometric evidence on labor supply among low-wage workers does not resolve this uncertainty (see Levy 1979; Moffitt 1985; and Burtless 1987: 40–43).

In addition to reducing the financial attractiveness of welfare, President Reagan also sought to change the terms under which assistance benefits could be received. In both the food stamp and AFDC programs, his administration attempted to require able-bodied adult recipients to work in exchange for benefits. The President was unsuccessful in persuading Congress to impose this requirement in all cases, but he did succeed in imposing the requirement on some classes of assistance recipients. If his policies worked, there should have been a rise in the employment rate of low-income breadwinners most likely to be dependent on welfare, particularly single mothers.

LABOR SUPPLY IN THE 1980s

Previous Estimates of Reagan Policy Effects

The labor supply effects of Reagan administration reforms can be analyzed using a variety of methods. Probably the soundest approach is to estimate labor supply functions for the major demographic groups and then to use the resulting parameter estimates to predict aggregate supply responses. If a suitable longitudinal microdata base (e.g., the Panel Survey of Income Dynamics) is used, predicted responses can be compared with actual changes in labor supply over time.

Several analysts have estimated supply functions for the U.S. labor force. But no one, to my knowledge, has predicted the effects of the Reagan administration reforms and then compared those predictions with actual labor market trends. In the early 1980s, Jerry Hausman (1981a, 1981b, and 1983) used empirical estimates of the supply behavior of prime-age husbands and wives to predict the effect of the Kemp-Roth tax proposal. The original Kemp-Roth proposal called for a 30 percent reduction in marginal tax rates, rather than the 23 percent reduction actually enacted in 1981. Hausman's estimate of response is also raised by his assumption that the reform will be fully implemented with no delay. In fact, the reform was phased in over four years. Since tax brackets were not indexed over that period, wage inflation pushed workers into higher brackets, and the tax rate reduction turned out to be less than 23 percent. Nonetheless, Hausman's predictions are interesting. He found that a 30 percent rate reduction would lead to a 2.7 percent increase in the labor supply of husbands and a 9.4 percent increase for wives. A 10 percent tax cut—smaller than the one actually enacted—would lead to a 1.1 percent rise in labor supply among husbands and a 4.1 percent rise among wives. Hausman (1981: 194–96) found no justification for the claim of some supply-side enthusiasts that the supply response would cause tax revenues to rise. A 30 percent rate reduction would lead to a 22.6 percent fall in revenue from husbands and a 16.2 percent decline for wives; the 10 percent rate reduction would cause tax revenues to fall by 7.4 percent for husbands and a 3.8 percent for wives. So far as I know, Hausman's predictions have never been compared with actual labor supply changes over the 1980s.

Trends in Work Effort

Another approach to estimating labor supply responses is to measure long-term trends in aggregate supply and then determine whether the 1980s have witnessed a break with past trends. That approach will be followed here by examining supply trends separately in different demographic groups. Trends among men and women have been quite different over the past four decades, and so it seems prudent to examine these two groups separately. In addition, there have been major differences between trends among older and younger workers. For that reason, older and younger men are examined separately. One group that deserves special attention is single mothers. These women have been disproportionately affected by changes in the nation's welfare system. If President Reagan's supply-side policies have affected behavior, the effects should be especially pronounced among single women who are rearing children.

Table 3.2 shows trends in six measures of supply as separated for men and women age 16 and older. All numbers in the table are calculated from survey responses in the Census Bureau's March CPS. Some of the statistics are published by the Census Bureau or the Bureau of Labor Statistics, but most must be tabulated using the public-use version of the March CPS tapes, which contain survey responses for over 100,000 individuals each year. The labor force participation rate (LFPR) is arguably the most inclusive measure of labor supply on offer. It includes not only work effort actually supplied, but also people available for work who cannot find employment. Labor force participation has been slowly declining among men, particularly at older ages. If there has been

Table 3.2
Labor Supplied by U.S. Men and Women 16 and Older, 1968–88

Year	Labor force participation rate	Employment/ population rate	Average weekly hours-- workers	Average weekly hours-- population	Average annual earnings-- workers[a]	Average annual earnings-- population[a]
Men						
1968	79.0%	76.4%	43.0	31.1	$19,580	$16,778
1971	78.1	73.5	42.1	29.3	20,382	17,108
1974	77.9	74.1	42.1	29.5	20,802	17,264
1977	76.6	70.9	41.9	28.1	21,090	17,184
1979	77.1	72.7	42.1	29.0	21,319	17,322
1982	76.7	68.4	41.2	26.7	19,999	15,694
1985	75.6	69.8	41.9	27.8	21,345	16,857
1988	75.3	70.6	42.3	28.4	22,063[b]	17,414[b]
Women						
1968	41.2	39.3	34.6	13.1	8,364	4,222
1971	43.0	40.1	33.9	13.0	9,024	4,521
1974	45.2	42.5	34.1	13.9	9,146	4,821
1977	47.9	43.7	33.6	14.2	9,622	5,245
1979	50.6	47.2	34.2	15.6	10,043	5,752
1982	52.1	47.4	34.0	15.6	10,392	5,851
1985	54.5	50.4	35.0	16.9	11,387	6,733
1988	55.9	52.9	35.5	18.1	12,192[b]	7,418[b]

Source: Author's tabulations of March Current Population Survey tapes, various years.

a. Measured in constant 1986 dollars deflated using CPI-UX.

b. 1987.

any weakening of this trend in the 1980s, it is not apparent in Table 3.2. Participation among men fell by 0.17 percent a year from March 1968 through March 1979; it fell 0.20 percent a year in the nine years after March 1979.[4] By contrast, participation among women has been rising sharply. However, the rise in participation has not accelerated during the 1980s; rather, it has slowed. The female participation rate rose 0.85 percent a year from 1968 to 1979, but just 0.59 percent between 1979 and 1988.

Trends in the employment/population ratio (EMPR) are similar. The male employment rate fell 0.34 percent a year in the 11 years before March 1979. The rate of decline fell a bit to 0.23 percent a year in the nine years after 1979. Among women, the employment rate rose 0.72 percent per year between March 1968 and March 1979, but just 0.63 percent a year between 1979 and 1988.

Both the participation rate and employment rate provide indicators of the number of potential or actual workers on offer. Neither series provides an indication of the level of supply that an average worker is willing to provide. As noted earlier, the tax reforms enacted during the Reagan years had their largest proportional effect on the tax burdens of the affluent, most of whom were already at work when President Reagan came to office. It is unlikely that tax reform substantially raised the participation or employment rates of the affluent, except possibly the spouses of affluent men. It seems more plausible to believe that the reform induced the affluent to work longer hours. The third column in Table 3.2 shows the reported weekly work effort of CPS respondents who were at work during the March reference week. There seems very little trend in the series for men. Most of the movement seems related to the business cycle. Nonetheless, weekly work effort in March 1988 is higher than in any other year after the late 1960s. For women, the trend in weekly hours appears much stronger. Whereas hours fluctuated with business conditions over the 1970s around a fairly stable level, the rise in weekly hours during the 1980s is quite striking. Average work effort rose 1.3 hours—nearly 4 percent—after 1979.

A more accurate indicator of the actual supply of labor is average weekly hours within the entire relevant population, including persons at work, absent from their job, unemployed, or out of the labor force. This average is shown in the fourth column. Among men there has been some moderation in the rate at which average weekly hours is falling. Between March 1968 and March 1979, the overall average work week of men fell by 0.19 hours per year. In the nine years ending in March 1988, it fell only 0.07 hours a year. Among women, there has been an acceleration in the growth of average hours. In the 11 years up to March 1979, overall hours rose 0.23 hours a year; in the nine following years, average weekly hours rose 0.28 hours a year.

The last two columns in Table 3.2 show the average wage, salary, and net self-employment earnings of two categories of people. The fifth column shows average earnings among persons reporting annual earnings of $1 or more, while the sixth shows average earnings in the entire population, including people reporting no earnings. Neither column represents a good measure of labor supply, since both include the effects of productivity movements, variations in the price level (earnings are measured in constant 1986 dollars), and fluctuations in the market price of labor—that is, the real wage. However, respondents' reports of average hours of work are often held to be suspect, while CPS responses on earnings—particularly wage and salary earnings—have been found to be reasonably accurate. A surge in average earnings growth above and beyond the part that can be explained by productivity movements and price changes might indicate that labor supply is rising.

Neither column 5 nor column 6 provides much evidence for an unexpected surge in male earnings, though there is a suggestion that women's earnings growth has accelerated in the 1980s. Earnings among women who had earnings grew at a compound annual rate of 1.4 percent between 1968 and 1979; they grew at a 2.5 percent compound rate after 1979. Average earnings growth in the entire population of women also accelerated after 1979. This could be explained by either a spurt in hours or a change in the composition of female workers, with rising hours contributed by women with greater skills and higher wages.

Controlling for Cyclical Effects

The numbers reported in Table 3.2 may be suggestive, but they ignore the influence of business cycle movements on labor supply. The level of employment, weekly hours, and average earnings are jointly determined by aggregate demand and the willingness of potential workers to contribute to labor supply. Even labor force participation is known to be affected by demand conditions in the labor market. As job finding becomes easier, more potential workers join the labor force to seek jobs.

While it is beyond the scope of this chapter to attempt joint time-series estimation of aggregate supply and demand functions, it seems essential to adjust aggregate trends in labor supply to reflect business cycle movements. A straightforward way to adjust the series is to include the unemployment rate or some other cyclically sensitive variable in a time-series regression on labor supply. Since the unemployment rate itself measures one component of supply, it is useful to test the sensitivity of the specification to alternative cyclical variables. In the regressions below, I estimate supply trends using the Commerce Department's estimate of GNP gap as well as the unemployment rate.[5]

Tables 3.3 and 3.4 show regression coefficients for a variety of labor supply variables across six demographic groups. Three sets of estimates are displayed for males and females. For males I estimated supply trends among all men over age 15, men aged 25 to 54, and men aged 55 to 64. Supply trends were estimated among women 16 and older, women 25 to 54, and single women with children.[6] For each group I estimated trends in the labor force participation rate, the employment/population ratio, and average hours in the entire population, including persons at work, employed but absent from work, unemployed, or out of the labor force. Average hours were measured in two different ways. I calculated average hours during the March reference week for the years 1968–88. And I obtained an estimate of average annual hours at work during the previous calendar year, that is, during the years 1967–87.

The basic specification includes two time trend variables: The first, T, rises over the entire span of years covered by the regression (1968 through 1988), and the second, labelled $T80$, begins in 1981 and rises through 1988. The coefficient on the latter variable should capture the difference, if any, between labor supply trends during the Reagan years and trends that were already well established when Reagan came to office. This seems to me a simple yet sensible specification of the potential effect of the Reagan-era policies. The policy effects would have been small early in the administration, but should have grown over time as new legislation was implemented and people were provided an opportunity to respond. Of course, the specification also depends on the unprovable assumption that supply trends over the 1967–80 or 1968–80 periods would have continued unchanged over the 1980s.

As noted earlier, two regression specifications are used for each dependent variable. The first uses the seasonally unadjusted civilian unemployment rate

Table 3.3
Regression Results for Men, 1967–88[a]

	Labor Force Participation Rate[b]		Employment-Population Ratio[b]		Hours of Work per Week[b] (All Persons)		Hours of Work per Year[c] (All Persons)	
	(1)	(2)	(3)	(4)	(5)	(6)	(7)	(8)
Men Aged 16 and Over								
UR	-0.18	...	-1.05	...	-0.60	...	-25.23	...
	(-3.65)		(-29.91)		(-25.99)		(-5.36)	
GNP gap	...	-0.07	...	-0.45	...	-0.27	...	-12.29
		(-2.73)		(-11.04)		(-14.93)		(-8.25)
T	-0.16	-0.21	-0.15	-0.39	-0.08	-0.22	-4.67	-9.04
	(-6.48)	(-9.37)	(-8.78)	(-11.59)	(-7.01)	(-15.25)	(-2.28)	(-8.52)
T80	-0.01	0.05	-0.07	0.22	0.04	0.20	6.01	10.62
	(-0.14)	(0.93)	(-2.10)	(2.82)	(1.72)	(6.15)	(1.43)	(3.89)
R²	0.96	0.94	0.99	0.96	0.98	0.96	0.87	0.93
ρ	0.06	0.07	-0.25	-0.13	-0.50	-0.35	-0.05	-0.10
Men Aged 25–54								
UR	-0.04	...	-1.00	...	-0.65	...	-26.02	...
	(-0.95)		(-22.24)		(-13.22)		(-4.28)	
GNP gap	...	-0.01	...	-0.44	...	-0.29	...	-12.85
		(-0.59)		(-12.64)		(-11.35)		(-5.92)
T	-0.19	-0.20	-0.15	-0.38	-0.09	-0.24	-6.52	-10.91
	(-5.14)	(-5.62)	(-6.66)	(-13.49)	(-3.70)	(-11.34)	(-2.42)	(-6.79)
T80	0.13	0.15	-0.06	0.21	0.02	0.20	5.75	10.31
	(1.78)	(1.97)	(-1.33)	(3.31)	(0.48)	(4.09)	(1.02)	(2.50)
R²	0.94	0.94	0.99	0.96	0.96	0.95	0.86	0.91
ρ	0.72	0.72	-0.09	-0.27	-0.14	-0.20	0.06	0.02
Men Aged 55–64								
UR	-0.18	...	-0.76	...	-0.44	...	-21.18	...
	(-1.17)		(-4.72)		(-4.51)		(-3.26)	
GNP gap	...	-0.04	...	-0.29	...	-0.17	...	-9.83
		(-0.49)		(-3.41)		(-3.37)		(-3.53)
T	-1.05	-1.10	-0.95	-1.13	-0.44	-0.55	-19.19	-22.67
	(-10.79)	(-12.76)	(-10.43)	(-13.24)	(-7.72)	(-10.72)	(-6.51)	(-9.57)
T80	0.43	0.50	0.24	0.47	0.16	0.29	5.51	8.94
	(2.14)	(2.59)	(1.30)	(2.40)	(1.34)	(2.51)	(0.89)	1.48
R²	0.98	0.98	0.98	0.98	0.97	0.96	0.96	0.96
ρ	0.40	0.41	0.25	0.23	0.30	0.22	0.14	0.28

a. First-order autocorrelation estimation results; constant terms estimated but not reported. Numbers in parentheses are t-statistics.

b. Twenty-one observations, March reference week, 1968–88.

c. Twenty-one annual observations, 1967–87.

(UR), either for March or for the previous calendar year, to control for business cycle effects; the second includes the first quarterly or annual observation of the Commerce Department's GNP gap. All regression equations include first-order autocorrelation error correction. The estimate of ρ as well as corrected R^2 is reported for each equation.

Under the assumptions of this analysis, the effects of Reagan administration

Table 3.4
Regression Results for Women, 1967–88 [a]

	Labor Force Participation Rate[b] (1)	(2)	Employment-Population Ratio[b] (3)	(4)	Hours of Work per Week[b] (All Persons) (5)	(6)	Hours of Work per Year[c] (All Persons) (7)	(8)
Women Aged 16 and Over								
UR	-0.14 (-1.97)	...	-0.54 (-8.53)	...	-0.23 (-7.99)	...	-5.80 (-2.23)	...
GNP gap	...	-0.05 (-1.45)	...	-0.23 (-5.31)	...	-0.10 (-5.74)	...	-3.41 (-3.23)
T	0.87 (16.33)	0.84 (17.06)	0.82 (15.87)	0.70 (14.72)	0.27 (11.49)	0.22 (10.85)	12.09 (7.68)	11.45 (9.86)
T80	-0.23 (-2.10)	-0.19 (-1.74)	-0.17 (-1.59)	-.02 (-0.15)	0.03 (0.60)	0.09 (1.97)	4.71 (1.30)	5.28 (1.81)
R^2	0.99	0.99	0.99	0.99	0.99	0.98	0.98	0.98
ρ	0.57	0.55	0.64	0.36	0.65	0.40	0.59	0.53
Women Aged 25–54								
UR	-0.11 (-1.09)	...	-0.57 (-6.54)	...	-0.25 (-7.19)	...	-4.79 (-1.37)	...
GNP gap	...	-0.02 (-0.35)	...	-0.22 (-3.86)	...	-0.11 (-5.01)	...	-3.31 (-2.28)
T	1.39 (12,45)	1.36 (12.17)	1.34 (13.70)	1.23 (13.19)	0.48 (11.84)	0.43 (11.47)	21.37 (8.29)	21.10 (9.86)
T80	-0.29 (-1.32)	-0.25 (-1.12)	-0.26 (-1.32)	-0.07 (-0.33)	0.01 (0.15)	0.09 (1.11)	5.43 (0.92)	5.48 (1.08)
R^2	1.00	1.00	1.00	0.99	1.00	0.99	0.99	0.99
ρ	0.83	0.83	0.82	0.63	0.83	0.67	0.73	0.71
Unmarried, Divorced, and Separated Women with Children								
UR	-0.22 (0.99)	...	-1.04 (-5.07)	...	-0.46 (-5.68)	...	-8.31 (-1.17)	...
GNP gap	...	-0.10 (-0.98)	...	-0.43 (-4.04)	...	-0.20 (-5.10)	...	-5.81 (-1.94)
T	0.85 (4.36)	0.81 (4.51)	0.72 (5.38)	0.48 (4.44)	0.33 (5.44)	0.24 (5.13)	11.33 (2.86)	10.79 (3.65)
T80	-0.67 (-1.65)	-0.61 (-1.58)	-0.55 (-2.00)	-0.24 (-0.98)	-0.21 (-1.70)	-0.10 (-0.96)	-0.70 (-0.08)	-0.41 (-0.05)
R^2	0.93	0.93	0.86	0.81	0.91	0.89	0.82	0.84
ρ	0.70	0.69	0.45	0.27	0.57	0.39	0.51	0.44

a. First-order autocorrelation estimation results; constant terms estimated but not reported. Numbers in parentheses are t-statistics.

b. Twenty-one observations, March reference week, 1968-88.

c. Twenty-one annual observations, 1967-87.

policies are estimated by the coefficients on *T80*. These coefficients are often sensitive to the cyclical control variable included in the specification. As a rule, specifications including the unemployment rate show a smaller break in work-effort trends during the 1980s; in a few cases, the sign of change is even reversed. Judged in terms of the fraction of variance explained, the specification including the unemployment rate is usually somewhat preferable to the alternative, but the difference is seldom large.

The findings for the seven demographic groups will be considered in turn. Results for men are shown in Table 3.3. The top panel shows results for all men over age 15. There is little evidence that the 1980s have witnessed an unexpected rise in labor force participation among men 16 and older, and the evidence for an effect on employment rates is mixed. The two specifications agree, however, in showing an effect on hours of work. Unfortunately, the range of uncertainty in the estimates is fairly wide. The specification that includes the GNP gap (column 6) suggests that overall weekly hours in 1988 are 6 percent above the level they would have attained if work-effort trends had maintained their pre-1980 trend. The alternative specification (column 5) suggests that overall hours rose just 1 percent above their previous path.

The percentage effect on annual hours of work, shown in columns 7 and 8, is similar to the estimated effect on weekly hours of work. Among all males 16 and older, average work effort in 1987 was approximately 1,360 hours per year. The coefficients on $T80$ in columns 7 and 8 imply that this level of work effort was 3.2 percent to 5.9 percent higher than it would have been if previous trends had continued.

Not surprisingly, a similar range of uncertainty is also found among males aged 25 to 54, who constitute the most important group of male workers. (Results for this group are displayed in the middle panel.) The gain in overall weekly hours in 1988 among this group is estimated to be about 4 percent in the specification that includes GNP gap (column 6), but just 0.5 percent in the specification that includes the unemployment rate (column 5). Average work effort among 25- to 54-year-old men was slightly more than 1,840 hours a year in 1987. According to the coefficients in columns 7 and 8, this average is 2.3 percent to 4.1 percent greater than average hours would have been without the break in trend after 1980. For purposes of comparison, recall that in simulating the impact of a 30 percent marginal tax reduction, Jerry Hausman (1981b) predicted a 2.7 percent rise in labor supply among 25- to 59-year-old husbands. The estimates of response in the middle panel of Table 3.3 are thus roughly consistent with Hausman's prediction.

Interestingly, both econometric specifications imply a similar, and sizable, rise in labor force participation among prime-age men. The actual labor force participation rate among 25- to 54-year-old males was 93.4 percent in March 1988. In the absence of the break in trend in 1981, the participation rate would have been 1.1 to 1.2 points lower. For reasons alluded to earlier, it seems implausible that Reagan tax policies would have caused major changes in the participation of prime-age men, most of whom were already working in 1980. In fact, the specification that includes the unemployment rate shows no change in trends in the employment-population rate of this group.

Labor supply among older men had been declining for many years before

President Reagan took office. The results in the bottom panel of Table 3.3 show that labor market trends in the 1980s did not reverse this decline, but may have slowed it down. Under either statistical specification, there has been a significant slowing in the decline of labor force participation, employment, and average weekly hours among this group. For example, in 1988 the employment-population rate for this group was 64 percent. If the pre-Reagan trends had continued, the rate in 1988 would have been 1.9 to 3.7 percentage points lower. It should be noted that not all of this change is attributable to reforms passed during the Reagan years. Part of the reason for the rapid decline in participation and employment among older males in the 1970s was the rapid rise in Social Security retirement benefits during the early part of that decade. Benefit growth slowed in the 1980s because of changes in the benefit formula that were passed by Congress in 1977 but were not fully effective until the early 1980s. Nonetheless, the results at the bottom of Table 3.3 suggest that the decline in work effort among 55- to 64-year-old men has slowed perceptibly over the past decade.

Surprisingly, the results for women suggest that participation and employment rates in the 1980s have actually *fallen* relative to their trend rates in the 1960s and 1970s (see Table 3.4). This conclusion is mildly astonishing, since one of the goals of tax policy changes in the 1980s was to reduce marginal tax burdens on secondary family earners. Evidently, this reform did not bring in large numbers of new female entrants, and may have even reduced labor market entry. (The latter effect could occur if significant numbers of families experienced sizable after-tax income gains as a result of the reform.)

Even though the probable effects on participation and employment were negative, other regression estimates (not shown in Table 3.4) suggest that all groups of women at work except single mothers registered strong gains in average weekly hours. These gains were large enough to offset the effects of employment declines, so average work effort among U.S. women (measured by weekly and annual hours among all persons) rose relative to past trends. The positive effect on overall hours is found to be statistically significant in only one of the two specifications, however, and the effect is not apparent in the largest group of potential workers—women aged 25–54. For women as a whole, the effect of the Reagan-era reforms may have been to reduce the proportion of women at work, but to raise the intensity of work effort among those at work.

The effect on annual hours among women can be seen in columns 7 and 8 of Table 3.4. The coefficients on *T80* imply that female labor supply in 1987 was 4.3 percent to 4.8 percent higher than it would have been in the absence of the break in trends. Among women aged 25–54 (middle panel), the proportional effect is somewhat smaller—about 3.5 percent. Among older women (not shown) the effect is somewhat larger—5.0 percent to 6.3 percent. For none of these groups, however, is the effect reliably estimated at conventional significance levels. By comparison, Jerry Hausman (1981b) predicted that labor supply among prime-age wives would rise 9.4 percent in response to a 30 percent tax rate cut. Estimated responses among prime-age women appear to be substantially below this prediction.

Responses among single mothers appear perverse. Instead of rising, labor supply fell (see bottom of Table 3.4). The participation, employment, and overall hours of single women are below the levels that would have been predicted from past trends in their behavior. Although participation and employment continued to climb in the 1980s, the rate of increase is between one-quarter and two-thirds of a percentage point per year below the pace of the late 1960s and 1970s. The labor force participation rate of single mothers was 67 percent in March 1988. According to coefficients shown at the bottom of Table 3.4, the rate would have been 69 percent if participation growth had continued at the pace observed in the 1960s and 1970s. The employment rate would have been one point higher, and overall labor supply 1 percent higher.

Distribution of Earnings Gains

The results thus far suggest that labor supply among men is somewhat above the level that would have been predicted if trends of the 1960s and 1970s had continued through the 1980s. Average work effort among women may also be above the level that would have been attained in the absence of a break in trends, although the magnitude and statistical significance of this gain is not clear. If labor supply trends during the 1980s were attributable to Reagan administration policies, we would anticipate that the largest work responses occurred among groups facing the largest change in tax or transfer policy. In the previous section, I argued that the largest changes in average and marginal tax rates were experienced by earners near the top of the earnings distribution and single mothers near the bottom. We have already seen that single mothers failed to raise their labor supply during the 1980s; they may have reduced it. It remains to be seen whether large responses are detectable for earners near the top of the earnings distribution.

An indirect way to see whether labor supply has risen fastest among the most affluent workers is to measure trends in earnings growth at different points in the earnings distribution. If earnings gains have been disproportionately concentrated among earners near the top of the distribution, there is an suggestion that those workers may have been more responsive to Reagan administration policies than workers near the bottom.[7] To see whether this is true, I tabulated the annual earnings distribution for persons with wage and salary earnings for each year from 1967 through 1987. The earnings distribution was tabulated separately for men and women aged 25-64. I then calculated real earnings levels at selected points in the earnings distribution.[8] Real earnings growth at each point in the distribution is strongly influenced by the state of the economy. To control for the effects of the business cycle, I regressed the logarithm of real

Figure 3.1
Annual Growth in Wage and Salary Earnings at Selected Points in the Earnings Distribution, 1967–81 and 1981–87

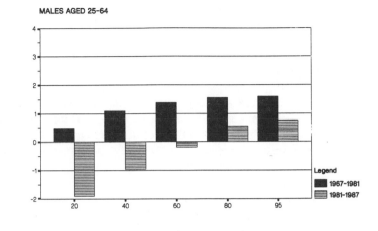

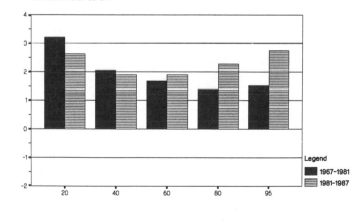

annual earnings on the unemployment rate and separate time-trend variables for the periods 1967–81 and 1981–87.

The results of these regressions are shown in Figure 3.1. The top panel in Figure 3.1 shows the pattern of real earnings growth among 25- to 64-year-old men. I display real wage growth at five points in the earnings distribution: the twentieth, fortieth, sixtieth, eightieth, and ninety-fifth percentiles. The solid bars measure the annual rate of real earnings growth between 1967 and 1981;

the lightly colored bars measure real earnings growth between 1981 and 1987—
that is, over the Reagan era. The panel shows that earnings growth has been
substantially slower since 1981. For earners at the twentieth percentile, earnings growth averaged 0.5 percent a year before 1981. It has averaged -1.9
percent since 1981. At the eightieth percentile, earnings growth averaged 1.4
percent before 1981. It has averaged just 0.5 percent since that year. Even
though average hours of work among men actually declined more slowly in the
1980s than they did during the 1960s and 1970s, average earnings for most
male workers have shrunk. Interestingly, earnings at the top of the earnings
distribution have resisted this trend: They have continued to rise through the
1980s. Thus the top panel of Figure 3.1 provides weak evidence that male
earners may be responding as predicted to the incentives embedded in the Reagan-era tax reforms. Earners at the top are relatively more responsive than
earners in the middle or at the bottom.

Similar results are shown in the bottom panel for female wage and salary
earners. Unlike men, women at all points in the earnings distribution have
continued to enjoy real wage gains through the 1980s. For women in the bottom half of the earnings distribution, these gains are slower than they were
before 1981. For women in the top half of the distribution, the rate of earnings
gain has risen over the 1980s. Among women at the ninety-fifth percentile, for
example, earnings growth averaged 1.5 percent a year in the 1960s and 1970s;
however, it has averaged 2.8 percent a year since 1981. As in the case of men,
there is weak evidence that the effects of Reagan administration policy, if any,
have been concentrated on earners in the top half of the distribution. This pattern of response would be anticipated if the earnings response is roughly proportionate to the magnitude of the tax rate change.

CONCLUSIONS

President Reagan proposed major reforms in welfare policy and the individual income tax during his two terms in office. He persuaded Congress to adopt
many of them. These reforms brought significant reductions in the generosity
of welfare benefits available to low-income families and substantial cuts in the
average and marginal tax rates faced by affluent taxpayers. Part of the justification for the reforms was an expectation that tax and benefit changes would
spur a rise in work effort, entrepreneurship, and private investment. If the supply-side effects were large enough, some or all of the direct consequences of
the income tax reduction would be offset by rapid growth in the size of the tax
base.

This chapter has examined potential effects of the Reagan-era reforms on
aggregate labor supply in the United States. The effect of the Reagan reforms
is inferred from the presence or absence of breaks in aggregate work-effort
trends between the periods 1967–80 and 1981–88. On the whole, my analysis
suggests there has been a break in labor supply trends between these two pe-

riods. The break is more reliably estimated in the case of men than women, and it is proportionately larger among older workers than among workers in their prime working years, ages 25-54. A notable exception to this pattern is labor supply among single mothers, a group that was a particular focus of Reagan administration policy. Labor supply in this population rose a bit less rapidly during the 1980s than it did during the late 1960s and 1970s. The supply-side revolution has evidently passed this population by.

The two most inclusive measures of labor supply analyzed in the chapter are average hours per week during a March reference week and annual average hours of work in the population. Fortunately, the trends in these two variables show a roughly consistent pattern. Among men in their prime working years, average weekly hours during the March reference week rose 0.5 percent to 4.0 percent relative to their previous trend rate, while average annual hours rose 2.3 percent to 4.1 percent. Among women between 25 and 54, average weekly hours rose 0.4 percent to 3.0 percent and average annual hours rose about 3.5 percent. The proportionate rise in labor supply is somewhat larger among older men and women.

Curiously, the rise in labor supply may not have been matched by a rise in the income tax base. Regressions on real annual earnings per person show no rise in the trend of earnings growth. Among male wage and salary workers, there has probably been a *decline* in the rate of growth of real earnings. The conclusion appears inescapable that income tax revenues from labor earnings are substantially lower than they would have been if tax rates had been kept constant over the 1980s. Of course, trends in real annual earnings are affected by trends in productivity and market wage rates as well as aggregate labor supply. Even though the 1980s have witnessed no surge in the growth of earnings trend, average annual earnings may nonetheless be above the level they would have attained in the absence of the Reagan reforms. The rise in aggregate work effort may have offset part of the loss in earnings that otherwise would have occurred as a result of anemic productivity growth or declining real wages.

All of the effects of the Reagan-era reforms have been calculated under the assumption that observed trends in labor supply from 1968 through 1980 would have continued unchanged after 1980 if the Reagan administration had not taken office. That is, deviations from past trends are wholly attributed to Reagan administration policies. This assumption is questionable, although it is not clear what alternative assumption could be adopted. Even though the analysis is based on tabulations of about 2.5 million survey responses, the available data series on hours of work and real earnings contain only 21 annual observations. It is thus impossible to test more than a couple of alternative specifications.

The two specifications examined in this chapter contain independent variables to measure the extent of demand for labor. Thus all estimates of Reagan policy effects should be interpreted as effects that hold the state of the economy fixed. The state of labor demand is implicitly assumed to be beyond the control of the administration. This assumption has a subtle but significant implication for interpreting the response estimates reported earlier. Even though trends in labor demand have been favorable since 1983, the average unemployment rate during the Reagan years was higher than the rate during any other postwar administration. The March unemployment rate was 6.1 percent from 1968 through 1980, but 8.0 percent from 1981 through 1988. The 1.9 percentage point difference between the two periods reduced the labor supply of prime-age men by about 3.5 percent and the supply of prime-age women by almost 2 percent. If the high unemployment rate of the 1980s is attributable to Reagan administration policy, higher unemployment has just about offset the supply-enhancing effects of its tax and transfer policies.

President Reagan's tax policies are probably responsible for a modest increase in the U.S. labor supply. They have not brought the nation a supply-side miracle.

NOTES

This chapter was prepared with support from the Brookings Center for Economic Progress and Employment. The views expressed are the author's alone and should not be ascribed to the staff or trustees of the Brookings Institution.

I gratefully acknowledge the exceptional research assistance of Stephen Kastenberg and Paul R. Bergin and the helpful comments of Barry P. Bosworth, Joseph A. Pechman, and George L. Perry.

1. U.S. households could also respond to a reduction in taxes by changing their saving behavior. It seems doubtful, however, that Reagan-era policies had a beneficial impact on savings. Saving out of personal income fell from an average rate of 7.9 percent between 1971–80 to a rate of just 3.9 percent between 1985 and 1988. Even including savings in the corporate sector, the private saving rate reached new lows in the middle and late 1980s.

2. The new tax schedule became fully effective in 1988. In 1987 federal taxpayers faced an interim tax formula containing five brackets with associated marginal tax rates ranging from 11 percent up to 38.5 percent (see Pechman 1987: 317–20).

3. For a detailed description of the specific reforms proposed by President Reagan and adopted by Congress, see U.S. Congress, Committee on Ways and Means 1989; for a more general description, see Haveman 1984: 93–103.

4. The year 1979 is selected as a comparison year because, like 1968 and 1988, it was a period of relatively robust economic expansion. The following year, 1980, was a recession year, and 1981 was a year of weak economic recovery followed by recession later in the year.

5. The Bureau of Economic Analysis has estimated a series of middle expansion trend GNP to reflect potential GNP since 1955. The GNP gap is the difference between potential and actual GNP measured as a percentage of potential GNP (*Survey of Current Business* 1983: 30, and 1988: 21). Since this concept of the GNP gap is based exclusively on measured output and ignores labor input, I slightly prefer it to other cyclically sensitive variables. However, use of the Federal Reserve Board's capacity utilization rate in the regressions produced very similar results to those obtained using the GNP gap.

6. Throughout this chapter I use the phrases "unmarried" and "single" interchangeably when speaking of mothers. Single mothers are defined as divorced, separated, widowed, or never-married women older than age 15 who are classified by the Census Bureau as heads of families with child dependents under the age of 18. This definition unfortunately excludes one group of single mothers—those not classified by the Census Bureau as heads of families.

7. An alternative explanation is that market wage rates have risen faster for high-wage than for low-wage workers.

8. Nominal earnings were translated into constant 1986 dollars using the CPI-UX deflator.

"The Supply-Side Legacy of the Reagan Years": *Comment*

Augustin Kwasi Fosu

The Burtless chapter examines the extent to which the Reagan administration policies of the 1980s may have augmented labor supply in the U.S. economy. It first reviews possible labor-supply implications of the administration's tax and welfare programs. The policy effects on labor supply are then estimated by employing in a time-series, single-equation econometric model a linear time trend beginning in 1981, along with other explanatory variables measuring previous trends and the business cycle.

Burtless first observes that federal marginal tax rates have fallen for all major income groups as a result of the Reagan-era policies, but that the magnitude of the cut clearly increases with income. The most telling aspects of the reforms were a significant abatement in the generosity of welfare benefits to low-income families and substantial reductions in both average and marginal tax rates of affluent taxpayers. Assuming equal responsiveness across income groups, low-income families and the affluent should exhibit the greatest labor-supply effects of these policies.

The empirical analysis shows little or no evidence in favor of positive impacts of Reagan-era policies on labor force participation rates of men or women overall. Indeed, the effect is negative for women as a group. However, there appears to be a positive impact on the intensity of work effort measured as hours per week or per year, but even here the statistical significance of the evidence rests crucially on the variable employed to control for the business cycle. The evidence of a positive effect is stronger when the GNP gap, instead of the unemployment rate, is used.

Unfortunately, the usual econometric statistics cannot be relied on to select between the above two regression specifications. In several instances, the equation containing the unemployment rate exhibits better overall goodness of fit according to the corrected R^2, yet the statistical significance of the trend variable is worse than the specification with the GNP gap. Nevertheless, I agree with Burtless's remark that he prefers the GNP gap as a measure of the business cycle, since this concept is "based exclusively on measured output and ignores labor input" (Note 5). He does not, unfortunately, elaborate on this issue, which seems rather critical to the appropriate interpretation of his results.

I suspect that the unemployment rate incorporates significant supply as well as demand conditions, and that it may be picking up portions of the labor supply trends not appropriately captured in the linear trend variables. Concurrently, if its correlation with the trend variables is relatively high (the correlation matrix is not reported), then not only might the post-1980 trend estimate be biased, but also its statistical significance would be reduced. Such an outcome should be more likely in those demographic groups in which the overall unemployment rate has relatively little cyclical effect on labor supply. It is perhaps not surprising, then, to observe such comparatively large differences in results between the two alternate specifications reported for men.

Assuming that the equation containing the GNP gap is preferable, at least in the case of men, then Burtless's empirical results become easier to interpret. For men, possibly with the exception of youths (16-24 years of age), the Reagan administration reforms positively affected labor supply, whether measured by participation rates, unemployment ratios, or by hours per week or per year.

In the case of women, however, it is difficult to argue on the basis of Burtless's reported empirical results that the Reagan-era policies have augmented labor supply, irrespective of the regression specification. Not only do the results suggest negative partial impacts on participation rates and employment ratios, but there is also little reported evidence in support of Burtless's assertion for the 1981–87 period that, *ceteris paribus,* "all groups of women at work except single mothers registered strong gains in average weekly hours." At best, what the results show is that among working-age women, the Reagan years may have contributed five additional working hours per year on average, which represents only about one-half of that reported for men and is, furthermore, subject to rather low statistical significance. And the results for unmarried, divorced, and separated women with children point to a perverse influence on their labor supply, contrary to what one would expect in terms of the work incentive implications of the reforms for this "targeted" group.

Burtless's finding that annual growth in wage and salary earnings grew relatively faster in the 1980s than previously for women and higher income groups may be attributable to increases in relative wage rates rather than work effort. Unfortunately, the reported evidence does not shed light on this issue. Recursive-equation estimation involving the inclusion of the employment ratio in the hours equation should help untangle this conundrum.

Perhaps the finding of the weak effect of Reagan-era policies on labor supply resulted in part from the concurrent higher social security tax rates and potentially larger state and local tax burdens. Inclusion of these in Burtless's calculations might have dampened any expected positive impacts of the policies.

Nevertheless, there is reason to believe that Burtless's basic assumption underlying his econometric estimation that previous labor force trends continued into the 1980s may be untenable, especially in the case of women. Fosu (1989), for example, argues that the tremendous rise in married female labor force participation rates in the 1960s and 1970s was likely attributable in large part to the heightened feminism of the times, and that trends in the 1980s would once again be receptive to traditional economic variables. If so, then trends in female participation would probably be lower in the 1980s than previously. Thus Burtless's estimates of the Reagan-reforms impacts that do not account for such a change would be biased downward. A simple way to correct this possible defect is to introduce an additional higher-order term into the pre-1981 time trend.

Major declines in the inflation rate in the 1980s from its 1967–80 trends may have similar implications for trends in labor force participation and hence for the accuracy of Burtless's estimates of the Reagan-era impacts. There is some evidence that participation of married females, for example, is positively correlated with the cost of living (Fosu 1990). Hence, the failure to account for cost-of-living differences over time, coupled with the lower inflation of the 1980s, portends a negative bias in the Burtless estimates of the effects attributable to the Reagan tax and welfare policies, at least in the case of women.

The Burtless study is nonetheless path-breaking in that it is the first to estimate the impact of the Reagan-era policies based on actual labor market trends. It is hoped that future work incorporating the above suggestions into Burtless's insightful study will help to assess more fully the labor-supply dimension of the legacy of the Reagan years.

4

Two Revolutions in Economic Policy: Growth-Oriented Macro Policy in the Kennedy and Reagan Administrations

Laurence H. Meyer,
Joel L. Prakken, and
Chris P. Varvares

The inspiration for this chapter is the interesting volume edited by James Tobin and Murray Weidenbaum, *Two Revolutions in Economic Policy*. *Two Revolutions* brings together the first *Economic Report of the Council of Economic Advisors* in the Kennedy and Reagan administrations, along with earlier papers written by the respective Council of Economic Advisors (CEA) staffs summarizing the economic policy initiatives of the new administrations and later analyses written for the volume evaluating the policies with the benefit of some historical perspective. It is apparent from *Two Revolutions* that the Kennedy and Reagan administrations shared an emphasis on growth-oriented macro policy, while advocating sharply different policies for promoting growth. The Kennedy CEA stressed the role of the mix of monetary and fiscal policies in promoting growth, while the Reagan CEA emphasized the role of supply-side tax incentives.

The theoretical analysis and empirical evidence in this chapter provide support for both administrations' views of the role of policy in promoting growth: both the policy mix and supply-side tax cuts are theoretically legitimate and empirically supported ways of enhancing intermediate-term economic growth. The puzzle that motivates this chapter, however, is the failure of fiscal policy in the Reagan administration as growth-oriented policy despite the promises of supply-side economics. The rate of growth of potential output during the Reagan years was about 2.5 percent per year, about the same as that recorded in the Carter years.

The failure of Reaganomics to promote growth can be understood as resulting in part from the perhaps unintended combination of a pro-growth supply-side tax policy with an anti-growth policy mix, and in part from the inconsistency with which supply-side tax policy was implemented during the Reagan years. The increase in real interest rates associated with the large Reagan budget deficits provided a powerful offset to supply-side tax cuts. The power of the supply-side cuts in personal tax rates, in turn, was substantially undermined by the reduction in investment incentives as part of tax reform. The net effect was that supply-side tax policy in the Reagan years, even in the absence of the adverse move in the policy mix, would have made only a small contribution to raising the rate of economic growth.

This chapter presents both an analytical framework in support of these themes and empirical evidence, based on simulations of the Washington University Macro Model. The analytical evidence derives from a simple model in which potential output is endogenous and can be affected by both the policy mix and supply-side tax policies. The Washington University Macro Model, a 350-equation structural macroeconometric model, is consistent with this theoretical framework. Its properties include a high degree of sensitivity of aggregate demand to interest rates, making the policy mix a powerful force affecting investment and hence capital accumulation and potential output, and the incorporation of "supply-side" effects through the influence of marginal personal tax rates on labor supply and investment incentives on investment. It therefore provides a particularly promising vehicle for attempting to isolate the respective influences of policy mix and supply-side tax policies and the relative effect of supply-side incentives operating through the personal and corporate tax codes.

GROWTH-ORIENTED FISCAL POLICIES IN THE TWO ADMINISTRATIONS

The two CEAs and their reports are interesting because these two periods were "watersheds in federal economic policy" that brought new ideas, in each case growing out of dissatisfaction with the economic performance over the previous decade.[1] The Kennedy Council brought a well-developed neo-Keynesian theoretical framework (labelled the "New Economics," although, as Solow and Tobin note, "it followed well-trodden Keynesian paths"[2]) along with a confidence in the potential for an activist stabilization policy. The Reagan Council brought an intellectual counterrevolution against that neo-Keynesian mainstream—with supply-side, monetarist, and neo-classical approaches providing the components of the alternative paradigm.

The Kennedy Council: "Short-Run Policies Should . . . Serve Long-Term Ends"

The Kennedy Council afforded a high priority to the use of stabilization policy to move the economy toward full employment. While there was considerable emphasis by the Kennedy Council on fiscal policy—both automatic stabilizers and discretionary or activist policy—there was also a clear appreciation of the importance of the "policy mix"—the mix of monetary and fiscal policies. The Kennedy Council indeed viewed monetary and fiscal policies as *substitutes* for stabilization policy and suggested that the appropriate mix of the policies should be based on other considerations, the most important of which was the encouragement of the long-term growth of the economy. As a result, the Council emphasized the design of a set of policies to deal with stabilization policy which also contributed to promoting growth. In the 1961 policy paper, the Kennedy CEA wrote, "Short-run policies should, as far as possible, also serve long-run ends."[3] Concern about deteriorating trade deficits quickly put a constraint on the implementation of the policy mix strategy and the principal pro-growth components of the Tax Act of 1964 were the investment incentives—the Investment Tax Credit and the acceleration in depreciation schedules—both subsequently eliminated in the Reagan years as part of the Tax Reform Act of 1986.

The Reagan Administration's Combination Policy

In its first *Economic Report,* the Reagan Council presented a legislative program that featured a deceleration in the rate of growth in federal spending, a decline in marginal personal tax rates, and an increase in tax incentives favoring investment. The Reagan CEA clearly deemphasized stabilization policy and stressed the growth objective in the design of fiscal policy.

The Role of Spending Restraint (Policy Mix): Plan and Practice

The Reagan team appeared sincere in its commitment to spending restraint, referring to it as "the leading edge of our program."[4] It was spending restraint that made supply-side tax cuts compatible with a move to a balanced budget. The following objectives were set out in the 1981 blueprint by the Reagan CEA:

From a high of 23 percent of the gross national product (GNP) in fiscal 1981, Federal outlays are now scheduled to decline to 21.8% in fiscal 1982 and to reach approximately 19% beginning in 1984. From deficit of $59.6 billion in 1980, . . . Federal expenditures are now estimated to exceed revenues by $45.0 billion in fiscal 1982 and $23.0 billion in fiscal 1983. By fiscal 1984 . . . the Federal budget should be in balance.[5]

Spending restraint was not in fact carried out in the early Reagan years. Figure 4.1 depicts the pattern in the ratio of cyclically adjusted expenditures and revenue to cyclically adjusted GNP from 1977 through 1987. Note that the ratio of government expenditures to GNP increased by two percentage points during the Reagan years, instead of declining by four percentage points. This six-percentage-point gap between plan and practice more than accounts for the increase in the cyclically adjusted budget deficit in the Reagan years. The failure to implement spending restraint was partly due to the tension between the desire to sharply raise defense spending and the plan to restrain overall spend-

Figure 4.1
The Sources of the Budget Deficit: Taxes vs. Expenditures

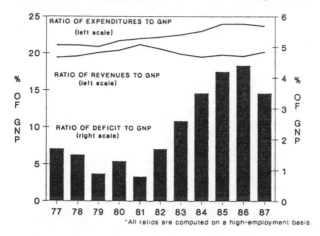

*All ratios are computed on a high-employment basis.

ing. However, it also reflected a serious miscalculation in the Reagan plan. Given the tax cuts, the defense spending targets, and the unwillingness to cut significantly into entitlements, there was too little elsewhere in the budget to produce both overall spending restraint and a balanced budget.

Supply-Side Tax Policy in the Reagan Administration

According to the *Economic Report of the President* (1982), "Structural tax policy probably constitutes the Federal Government's most powerful tool for influencing economic growth."[6] The Reagan policy team emphasized the role of supply-side tax incentives in promoting economic growth, through their effect on household decisions about saving and work effort and business capital spending decisions. While the Kennedy Council had been concerned about providing firms enhanced incentives for investment to spur growth, the unique feature of supply-side economics was the importance attached to the effect of tax rates on household decisions and the contribution that such tax changes were expected to make to economic growth.

The tax policy of the Reagan years can be usefully separated into four components. The first is the Economic Recovery Tax Act of 1981 (ERTA), implementing the cuts in personal and corporate marginal tax rates and enhancing investment incentives. The second component is the series of tax increases that partially reversed the generosity of the 1981 tax cuts. The third component is the social insurance tax increases legislated in accord with the recommendations of a bipartisan commission on social security chaired by Alan Greenspan. While these tax increases were not a part of the Reagan fiscal policy per se, they help explain why the Reagan tax cuts merely helped to stabilize the ratio of tax revenue to GNP. The fourth component is the Tax Reform Act of 1986. This in part extended and in part reversed the thrust of the 1981 tax act. Tax reform extended the cuts in marginal and average personal tax rates, thereby further enhancing the supply-side effects on work effort and saving. But tax reform also shifted the tax burden sharply from households to corporations and eliminated not only the enhanced investment incentives that had been legislated as part of the 1981 tax act, but also substantially reversed the liberalization of investment incentives that had begun in the Kennedy administration.

Tax Cuts and the Reagan Deficits

The Reagan tax cuts were followed by a sharp escalation in the deficit. However, note that the average tax rate (measured as the ratio of cyclically adjusted revenue to cyclically adjusted GNP) in the Reagan years (20.1 percent) was virtually identical to that during the Carter years (19.9 percent). The Reagan deficits must be due to more than the 1981 tax cut. The Reagan deficits clearly also reflect the failure to implement spending restraint. The failure to limit spending, in turn, likely reflected the excessive optimism of the Reagan team about the effect of supply-side policies on the economy's rate of growth. The Reagan CEA *Report* projected that "the economy . . . should break out of its anemic growth patterns to a much more robust growth trend of 4 to 5 percent per year."[7] Although the Reagan projections never assumed that the tax cut would be self-financing (as was possible, according to the Laffer curve), the immediacy and magnitude of the projected effects probably led the Reagan team to downplay the difficulty of balancing the budget, encouraging the belief that the economy would rapidly grow its way out of the early deficits.

THE ANALYTICS: FISCAL POLICY AND TREND GROWTH

Reaganomics and Trend Growth

Before discussing the analytics of trend growth and the effect of Reaganomics on trend growth, we review the record of economic growth in the Reagan years. Figure 4.2 reports the pattern of trend growth from 1955 through 1988. Trend growth is measured using the growth in the mid-expansion series for real GNP developed by the Commerce Department and reported periodically in the *Survey of Current Business*. The peak growth rate, 3.65 percent per year, occurred in the 1960s. The growth rate slowed to 2.92 percent in the 1970s and to 2.5 percent in the 1980s. In both the Carter and the Reagan years, growth was a dismal 2.5 percent per year.

Growth Theory and Growth-Oriented Fiscal Policy

Neoclassical growth theory provides a framework for assessing the effect of both policy mix and supply-side tax policies on the rate of economic growth. In a simple neoclassical one-sector growth model with labor-augmenting technical change, the economy gravitates toward a steady-state rate of growth equal

Figure 4.2
Reaganomics and Trend GNP

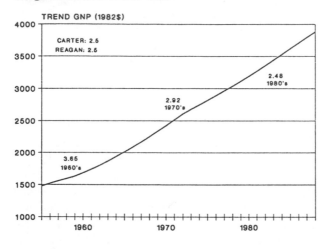

to the sum of the exogenous rate of population growth and the exogenous rate
of labor-augmenting technical change. The steady-state rate of growth is independent of the exogenously determined saving rate. This immediately suggests
a limited potential for fiscal policy to affect steady-state growth.

Fiscal policy can nevertheless affect intermediate-term economic growth by
encouraging an increase in the level of the labor force and/or capital stock and
hence the level of productive capacity. As the economy gradually moves to this
higher level of productive capacity, the observed growth rate will exceed the
steady-state rate of growth. Once the full adjustment has been achieved, observed growth will return to the original steady-state rate, although the level of
output will be permanently higher than it would have been in the absence of
the growth-oriented fiscal policy change. A change in the saving rate in this
model proxies conveniently for growth-oriented fiscal policy. An increase in
the saving rate via an increase in government saving (a decline in the budget
deficit) would be consistent with a change in the policy mix toward tighter
fiscal and looser monetary policies. An increase in the saving rate could also
be interpreted as reflecting supply-side tax policy, via the effect of lower marginal personal tax rates on the saving rate.

Fiscal Policy and the Level of Productive Capacity

The above analysis suggests that the key effect of growth-oriented fiscal policy is on the level rather than the growth rate of productive capacity. This
allows us to employ a comparative static analysis to demonstrate the long-run
output effects of both the mix of monetary and fiscal policies and supply-side
tax policies.

*A Modified IS-LM Model with Endogenous Level of Full
Employment Output*

We modify a simple IS-LM model to allow for the long-run effect of fiscal policy. A model of this variety was introduced by Prakken (1987) and a simplified version is presented below.

1. *The IS and LM curves.* We begin with standard IS and LM curves:

$$X = C(Y, (1-t)r) + I(c) + G \qquad (4.1)$$

$$m = L(r, X) \qquad (4.2)$$

where X = output (GNP), Y = disposable personal income, t = personal tax rate (assumed for simplicity to be both average and marginal tax rate), r = interest rate (real and nominal, as we assume there is no inflation to further simplify the analysis), c = cost of capital, G = government purchases, and m = money supply. We included the after-tax rate of interest in the consumption function and the cost of capital rather than just the interest rate in the investment function to anticipate the use of this model to study supply-side tax policies. The following identities are required to complete the basic IS-LM system:

$$Y = X - T \qquad (4.3)$$

$$c = (1 - k - qz)\{(1-q)r + d\}/(1-q) \qquad (4.4)$$

where T is tax revenue, k = the investment tax credit, q = corporate marginal tax rate, z = the present value of the depreciation allowance, and d = the rate of economic depreciation. The cost of capital thus depends on both the interest rate and a variety of tax rates and other tax parameters, including the investment tax credit and tax depreciation.

2. *The long-run aggregate supply (AS) curve.* Given that we are only interested in the long-run effect of fiscal policy here, we will assume the economy is initially in equilibrium at full employment and consider the effect of a change in fiscal policy on the full employment or equilibrium level of output. The point of departure is the production function that relates the level of production *(X)* to the level of labor input *(N)* and the capital stock *(K)*. To transform the production function into an aggregate supply curve, the level of labor input and capital stock are replaced by the equilibrium level of labor input $(N_f$, the full employment level) and the profit-maximizing level of the capital stock. The equilibrium level of labor input, in turn, is a function of the marginal personal tax rate, assuming that labor supply is positively related to the after-tax real wage rate. The optimal level of the capital stock, in turn, is a function of the

Figure 4.3
The Policy Mix, Supply-Side Tax Policy, and Productive Capacity

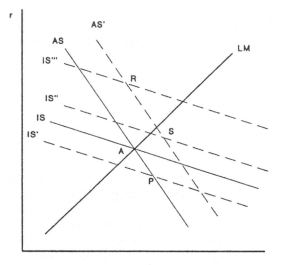

cost of capital. The aggregate supply equation can therefore be expressed as equation (4.5), where X_f is the equilibrium or full-employment level of output.

$$X_f = F(K(c), N_f(t)) \tag{4.5}$$

The aggregate supply curve (the AS curve in Figure 4.3) is negatively sloped (a higher level of productive capacity is associated with a lower interest rate) and shifts with supply-side tax changes. A change in the policy mix thus involves a movement along the AS curve while supply-side tax policies shift the curve (with the exception of saving incentives, which result in movements along the curve via the induced change in the interest rate).

The Long-Run Effects of Policy Mix and Supply-Side Tax Policies
in the IS-LM-AS Model

The set of IS, LM, and AS curves is depicted in Figure 4.3. The AS curve is steeper than the IS curve, as required for model stability. We will now use this diagram to illustrate the effect of policy mix, supply-side tax policy, and fiscal policy in the Reagan years.

1. *The policy mix and the level of potential output.* A change in the rate of government expenditures shifts the IS curve in this diagram leftward for a decline in expenditures. The intersection of the IS and AS curves identifies the equilibrium level of output and of the real interest rate. The LM curve then adjusts to intersect the IS and AS curves at the same point, the adjustment in the real money supply occurring either via price flexibility or an explicit change in monetary policy. In either case, the result is a change in the mix of monetary

and fiscal policy, with a tighter fiscal policy being complemented by a looser monetary policy. In the three experiments detailed in this section the LM curve is not adjusted in Figure 4.3 simply to avoid cluttering the diagram.

The initial equilibrium in Figure 4.3 is shown at point A. A decline in government purchases (complemented by an increase in the money supply) results in a new equilibrium at P. The result is a decline in the (real) interest rate and an increase in the full employment level of output, consistent with the effect of the policy encouraging investment and hence capital formation.

2. *Supply-side tax policy and the level of full employment output.* We now assume that tax incentives for saving, work, and investment are increased, but that there are also offsetting changes in the level of government purchases so that the budget deficit remains unaffected. We refer to this as a *pure* supply-side tax policy. It conforms closely to what Reaganomics proposed, though not to what was in fact implemented. The effect of this policy on the IS curve depends on the particular supply-side changes implemented. Assuming in each case that any tax cut is offset by a spending reduction, an increase in investment incentives, for example, shifts the IS curve rightward, an increase in saving incentives shifts it leftward, and an increase in labor supply incentives leaves the IS curve unchanged. Because of the large increase in investment incentives under the Reagan plan, we will assume that the IS curve shifts slightly rightward to IS''. Investment incentives and labor supply incentives shift the AS curve rightward to AS'. The net effect is an increase in equilibrium output from that corresponding to point A to that associated with point S in Figure 4.3. Pure supply-side tax policies thus unambiguously increase productive capacity and hence raise the intermediate-term rate of economic growth.

3. *Economic policy in the Reagan years: The combination of supply-side tax policy and policy mix approaches.* The Reagan era brought us a combination of the policy-mix and supply-side approaches developed above. Unfortunately, the combination involved pairing a pro-growth supply-side policy with an anti-growth policy mix. This case is shown as movement from the initial equilibrium at A to point R in Figure 4.3. The IS curve shifts rightward, in the opposite direction of what an appropriate policy-mix strategy would have dictated. This illustrates the effect of the sharp increase in the structural budget deficit. Taken by itself, this would lower full-employment output. Supply-side tax policies, however, result in a shift in the AS curve rightward, the same shift to AS' used above. Taken alone, we found this would unambiguously increase full employment output. The net effect of this combination policy is ambiguous and depends on the relative importance of the policy mix and supply-side elements of the policy, which in turn depend on the empirical parameters of the model and the precise specification of the policies.

THE EMPIRICS: POLICY SIMULATIONS WITH THE
WASHINGTON UNIVERSITY MACRO MODEL

We are left with the task of isolating the relative importance of the policy mix and supply-side tax components of Reaganomics. The simple analytical model only provides qualitative results and these turned out to be ambiguous. Quantitative results require estimates of the various model parameters. To provide empirical evidence we use simulations with the Washington University Macro Model (WUMM). We begin by describing the relevant properties of WUMM, then outline the simulations performed, and finally, report and interpret the results.

The Washington University Model

The underlying philosophical core of the model is the neo-Keynesian synthesis. In this view, output is demand-determined in the short run and supply-determined in the long run. That is, the model has long-run neoclassical properties, but is Keynesian in the adjustment process. The neoclassical long-run properties include an effect of the policy mix on the composition of output and hence on the capital stock and the intermediate rate of economic growth. Policies that affect the deficit definitely have significant effects on the long-run equilibrium level of output in WUMM. In the short run, for example, an increase in government purchases raises aggregate demand (based on the short-run Keynesian features of the model), but in the long run such a policy would actually lower the equilibrium level of output. Thus, long-run multipliers for increases in government spending are in fact negative in WUMM.

The model also incorporates many of the insights of supply-side economics. The labor supply, for example, depends on the after-tax real wage rate (through the participation rate equation and the equation for the average workweek). The demand for capital depends on a cost of capital variable in which investment incentives enter importantly. Saving depends on the interest rate, but only via the interest-induced wealth effect and the effect of a cost of capital-type variable on the demand for consumer durables.

The Policy Simulations

In a policy simulation, the solution values of the model variables in a base case (lined up on the historical data) are compared with the solution values from a simulation in which some policy instrument or a combination of policy instruments is altered relative to its historical values. The difference between the values of the endogenous variables in the base and policy runs is a measure of the impact of the policy.

Policy Simulations: Not as Simple as It Sounds

This procedure sounds simpler and more mechanical than it generally is. The main problem we encounter is that the exchange rate equation does not track well enough to give us confidence that the unadjusted model would provide a plausible account of how different the exchange rate would be in a policy run. Our approach is to make some judgmental adjustments to the exchange rate in the policy run to provide what we believe is a more reasonable picture of the likely effect of the policy. But our judgment clearly might not be the same as that of some other careful researchers. Our point is that these policy simulations have a judgmental element, an aspect we do not wish to hide.

The Concept of an "Accommodated" Change in Fiscal Policy

The fiscal policy simulations reported below were constructed such that the effect of the fiscal policy change on aggregate demand is offset by imposing a complementary monetary policy. In other words, the fiscal policy change is simulated as a shift in the policy mix, not as an isolated fiscal policy change. Alternatively, monetary policy is said to accommodate the fiscal policy change so as to leave the unemployment rate unchanged from the base simulation.

Why the unemployment rate? Since we are attempting to determine if there is an effect of the policy on the level of productive capacity, it is essential not to attempt to use monetary policy to maintain output at the same level as in the base case. Instead, we accommodate to the level of the unemployment rate. However, even if the unemployment rate is the same in the base and policy runs, output may differ if policy mix or supply-side policies affect the level of the labor force, average hours per worker, or the capital stock.

Specific Policy Simulations

We ran two sets of policy simulations, the first to quantify the effect of deficits on trend growth, and the second to provide quantitative evidence on the role of supply-side tax effects.

1. *Deficits and trend growth.* To quantify the effect of the large deficits on trend growth in the Reagan years, we left the supply-side tax policies in effect, but lowered the path of government expenditures, offsetting the effect on aggregate demand via looser monetary policy. There is still a sizable deficit during the early 1980s. No attempt is made to reduce the cyclical deficit associated with the 1981–82 recession. However, the restraint imposed on federal expenditures ensures that the deficit is eliminated once the economy reaches full employment.

2. *Supply-side tax policies and trend growth.* In this simulation the Reagan structural deficit is eliminated by removing the tax cuts with an accommodating monetary policy. That is, the tighter fiscal policy is implemented by eliminating from the simulation changes in tax rates, depreciation, and so on that took effect over the last eight years. Thus this simulation removes the "supply-side"

policy changes and implements the shift in the policy mix via "tax increases" (relative to history) accompanied by looser monetary policy. This provides a good test of the Reagan team's proposition that the manner in which the deficit is closed may be as important as whether or not the deficit is closed.

The Results

An Accommodated Cut in Federal Government Expenditures: The Effect of the Policy Mix on Trend Growth

The first simulation imposes the planned fiscal restraint to complement the supply-side tax policies of the Reagan years. The effect of the shift in the policy mix was to move the budget from substantial deficit to surplus by 1990. Figure 4.4 shows the pattern in some of the key variables in the base as compared with the policy simulation. Note that despite the fact that the unemployment rate is returned to its initial level in 1990, the level of output is one percentage point higher by 1989 and 1990, indicating a positive effect on productive capacity from the shift in the policy mix. Underlying the higher level of productive capacity are increases in both the levels of the capital stock and the labor force. The higher capital stock reflects the two-percentage-point decline in the real interest rate in the policy run. The higher level of the labor force reflects the effect of a decline in transfer payments on labor force participation in the model. Note that the 1 percent increase in GNP in the simulation fits perfectly with the contribution of the 0.5 percent increase in the labor force and the 2.5 percent increase in the capital stock, weighted by their appropriate shares in national income (0.73 for the labor force and 0.27 for the capital stock). The 1 percent increase in the level of GNP by the end of the period translates into a 0.1 percentage point increase in the growth rate over the period.

The full adjustment to the change in the policy mix is not, however, complete by the end of the simulation period. We find that a 20-year simulation is generally required to approximate the full equilibrium response. This is an even more serious problem with the second policy simulation reported below. In each case we estimate the long-run response of the capital stock, and hence output, by combining the effect on the percentage decline in the labor force at the end of the ten-year simulation period with the percentage decline in the capital stock implied by the percentage difference in the cost of capital at the end of the ten-year simulation. The percentage changes in labor force and capital stock are then used to compute the percentage change in the level of output by applying the weights on labor and capital in the model's production function (0.27 for capital and 0.73 for labor). The results of these calculations are reported in Table 4.1.

By the end of the ten-year simulation period, the real interest rate was two percentage points lower and the cost of capital was 7.5 percentage points lower

Figure 4.4

Accommodated Decline in Government Expenditures

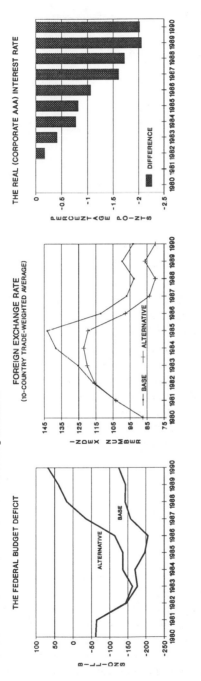

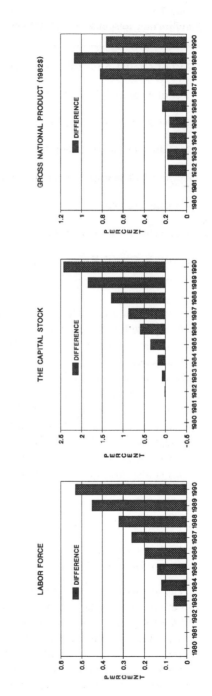

Table 4.1
Equilibrium Response of Capital and Output

Cost of Capital, 5.5% Real Interest Rate:	0.216
Cost of Capital, 3.5% Real Interest Rate:	0.197
% Change in Cost of Capital:	-8.8%
% Change in Capital/Labor Ratio:	+8.8%
Weight of Capital in Production Function:	0.27
% Change in Output:	+2.4%
# of Years for Full Adjustment:	20
Impact on Growth Rate:	+0.12%

than in the base case. It is clear from Figure 4.4 that the capital stock had not fully adjusted to the decline in the cost of capital. The 7.5 percent equilibrium increase in the capital stock implied by a 7.5 percent decline in the cost of capital would contribute two percentage points (using the 0.27 weight for capital) to the level of equilibrium output. This full effect would take about 20 years to be complete, implying a 0.1 percentage point increase in the growth rate for GNP over this period. The effect via the higher labor force must be added to this to get the full equilibrium effect on the level of output. Most of the adjustment of the labor force occurs relatively quickly. Assuming that the 0.5 percent increase in the labor force after ten years in the first policy simulation is also the equilibrium response of the labor force, the higher labor force contributes 0.36 percentage point to the equilibrium level of output. The full equilibrium increase in output is therefore 2.4 percent, translating into a 0.12 percentage point increase in the rate of growth over the 20-year period.

An Accommodated Increase in Federal Tax Revenues: Does It Matter How the Deficit Is Reduced?

The second simulation also eliminates the deficit, but by raising tax revenue rather than by cutting government expenditures. It represents an attempt to back out the Reagan tax cuts. In implementing this simulation, the pre-1981 tax code was retained, and the effects of both the 1981 tax cut and of tax reform were thereby removed. The result is higher marginal and average personal and corporate tax rates. Depreciation is initially much less generous than under Reagan until 1986, after which depreciation is slightly more generous than under Reagan. The investment tax credit is retained. Hence, investment incentives on net are initially less generous than under Reagan, but after 1986 are significantly more generous than under Reagan.

The removal of the significant reductions in personal marginal income tax rates has a profound effect on the labor force. Whereas the Reagan tax cuts reduced the average effective marginal rate from 24.9 percent in 1980 to 22.3 percent in 1990, this simulation assumed a modest upward drift, with the marginal rate reaching 32.3 percent. As a result, the labor force ends this simulation nearly 2 percent lower.

With respect to investment, removal of Accelerated Cost Recovery System (ACRS) initially raises the cost of capital for equipment relative to the base. Subsequently, the impact of lower real interest rates pushes the cost of capital modestly lower. The retention of the ITC in this policy simulation results in a sharp decline in the cost of capital for equipment relative to the base case after 1986. The cost of capital for structures also initially rises well above the base case as ACRS is removed, and subsequently falls below the base case as real rates decline. However, the effective ITC for structures was much smaller than that for equipment and thus its removal had a much smaller impact. Thus, while the cost of capital for structures is also lower than in the base case, the decline is not nearly as much as for equipment. By the end of the ten-year simulation period, the cost of capital is 11.3 percent lower after removal of Reagan's supply-side tax policies, providing a significant offset to the effect of higher tax rates on labor income.

At the end of the ten-year simulation, the policy of eliminating the Reagan deficit by reversing its tax policies results in a lower level of GNP. The results for this simulation for labor force, capital stock, output and several other variables is shown in Figure 4.5. The higher the marginal personal tax rates, the lower the labor force. The capital stock is lower through most of the ten-year period, reflecting the initially less generous investment incentives only partially offset by lower real interest rates. However, backing out of tax reform in 1986 leaves investment incentives substantially more generous later in the period, with the result that the capital stock ends the ten-year period higher in the absence of Reagan's supply-side tax policies. Nevertheless, the capital stock has not at this point fully adjusted to the improvement in investment incentives relative to the base case.

We use the same approach as applied in the case of a change in the policy mix to estimate the long-run response of capital and output. By the end of the ten-year period, the cost of capital is 11.3 percent lower after eliminating Reagan's supply-side tax policies. This should raise the equilibrium capital stock by 11.3 percent, contributing 3.1 percentage points to the level of output in the long run. This would more than offset the effect of the 1.9 percent decline in the labor force associated with higher marginal personal tax rates. The net effect therefore would be a 1.7 percent increase in the level of output. How the deficit is reduced clearly does matter. Reducing the deficit by cutting government expenditures allows a 2.4 percent increase in output, the full effect of a

Figure 4.5
Accommodated Increase in Tax Rates

THE FEDERAL BUDGET DEFICIT

COST OF CAPITAL; EQUIPMENT

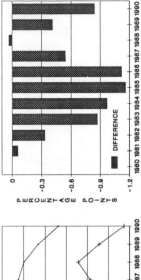

THE REAL (CORPORATE AAA) INTEREST RATE

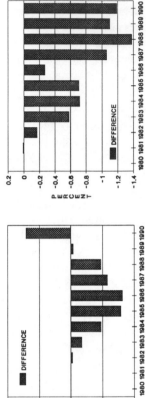

LABOR FORCE

CAPITAL STOCK

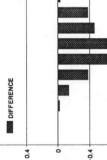

GROSS NATIONAL PRODUCT (1982$)

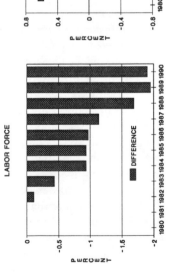

Table 4.2
The Long-Run Effects of Policy-Mix and Supply-Side Tax Changes on Output

	Capital Stock	Labor Force	Output
Policy Mix*	7.5%	0.5%	2.4%
Combination Policy#	11.3%	-1.9%	1.7%
Pure Supply Side@	-3.8%	2.4%	0.7%

* Policy Mix compares the first policy simulation with the base.
\# Combination Policy compares the second simulation with the base.
@ Pure Supply Side compares the first and second policy simulations.

change in the policy mix. Closing the deficit by raising tax rates also raises output but by a smaller amount, as the effect of a change in the policy mix is partially offset by the adverse supply-side effect of higher tax rates.

Comparing the First and Second Policy Simulations: Isolating the Effect of Supply-Side Tax Incentives

The difference between the results for the first and second policy simulations is interpreted as measuring the effect of changes in the Reagan supply-side tax incentives: the deficit paths are similar in the two simulations, but the first policy simulation balances the budget with expenditure cuts, thus preserving the Reagan supply-side tax incentives, while the latter balances the budget by tax increases, in effect reversing the Reagan supply-side tax incentives. Note, however, as we are backing out Reagan's supply-side tax policies, a finding that output would decline implies that Reagan's supply-side policies promoted economic growth.

The results for "pure" supply-side policies are summarized in Table 4.2. Backing out Reagan's supply-side tax policies lowers the labor force by 2.4 percent. This is simply the difference between the 0.5 percent increase in the labor force via the first policy (associated with the decline in transfer payments) and the 1.9 percent decrease in the labor force via the second policy (due to higher marginal personal tax rates).

The ten-year simulation period again masks the equilibrium response of the capital stock. At the end of the period, the capital stock is 1.7 percent lower with the removal of supply-side tax policies. However, the effect of the reversal of tax reform is still a rise in the capital stock. We estimate that the equilibrium capital stock would be 3.8 percent higher under the second policy (reflecting the differences in the cost of capital). This would raise the equilibrium level of output by 1 percent. This is more than offset by the effect of the 2.4 percent decline in the labor force. The net result is that the second policy would have lowered the equilibrium level of output by 0.7 percent relative to the first policy. Thus removing the supply-side tax policies, while maintaining the deficit unchanged, would have slightly lowered output. Supply-side tax policies therefore made a positive, but small contribution to economic growth.

CONCLUSION

This chapter has presented an analytical framework and policy simulations to compare two approaches to growth-oriented fiscal policy: the policy-mix approach favored in principle by the Kennedy administration, and the supply-side tax incentives favored by the Reagan administration. The analytical framework suggested that both policies could promote an increase in the economy's intermediate-term rate of economic growth.

The Reagan fiscal policy was interpreted as a combination policy: a mixture of pro-growth supply-side tax incentives and anti-growth policy mix. This combination was not planned, but reflected the failure to implement the spending restraint that was an integral part of the Reagan team's vision for economic policy. The combination of large structural deficits and supply-side tax cuts yields a theoretically ambiguous effect on economic growth and helps account for the failure of the Reagan policy to improve on the disappointing growth performance over the previous decade. However, the contrast between the unambiguous application of supply-side tax policy in the 1981 tax cuts and the ambivalence of further cuts in personal tax rates, combined with a reversal of investment incentives in the 1986 tax reform act, also contributed to the failure of Reagan fiscal policy to stimulate economic growth.

The following conclusions emerge from the analysis above and the policy simulations:

1. A change in the policy mix is an effective strategy for encouraging more rapid intermediate-term economic growth.

2. Supply-side tax policy can also be an effective strategy for encouraging more rapid intermediate-term economic growth.

3. How the deficit is reduced matters as well as whether the deficit is reduced. To cut the deficit by lowering government spending achieves the full effect of a change in the policy mix. Lowering the deficit by raising tax rates combines the positive influence of moving to a pro-growth policy mix with the anti-growth supply-side effect of higher tax rates.

4. The Reagan fiscal policy failed to stimulate economic growth for two reasons. First, the Reagan fiscal policy was ambivalent about supply-side incentives, enhancing personal tax incentives and reducing investment incentives in the corporate tax code. Second, the failure to implement the planned fiscal restraint resulted in an adverse shift in the policy mix, which served to more than offset the small positive stimulus

associated with the net effect of the 1981 tax cuts and the 1986 tax reform on supply-side incentives.

NOTES

1. James Tobin and Murray Weidenbaum, "Preface," in James Tobin and Murray Weidenbaum, eds., *Two Revolutions in Economic Policy* (Cambridge, Mass.: MIT Press, 1988), p. vii.

2. Robert M. Solow and James Tobin, "Introduction to the the Kennedy Economic Reports," in Tobin and Weidenbaum, *Two Revolutions,* p. 5.

3. Walter Heller, Kermit Gordon, and James Tobin, "The American Economy in 1961: Problems and Policies." Statement before the Joint Economic Committee, March 6, 1961, reprinted in Tobin and Weidenbaum, *Two Revolutions,* p. 37.

4. Murray Weidenbaum, "America's New Beginning: A Program for Economic Recovery." Statement issued by the White House on February 18, 1981, reprinted in Tobin and Weidenbaum, *Two Revolutions,* p. 292.

5. Ibid., pp. 301–2.

6. *Economic Report of the President,* February 1982, p. 132.

7. Ibid., p. 291.

Economic Efficiency in Recent Tax Reform History: Policy Reversals or Consistent Improvements?

Don Fullerton and James B. Mackie

Few areas of public policy have seen changes as frequent or as dramatic as those in tax policy, with major legislation in almost every year from 1980 to 1986. These tax revisions may reflect an evolving economic environment, changing views of individual leaders, or simply shifts in political coalitions. They may appear almost random, however, at least with respect to any one of the multiple and sometimes conflicting objectives of tax policy. We might ask whether these tax changes reflect any consistency with respect to revenue, economic efficiency, distributional effects, or any of a number of noneconomic objectives of tax policy.

Tax initiatives enacted during the Reagan administration might seem particularly inconsistent with respect to the economic efficiency of taxes on income from capital. The Economic Recovery Tax Act of 1981 (ERTA) reduced personal tax rates and depreciation recovery periods, but favored some assets more than others. It thus appeared to promote saving and capital formation at the expense of a level playing field. It also reinforced a trend in revenue sources away from taxes on capital such as the corporate income tax. Subsequent changes through 1985 retrenched somewhat on the generosity of depreciation allowances. Then the Tax Reform Act of 1986 (TRA) lowered personal rates, reduced the corporate rate from 46 to 34 percent, repealed the investment tax credit, lengthened depreciation lifetimes, and added $120 billion of revenue over five years to the corporate income tax. Birnbaum and Murray (1987) refer to cost-recovery provisions in an administration forerunner of the Tax Reform Act as "an abrupt about-face, a 180-degree reversal from four years earlier

This chapter was reprinted from the *National Tax Journal* 42(1), March 1989, with permission from the editor.

. . . a remarkable flip-flop'' (pp. 50–51). It may seem almost inconceivable that these changes were all part of a coherent plan.

There are, however, some unifying threads in these tax initiatives. Both ERTA in 1981 and TRA in 1986 were supported by claims of economic efficiency. In the former case, supply-side rhetoric about work effort and saving was reinforced by economists' measures of distortions in households' choices between labor and leisure or between present and future consumption. In the latter case, rhetoric about the level playing field was reinforced by economists' measures of distortions in firms' choices among investments. Moreover, all such measures of economic efficiency are enhanced by lower marginal tax rates. Birnbaum and Murray (1987) also note that "Reagan wanted to go down in history as the president who cut the top tax rate at least in half, from 70 percent to 35 percent or lower. If abandoning business tax breaks and raising corporate taxes was the price he had to pay to achieve that goal, so be it'' (p. 286).

Were these tax changes essentially random? Is there some set of prior beliefs about parameter values under which efficiency consistently increases? To address these questions, we measure the economic efficiency of capital tax provisions in this series of tax initiatives using a disaggregate general equilibrium model of the U.S. economy and tax system. This model can measure second-best efficiency effects of personal and corporate tax policies, including effects on overall capital formation, and on the allocation of resources among assets, between the corporate and noncorporate sectors, and among industries. We also point out the importance of key unknown parameters such as the elasticity of substitution among capital assets and the elasticity of savings with respect to the net rate of return. We have concentrated on capital income taxation; thus our results are not as sensitive to the labor supply elasticity or to the elasticity of substitution between labor and capital in production.

The generality of the model is important. For example, Fullerton and Henderson (1985) evaluate the 1981 Act using a more restricted model that concentrates on intertemporal distortions. In that model, firms use fixed combinations of assets, and ERTA always generates welfare gains. Here, we use a more general model developed by Fullerton and Henderson (1989) in which asset choices are endogenous. In this model, even with moderate substitution parameters, the less uniform taxation in ERTA can generate welfare losses. For another example, Auerbach (1983) and Gravelle (1981) concentrate on asset distortions but assume Cobb-Douglas production. Our more general functional forms allow us to show that the ranking of tax reforms can be reversed for nonunitary elasticities of substitution.

Using results of this model, we interpret recent tax reform history. We have no formal model of political decision-making, but it is interesting to see how beliefs about the relative importance of different efficiency effects might have supported policymakers' views about the ranking of alternative reforms. ERTA may have been supported by those who believed that capital formation is important (or, in this model, that the saving elasticity is high), but it increases economic efficiency only when the level playing field is unimportant (in this model, when the elasticity of substitution among assets is low). The aspects of the 1986 Act that reversed ERTA may have been influenced by changing beliefs about the relative size of those parameters or importance of those effects.

Results also depend on the assumed effect of dividend taxes. Under the "new view" that dividend taxes have little effect on investment incentives, there is no set of substitution and saving elasticities for which these tax initiatives led to consistent improvements in economic efficiency. Under the "old view," however, reduction of personal taxes on dividends does affect incentives. In this case, for quite reasonable bounds on elasticities in our model, every change in the 1980s led to improvements in efficiency. An interpretation is that policymakers adhere to incremental reform.

We emphasize that recent tax policy decisions were influenced by revenue considerations, distributional effects, and noneconomic objectives. Those effects are entirely ignored here in order to focus on efficiency. The second section summarizes the general equilibrium model used in this chapter, and explains the distinction between the old view and the new view in this model. The third section provides some new results on the efficiency effects of recent tax initiatives, and a fourth section discusses scenarios under which these initiatives could have led to consistent increases in efficiency. A fifth section discusses the implications of assumptions and limitations in the model, and a sixth section concludes.

A GENERAL EQUILIBRIUM MODEL FOR SECOND-BEST EFFICIENCY ANALYSIS

Model Structure

The consumption side of the model is taken from Fullerton, Shoven, and Whalley (1983), in which households have initial endowments of labor and capital and maximize utility by choosing among present consumption goods, leisure, and saving. The elasticity of substitution between consumption and leisure is specified exogenously to be consistent with an uncompensated labor supply elasticity (0.15 for these calculations). Similarly, the elasticity of substitution between present and future consumption is specified to be consistent with an uncompensated saving elasticity. This parameter is set to Boskin's (1978) estimate of 0.4 for most calculations, but it is varied between 0.0 and 0.8 for others.[1]

In deciding how much to save, households myopically use current prices as expected future prices (but see the section on "Saving and Wealth," p. 99). We then calculate a sequence of equilibria in which endogenous saving from one period augments the capital stock in the next period. Labor force growth is set exogenously to place the 1980 baseline equilibrium on a steady-state path. Domestic saving is the only source of investment funds, since the model is not open to international capital flows (but see the section on "International Capital Flows," p. 100).

As in the Fullerton, Shoven, and Whalley model, producers in each of 18 industries have fixed requirements of intermediate inputs but can substitute between labor and capital in constant elasticity of substitution (CES) value-added functions.[2] As in Fullerton and Henderson (1989), however, producers react to a marginal cost of capital. They each use a nested CES function to allocate capital between the corporate and noncorporate sectors (or, in housing, between the rental and owner-occupied sectors). The elasticity of substitution between sectors does not affect major points made in this chapter, so it is set to unity for all calculations reported.[3] In a final CES nest, for each sector of each industry, firms allocate capital among up to 38 assets, including 20 types of equipment and 15 types of structures, plus inventories and residential and nonresidential land. The elasticity of substitution among assets is varied in calculations below.

Following Hall and Jorgenson (1967), the cost of capital for each asset in each sector is the marginal pretax return needed to earn the equilibrium posttax return. We assume a 4 percent required real posttax return for the original (1980) equilibrium, a constant 4 percent inflation, no uncertainty, no churning, and sufficient tax liability to use all credits and deductions (but see section on "The Cost of Capital"). We assume all investments are financed one-third by debt and two-thirds by equity (but see section on "The Debt-Equity Ratio). These calculations include the effects of statutory tax rates, investment tax credit rates, particular depreciation rules, and the personal taxation of interest, dividends, and capital gains.

All assets provide the same posttax rate of return, but they must earn different pretax returns or marginal products in order to pay taxes that differ by asset. Differential tax rules thus give rise to interasset distortions. The "double taxation" of corporate source income (especially under the old view) and the nontaxation of imputed net rents in owner-occupied housing mean that capital in different sectors must earn different marginal products, giving rise to intersectoral distortions. Finally, all taxes on capital drive a wedge between the price paid by firms and the return received by savers. Taxes thus raise the price of future consumption and create intertemporal distortions.

To ensure comparability, we wish to abstract entirely from changes in government expenditure. In addition, we wish to concentrate on changes in capital taxes. Thus we make each regime "revenue neutral" relative to 1980 by the imposition of a lump-sum tax or rebate to households, and we omit changes in labor tax rates (but see section on "Other Distortions").

Given behavioral rules and parameters, the model searches for an equilibrium by iterating on a wage rate, a posttax rate of return, and the lump-sum tax (or rebate) needed to maintain real government expenditures. At each iteration the model finds the cost of capital for each asset in each sector and evaluates all demands. Equilibrium is found when the total demand for capital matches its fixed supply for that period, the total demand for labor matches its endogenous supply, and total tax revenue matches government expenditures. To calibrate the model, exogenous substitution parameters and tax rules are used together with a consistent benchmark equilibrium data set to solve for other parameters that allow the model to replicate the benchmark data set as an equilibrium solution. Tax changes then generate alternative sequences of equilibria that are compared to the benchmark by calculating the present value of equivalent variations. The dollar gain is thus the amount that could be paid to consumers that would be "equivalent" in terms of utility to the tax change under consideration.

Key Parameters

There are many assumptions and parameters that influence the results from this model, but three are most important for present purposes. First, the importance of intertemporal effects is related to the prespecified size of the elasticity of saving with respect to the net rate of return. We set this to 0.4 for most calculations but vary it from 0.0 to 0.8 for others.[4]

Second, the importance of interasset effects is related to the elasticity of substitution among assets in production. There is very little evidence on appropriate values for this parameter, so we set it to 1.0 for standard calculations and vary it from 0.0 to 2.0 for comparisons.[5]

Third, given that the 1986 Act increases the capital gains tax while decreasing the personal tax on dividends, the ranking of these reforms depends in an important way on the relative weights given to those two forms of corporate income. Here we distinguish between the "old view" and the "new view." The original distinction between these two views involves the perennial and still unresolved debate about why firms pay dividends. The old view assumes that dividends have some intrinsic value such that dividend tax reductions provide more incentive to invest (McLure 1979). When this intrinsic value is modeled as a reduction in the required rate of return, Poterba and Summers (1985) show that the cost of capital involves a traditional weighted average of the dividend rate and the capital gains rate. The new view assumes that firms face a constraint in their repurchase of shares at the margin, so the dividend tax must eventually be paid. It is therefore capitalized into the value of shares, and firms always rely on retained earnings (dividend reductions) as the marginal source of finance. In this case, the cost of capital depends on the capital gains rate and not on the dividend rate (see Auerbach 1979; Bradford 1981; and King 1977).

The new view has more theoretical appeal, perhaps, but it conflicts with simple observations such as firms that both pay dividends and issue new shares. In addition, the constraints on share repurchases do not seem to bind, as many firms are increasing this activity (Shoven 1987). In empirical tests, Poterba and

Summers (1983) find evidence against the new view, and Auerbach (1984) finds evidence against the old view.

The reason for dividends and the effect of taxes on financial behavior do not concern us in this chapter. We model only the effects of taxes on real investment. The important distinction for our purposes is just the implication for whether dividend taxes affect investment. Formally, in our model, dividend taxes affect incentives only for new share issues. In one set of calculations we assume that new corporate investment is financed in the same proportions as past investment: only 5 percent by new share issues. Because the resulting weight for dividend taxes is so low, we call this the "new view." In the other set of calculations, we assume that marginal corporate equity is evenly divided between retentions and new shares. Dividend taxes are more important, so we call this the "old view." In this case, observed financing is irrelevant because retained earnings may be exhausted; even if retentions are used to finance most observed investment, they may be unavailable to finance a firm's additional investment.

One interpretation is that we are concerned with the number of firms on each margin, and another interpretation is that we distinguish between the old view and the new view. The two interpretations are indistinguishable in this model because they have the same implications for whether dividend taxes affect the cost of capital.

THE EFFECTS OF TAX REFORMS

In 1980, when President Reagan was elected, the top statutory corporate tax rate was 46 percent, and personal rates extended up to 70 percent.[6] Most equipment received a 10 percent investment tax credit, and capital cost recovery periods were based on the Asset Depreciation Range (ADR) system. Besides lowering all personal rates, including the top rate from 70 to 50 percent, the Economic Recovery Tax Act of 1981 expanded the investment tax credit and created the Accelerated Cost Recovery System (ACRS), which shortened all depreciation lifetimes. Table 5.1 shows that the fully phased-in version of this bill would have lowered the cost of capital in the corporate sector from 7.0 to 5.9 percent under the new view (8.5 to 7.0 percent under the old view). ERTA also reduces the overall cost of capital, which includes the noncorporate sector and owner-occupied housing.[7]

To indicate tax differences across sectors or across assets, the table also shows the coefficient of variation of the cost of capital under each tax regime.[8] By reducing the taxation of depreciable assets in the corporate sector, ERTA brought overall corporate taxes more in line with other sectors and consequently reduced slightly the coefficient of variation across sectors. However, ERTA widened the difference between depreciable assets and other assets such as land and inventories.[9] Overall, ERTA has the largest coefficient of variation of the four tax regimes.

Table 5.1
The Cost of Capital and Its Coefficient of Variation for Each Tax Regime

| | Cost of Capital (%) | | Coefficient of Variation | | |
	Corporate Sector	Overall	Across Sectors	Across Corporate Assets	Overall
New View					
1980 Law	7.0	6.3	.10	.25	.21
ERTA 1981	5.9	5.8	.08	.37	.25
1985 Law	6.5	6.1	.09	.25	.20
TRA 1986	7.5	6.5	.09	.07	.14
Old View					
1980 Law	8.5	6.9	.15	.23	.27
ERTA 1981	7.0	6.2	.12	.34	.28
1985 Law	7.7	6.6	.13	.24	.24
TRA 1986	8.0	6.7	.10	.07	.17

Authors' calculations. All terms are defined in the text.

Further changes were enacted each year through 1985. The rate of declining balance for depreciation was reduced, and the depreciation lifetime for structures was increased. In addition, inflation eroded some of the personal rate reduction through bracket creep. By 1985, when brackets were to be indexed, the cost of capital in the corporate sector had risen back up from 5.9 under ERTA to 6.5 percent, using the new view (from 7.0 to 7.7 percent, using the old view). The coefficient of variation across assets fell back from 0.37 to 0.25, as shown in Table 5.1.

The Tax Reform Act of 1986 revamped rules again. Personal tax rates fell to a top marginal rate of 33 percent, and the statutory corporate rate was cut from 46 to 34 percent. The investment tax credit was repealed, and depreciable assets were divided into a larger number of categories intended to reflect differences in economic depreciation. Finally, the 1986 Act repealed the capital gains exclusion. Other provisions have only small effects on the cost of capital (see the section on "Other Provisions").

The table shows that these changes raise the corporate cost of capital from 6.5 to 7.5 percent under the new view, in which cuts in personal taxes on dividends are relatively unimportant (from 7.7 to 8.0 under the old view, in which cuts in dividend taxes are more important). Under the new view the cost of capital is higher than it was in 1980, but under the old view it is lower than in 1980. Under either view, the attempt to "level the playing field" was effective in the sense that the 1986 Act provides coefficients of variation that are lower than those of other tax laws.

General equilibrium results for all tax laws appear in Figures 5.1 through 5.4. The vertical axes show the present value of welfare gains, in 1984 dollars.

Figure 5.1
**The Present Value of Welfare Gains from the 1980 Law Baseline: Saving
Elasticity 0.4, New View**

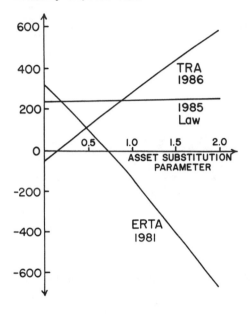

Figure 5.2
**The Present Value of Welfare Gains from the 1980 Law Baseline: Asset
Substitution Parameter 1.0, New View**

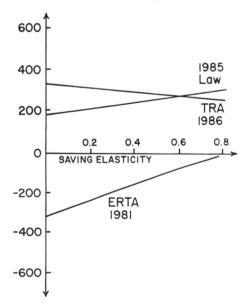

Figure 5.3
The Present Value of Welfare Gains from the 1980 Law Baseline: Saving Elasticity 0.4, Old View

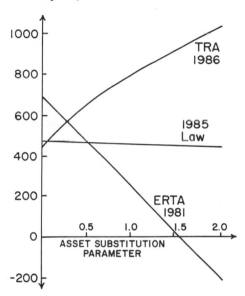

Figure 5.4
The Present Value of Welfare Gains from the 1980 Law Baseline: Asset Substitution Parameter 1.0, Old View

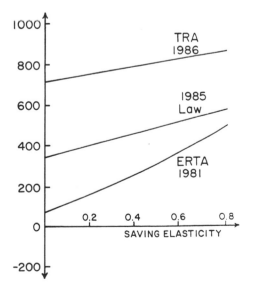

For comparison, each $200 billion of gain represents about 0.2 percent of total welfare, the present value of income plus leisure in the baseline of 1980 law. Figures 5.1 and 5.2 show the new view, while Figures 5.3 and 5.4 show the old view. In contrast, Figures 5.1 and 5.3 set the saving elasticity at 0.4 and vary the elasticity of substitution among assets, while Figures 5.2 and 5.4 set the asset parameter at 1.0 and vary the saving elasticity. These figures can be used to illustrate the following new results:

1. *The 1981 Act does not always generate welfare gains.* In previous studies, such as Fullerton and Henderson (1985), each industry was constrained to use assets in fixed proportions. That model thus captured the intertemporal welfare gains of ERTA but not the interasset welfare losses. Figure 5.1 shows that ERTA does indeed increase welfare when the elasticity of substitution is near zero (as when assets are used in fixed proportions), but intertemporal gains are completely offset if the interasset substitution parameter is 0.7 or greater. Under the old view, in Figure 5.3, ERTA's dividend tax cuts help to keep welfare gains positive until the substitution parameter is more than 1.5. Figures 5.2 and 5.4 show that ERTA's welfare gains increase with the saving elasticity.[10]

2. *It may be convenient to use Cobb-Douglas functional forms when substitution parameters are unknown, but results can be very misleading.* Given the dearth of information about the elasticity of substitution among disaggregate types of equipment and structures, Auerbach (1983) and Gravelle (1981) use the common Cobb-Douglas form. Figure 5.1 shows that the same unit elasticity assumption in this model would favor the efficiency of the level playing field in the Tax Reform Act of 1986. However, a slightly lower value would favor the 1985 tax law, and a still lower value would favor the 1981 Act. These elasticities are all within the range of possible estimates. Despite the apparently definitive results of a Cobb-Douglas model, we do not know which of the three tax regimes has the largest welfare gain.

CONDITIONS FOR CONSISTENCY

We consider consistency in terms of economic efficiency, and we investigate conditions in this model in which the reforms provide successive welfare improvements.[11] Efficiency gains depend on two key elasticity parameters, but a three-dimensional diagram quickly becomes unwieldy. Instead, Figure 5.5 varies the two key parameters under the new view and shows the area over which each reform dominates. ERTA 1981 dominates all other reforms in area A, the 1985 law dominates in area B, and TRA 1986 dominates in area C. Figure 5.6 varies the two key parameters under the old view and shows only the area in which the three reforms generate successive improvements. These figures help demonstrate the following two points:

Figure 5.5
Regions of Efficiency Dominance for Each Tax Regime, New View

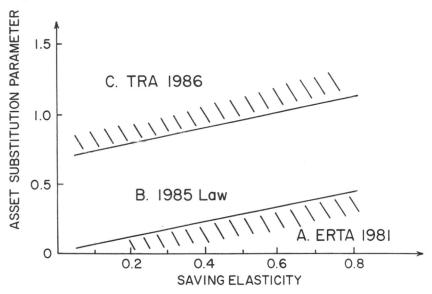

1. *Under the new view, there is no set of parameters for which tax initiatives during the Reagan administration led to successive welfare improvements.* Figure 5.5 confirms that the 1981 Act dominates the other tax regimes, in terms of efficiency, only when the elasticity of substitution among assets is small (for a wide range of values for the intertemporal substitution parameter). The 1985 law dominates when the asset substitution parameter is around 0.5, and the 1986 Act dominates when it is larger. The area in which the 1986 Act dominates is not one of successive improvements, because ERTA always generates welfare losses with this high degree of interasset substitution.

Under the new view, where dividend tax reductions are relatively unimportant, tax changes may seem random. In fact, randomness may cause additional welfare costs (Skinner 1986; Alm 1988) or benefits (Stiglitz 1982; Chang and Wildasin 1986) that are not considered in this chapter. The apparently random changes may arise from shifting political coalitions, despite well-ordered individual preferences.

Even under the new view, however, each change may have been a rational response to available information and consensus views.[12] First, debate in 1980–81 was heavily influenced by the supply-side school of thought, and the consensus view may have held that the saving elasticity was very high. In addition, policymakers may have been uninformed or unconcerned about interasset distortions. Certainly more of the discussion was about capital formation than about level playing fields. Thus ERTA may have been viewed as the highest-ranking reform on efficiency grounds.[13]

Figure 5.6
Region of Sequential Welfare Improvements, Old View

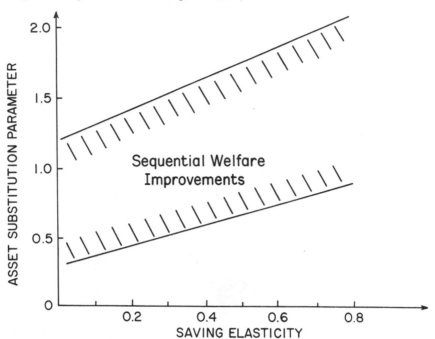

Second, changes in tax law through 1985 might be explained by changes in the actual or perceived importance of these distortions. Discussion of interasset distortions did not begin until Auerbach and Jorgenson (1980), Gravelle (1981), and Hulten and Wykoff (1981b). These papers were among the first to use Hall-Jorgenson-type formulas to calculate differences in the marginal effective tax rates among assets used in production. Also, the February 1982 *Economic Report of the President* included cost-of-capital calculations for different assets and discussion of negative effective tax rates in some industries. This research came too late to affect the 1981 legislation, but may have influenced subsequent changes.[14]

Finally, the policy environment was greatly influenced by stories about tax shelters and safe harbor leasing such as in the report on corporate tax avoidance by the Citizens for Tax Justice (McIntyre and Folen 1984). Indeed, a concern about the ''inequity'' of favoring certain kinds of corporations may have been the only popular support for the more diffuse concern about efficiency in the allocation of resources (e.g., Hendershott 1986). Popular studies may have combined with academic results on interasset distortions to raise the implicitly held elasticity of substitution among assets, making TRA perceived as most efficient.

Similarly, new estimates or other results on intertemporal distortions may have helped change the consensus view about the savings elasticity, moving beliefs in Figure 5.5 from area A, to B, to C.

2. *Under the old view, where dividend taxes matter, continued personal rate reductions led to successive efficiency gains throughout the 1980s for a wide range of parameters in this model.* When the saving elasticity is 0.4, Figure 5.3 shows that there is a wide band of values for the asset-substitution parameter (between 0.5 and 1.5) for which each tax change in the 1980s provides an additional welfare gain. When the asset-substitution parameter is 1.0, Figure 5.4 shows the same result for all values of the saving elasticity. With a systematic variation of both parameters, Figure 5.6 shows that as the savings elasticity is higher, successive improvements occur for a higher range of asset-substitution parameters.

The Figures demonstrate the possibility of a coherent agenda to achieve successive efficiency improvements. In fact, if a significant part of marginal corporate finance is new share issues, then recent tax policy has been consistent by this definition for a wide range of quite reasonable values of the two key elasticities.

This case also sheds some light on the theory of tax reform, which holds that optimal tax changes may result in a tax structure different from that of optimal *de novo* tax design. Feldstein (1976) analyzes a number of different implementation rules, including delayed effective dates to allow time for adjustment, and Zodrow (1981) demonstrates some advantages for immediate enactment of partial reform. If results for the old view are any indication, policymakers may adhere to incremental reform. Moreover, such steps may appear to take different directions. For example, some additional interasset distortions in ERTA may have been a necessary political price of achieving reductions of intertemporal distortions. Changes through 1985 and 1986 may then have addressed the interasset margin while trying to minimize losses on the intertemporal margin.

LIMITATIONS, ASSUMPTIONS, AND
THEIR IMPLICATIONS

This section reviews particular assumptions in the model, and discusses their importance for the results just obtained.

Saving and Wealth

Consumer saving reacts to the relative price of present and future consumption, an expected price that depends on the current net rate of return in this model. Saving during the transition might be less responsive if we were to replace these myopic expectations with perfect foresight, as in the multi-period overlapping generations model of Auerbach and Kotlikoff (1987). However, expectations do not affect the steady state in which relative prices are no longer changing. Ballard and Goulder (1985) allow variable foresight and find only moderate effects on present value welfare. We also ignore the effect of the interest rate on the present value of labor income. This wealth effect of Summers (1981) changes the responsiveness of saving, so its impact can be captured by altering the saving elasticity, as in our Figures 5.2 and 5.4.

International Capital Flows

We use a closed economy for simplicity, but we can see the effects of mobile capital in results of others. Mutti and Grubert (1985) and Goulder and Eichengreen (1988) show effects on savings, investment, and trade, but Goulder, Shoven, and Whalley (1983) include efficiency calculations similar to those of ours. Business tax cuts (like the 1981 Act) can have greater gains by attracting foreign capital that earns a marginal product greater than the net rate of return it is paid. Saving incentives can have negative effects by encouraging domestic saving to flow abroad.

The Cost of Capital

We assume that the asset is held forever, but Gordon, Hines, and Summers (1987) show that investors could sell a building, pay the capital gains tax, increase the basis for the new owner's depreciation, and pay less total tax. Churning can reduce the effective tax rate, narrow the difference between structures and equipment, and thus decrease the gain from a more level playing field. However, Gravelle (1987) indicates that the net effects on the cost of capital are small and depend on transactions costs. Also, we assume that firms can use all credits and deductions. Effects of uncertainty and imperfect loss offsets are discussed in Auerbach (1986). Finally, we exclude intangible capital that arises from advertising, research, and development. Summers (1987) suggests that the inclusion of these tax-favored assets would reduce the gain from removing the tax-favored status of equipment, but Fullerton and Lyon (1988) show that the 1986 Act still provides efficiency gains by reducing the effective tax rate on other assets, such as structures, land, and inventories.

The Debt/Equity Ratio

We assume the same financing for all assets. Gordon, Hines, and Summers (1987) note that structures might use more debt and thus have an effective tax rate that does not exceed equipment, but they provide no evidence on actual financing. Results in Gravelle (1987) support the assumption of equal financing.

Other Distortions

We ignore externalities, monopoly power, and other tax distortions such as in debt/equity ratios, dividend payout behavior, realization decisions, and the allocation of risk-bearing. The 1986 Act may have reduced some of these other distortions, especially by reducing statutory tax rates. The cost of noncompliance may also fall with rate reduction. In addition, there exist alternative models of the distortion between the corporate and noncorporate sectors (e.g., Gravelle and Kotlikoff 1989). Finally, we concentrate on capital taxation and abstract from labor tax distortions. Both the 1981 Act and the 1986 Act reduced personal rates on labor, but this issue is complicated by the implications of increased deficits for future personal rates. In any case, we have more simultaneous distortions than any other model, including those between assets, among sectors, and over time.

Other Provisions

The model includes all major tax provisions as well as considerable disaggregation and detail such as the half-year convention, the half-basis adjustment, LIFO inventory accounting, and noncorporate taxes. We ignore some specific provisions, however, such as the minimum tax, passive loss rules, and accounting changes in 1986. Lyon 1989 provides a full discussion of the minimum tax, and Fullerton, Gillette, and Mackie (1987) show that some of these other provisions have a very small effect on the cost of capital even though they raised noticeable revenue in the five-year budget period.

CONCLUDING REMARKS

Clearly, tax policy is not driven by any single criterion such as the measure of economic efficiency used in this chapter. Indeed, decisions are not made by any single political agent. The different policymakers in this process place different relative weights on revenue considerations, distributional effects, noneconomic objectives, and, perhaps, economic efficiency. The limited purpose of this chapter is to investigate how the last of these considerations may have affected tax policy decisions since 1980.

We employ a detailed general equilibrium model of the U.S. economy and tax system to evaluate the efficiency effects of recent tax law changes. This model is capable of second-best analysis of simultaneous distortions in households' saving decisions, firms' sectoral location decisions, and producers' asset-combination decisions. This simultaneity is important for analyzing the particular reforms considered here, but it may come at the expense of a better model for each distortion considered separately. Although this model is comprehensive, it is not without limitations. It adopts particular assumptions, for example, that there are no adjustment costs, noncompetitive behaviors, or distortions other than taxes.

One does not need to accept all the assumptions of the model, however, to follow the logic of the interpretations. With the new view that taxes on dividends are relatively unimportant, recent tax reforms appear inconsistent. Advocates of the Economic Recovery Tax Act of 1981 may have knowingly exacerbated interasset distortions in order to reduce intertemporal distortions, and subsequent legislation may have been a rational response to new information or to a new consensus about the relative importance of those distortions. Alternatively, in the old view, in which dividend taxes matter, these reforms may have been part of a coherent plan to achieve greater economic efficiency through incremental tax reform.

NOTES

We are grateful for helpful suggestions from Alan Auerbach, Jane Gravelle, Yolanda Henderson, Charles Hulten, William Johnson, James Poterba, Jonathan Skinner, and anonymous referees. The research reported here is part of the National Bureau of Economic Research's research program in taxation. Any opinions expressed are those of the authors and not those of the National Bureau of Economic Research or of the U.S. Treasury.

1. The saving elasticity is used to calculate the model's elasticity of substitution between present and future consumption, which is then fixed for simulations of alternative policies.

2. The model also assumes perfect competition, perfect mobility, perfect information, no externalities, and no involuntary unemployment.

3. No evidence is available on the elasticity of substitution between sectors. Indeed, little is known about the incorporation decisions of firms. The CES function is intended only as a representation of that decision, and of the possibility that taxes affect it.

4. Boskin's (1978) saving elasticity is about 0.4, but Howry and Hymans's (1978) estimate is near zero. Ballard et al. (1985) review these and other estimates.

5. Berndt and Christensen (1973) found a high elasticity of substitution between equipment and structures, but Mohr (1980) disputes their finding. These and other estimates are reviewed in Hulten and Wykoff (1981a) and Mackie (1985). Our elasticity of substitution among 38 assets has never been estimated.

6. For each tax law, the Treasury's individual tax file of 90,000 households was used to calculate the weighted-average personal marginal rate on interest receipts, dividends, capital gains, noncorporate business income, and mortgage interest deductions. Fullerton, Gillette, and Mackie (1987) report these rates and show that they are modified to account for taxes at the state level, the taxation of banks, insurance companies, and the holdings of tax-exempt institutions.

7. All calculations refer to the fully phased-in version of each law. Our model does not capture uncertainty about tax law changes, or the fact that these laws were never fully phased in. We only compare hypothetical cases in which each law is enacted and retained.

8. Coefficients of variation do not substitute for efficiency calculations reported below, but they might help anticipate and explain them.

9. The accelerated depreciation in ERTA may have been intended to offset the effects of high inflation. At our 4 percent inflation rate, however, the combination of the investment tax credit and ACRS means that equipment investment actually receives a net subsidy at the corporate level.

10. Note that ERTA has the largest revenue losses and lump sum tax replacement of any simulation; thus even these reduced efficiency gains may be overstated.

11. Because we use equivalent variations, results are transitive in the sense that the difference between the welfare gains of two reforms represents the welfare gain in baseline prices of moving from one reform to the other.

12. This discussion presumes that all three analyzed tax regimes were available as options in 1981, as, implicitly, they were. Explicitly, in fact, debate at the time included consideration of the Auerbach-Jorgenson (1980) first-year recovery system, a proposal to provide economic depreciation at replacement cost. Although a major point of that proposal was to remove the effects of inflation, its results in this model would look very similar to those of the 1986 legislation because we do not consider varying inflation.

13. Substitution elasticities are generally high in the supply-side view, however, and ERTA would reduce welfare with a high asset-substitution elasticity.

14. New rules in 1982 were set up specifically to prevent negative effective tax rates, as is clear from the Joint Tax Committee's *General Explanation* of the Tax Equity and Fiscal Responsibility Act of 1982 (pp. 35–40).

"Two Revolutions in Economic Policy" and "Economic Efficiency in Recent Tax Reform History": *Comment*

Ronald C. Fisher

Chapter 5 by Fullerton and Mackie and Chapter 4 by Meyer, Prakken, and Varvares center on four questions, which are also convenient for structuring my comments: Was the change in tax policy direction between 1981 and 1986 beneficial? Why did that change occur? What was the relationship between tax policy and monetary policy then and now? Finally, what is the long-run policy legacy of the Reagan tax changes?

There was clearly a substantial change in tax policy direction between 1981, when lowered marginal tax rates were accompanied by very uneven investment incentives in an attempt to spur supply-side growth, and 1986, when lowered and substantially flatter tax rates were tied to a broader and more uniform tax base. Was the change beneficial? The analytical part of the Fullerton and Mackie chapter provides the interesting, useful, and detailed results that arise from computational general-equilibrium tax analysis. In this model, Fullerton and Mackie have intertemporal, intersectoral, and interasset substitutions, although they focus on the tradeoff between the intertemporal and interasset substitutions. Except for the case of essentially a zero asset-substitution parameter—that is, no asset substitution at all—the 1986 Tax Reform Act always produces positive welfare gains, and for most of the tested parameters, welfare gains greater than from the 1981 Act. Indeed, under certain values of parameters the 1981 Act was actually a worsening of the situation. Fullerton and Mackie also show that for a reasonable set of parameters there were consistent improvements in economic efficiency over time from the tax changes. It is worth noting that they focus only on the capital market effects and do not allow for labor supply changes from the decrease in marginal tax rates, which presumably underestimates the gains from the 1986 Act.

That issue raises a question. Why were the policies embodied in the 1986

Tax Reform Act not adopted initially, thereby avoiding the inefficiencies caused by the uneven investment incentives and asset substitutions that resulted from the 1981 tax changes? One possible answer is that many of the changes adopted in 1981 were never intended. As control of the political process evaporated, the 1981 tax bill went well beyond the initially intended supply-side tax cuts. David Stockman (1986) has suggested that a trillion dollar package of liberalized depreciation and other "ornaments" was added to buy a trillion dollar supply-side tax cut. If one takes the point of view that the 1981 changes were not what the Reagan administration intended, but the result of a political process out of control, then there may not have been any change in perception or belief about the kind of tax policy to follow. The experience in 1981 did provide important information about structuring the process differently in 1986, and perhaps that is partly why revenue neutrality became an assumption in 1986.

A second possible answer, suggested by Fullerton and Mackie, is that individuals changed their opinions about the importance of intertemporal versus interasset substitutability in these years, partly because of the academic research that was going on and partly because of the political ramifications of firms using the incentives in various conspicuous ways solely to reduce taxes, sometimes to zero. In contrast, I believe that rather than people changing beliefs, it was more a case of changing people who always held different beliefs. The individuals holding tax policy positions changed substantially from 1981 to 1986 and I suspect that many of the new people (such as Charles McLure and others) had a different point of view from the beginning, essentially an appreciation for the Haig-Simons concept of the uniform income tax.

Interestingly, Henry Simons provided an efficiency argument in support of uniform taxation. Simons (1938: 231–24) wrote that

The system [his uniform income tax] would tend to alter as little as possible the course which would have been followed, if there had been no such taxes, in commercial and financial and in the management and distribution of private wealth. . . . It would minimize the diseconomies arising from the continuous and disturbing enactment of stopgap expedients for dealing with the inventions of tax-avoidance specialists.

I think these opinions are generally supported by the simulations of Fullerton and Mackie. It is not clear whether the experience with the 1981 Act and the resulting economic research led people to rediscover these opinions or whether previously held support of this position came to the fore.

Turning now to the Meyer, Prakken, and Varvares chapter, what about the macroeconomic implications of the relationship between tax and monetary policy? They use simulations of the Washington University Macroeconomic Model to analyze various combinations of tax, expenditure, and monetary policy in the Reagan years. One important simulation includes an increase in government expenditure with an offsetting change in monetary policy—a decline in the money supply. The result is an increase in interest rates and a resulting reduction in capital and long-run growth. The assumption is that increasing government expenditures reduce national output through a capital market effect, because of the higher interest rates resulting from the accommodating monetary policy.

Although this effect is part of the theory underlying the Washington model, it may not be consistent with the capacity problems and recession that existed in the 1981–83 period. But this viewpoint leads Meyer and his colleagues to the conclusion that an alternative policy mix would have been preferable. What they propose and simulate is avoidance of an increase in expenditures coupled with an increase in the money supply. Essentially, the simulations suggest that a reduction in tax rates without a planned reduction in revenue or an increase in spending along with monetary growth would have provided better long-run economic effects.

The concern with this policy mix is in what happens to the value of the dollar and domestic inflation. Indeed, the dollar does decline, but in the simulations domestic values are reported in real terms. If marginal tax rates are reduced and at the same time expansionary monetary policy is pursued, it seems to me that there is substantial danger of increasing inflation. Certainly at the present time (1989), that is the policy concern. And I suspect that was a major reason why an expansionary monetary growth/low interest rate policy was not pursued by the administration then.

What is the legacy of these Reagan tax changes overall? First, the tax structure has lower marginal rates, a broader base, and a number of the very poor completely out of the system. Those changes generally have been matched by the states. The states have lowered marginal tax rates on individuals, followed the broader federal tax base, and increased exemptions. Second, I think there has been a change in attitudes about the use of tax incentives. We have come to understand that tax incentives are often not as effective as some believed and that there can be severe problems with the nonuniformity that results from their use. Regardless of preference for a consumption or income tax, the emphasis on the value of uniformity that Henry Simons seemed to understand 50 years ago has been strengthened. The third aspect of the legacy is the budget deficit, which resulted partly from the loss of control of the tax reform process in 1981. The deficit has proved to be remarkably stubborn, and the question and danger is whether the tax structure changes from the Reagan era will survive the solution to the deficit problem.

6

The Reagan Economic Performance

Thomas Gale Moore

The performance of the U.S. economy under Ronald Reagan was excellent. Unemployment was and remains very low; growth has been robust. Contrast that with 1981, when Ronald Reagan came into office. At that time the inflation rate was 12 percent; the prime rate was 21 percent. Productivity growth was anemic; government spending and taxes were rising sharply. Reagan proposed a four-point program, dubbed ''supply-side economics,'' of lower marginal tax rates, smaller government spending, reduced regulation, and slower monetary growth to reduce inflation.

The idea was not simply to cut tax rates, but to lower marginal tax rates, which is quite different from cutting intramarginal tax rates. Reducing marginal tax rates was designed to encourage investment, savings, work, and additional growth. Reagan had success in each of the four areas, but more success in lowering marginal tax rates than in the others.

The supply-side tax cut initiative was not a new idea, though much of the media portrayed it as such. In fact, one of the chapters included in this volume talks about the Kennedy cuts. To go back further in history, Andrew Mellon, Secretary of the Treasury in the 1920s, engineered a series of tax cuts, reducing the top tax rate from 73 to 25 percent. The result was that during the 1920s, the U.S. economy grew vigorously while European economies largely stagnated, because they retained high marginal tax rates instituted during World War I.

In the first half of the 1960s, Kennedy, followed by President Johnson, reduced the top marginal tax rate from 91 to 70 percent. The economy during the 1960s boomed. A drop from 91 to 70 percent doesn't sound significant, but it meant that investors and workers were able to keep 30 cents instead of 9 cents of the marginal dollar; to put it in another way, the return from a marginal dollar increased 233 percent.

Ronald Reagan did almost as well as Andrew Mellon. President Reagan reduced the rate from 70 to 28 percent—a substantial cut. As a result, a high-income worker and investor now keeps 72 cents out of the marginal dollar rather than the 30 cents of 1980. Moreover, corporate rates have been reduced from 46 percent to 34 percent, yielding a 35 percent increase in the after-tax net profit.

Reagan's proposals to reduce government spending were less successful. His proposed cuts were largely ignored, except during his first year. Federal spending grew throughout most of his two terms. However, as a percentage of GNP, federal spending reached a peak in 1983. In 1987, for the first time in over a decade, real government spending actually declined. As a consequence, Reagan can claim a modest success in lowering spending and more success in reducing the rate of spending.

The third element of his program, deregulation, continued the Carter administration successes. As a student of the regulation-deregulation issue, I have been unhappy that Reagan did not reduce regulation more. Much more should have been deregulated. Transportation deregulation was continued, although further deregulation was only supported in the last term and without success. One of the first acts of the President was to remove controls over oil; instead of oil prices going up, they came down. He tried to eliminate the regulation of natural gas, but was not successful while in office. Natural gas was finally deregulated in 1989. The government did reduce regulation of the financial markets, but again, did not go far enough.

The result of the Reagan program, which was widely predicted to fail, has been the longest peacetime economic expansion since the United States began keeping records, that is since 1854. It is one of the most impressive economic performances in U.S. history. If growth is continuing today, as of January 1990, the economy is in its eighty-sixth month of continuous expansion—a very long expansion period.

Since 1982, the economy has added approximately 20 million new nonagricultural jobs. Recently, U.S. unemployment has been hovering around 5 percent—considerably lower than the lowest unemployment level under Jimmy Carter or Gerald Ford. European unemployment has been consistently higher. Traditionally, in the 1960s and 1970s European unemployment levels were well below those of the United States. In the 1980s, U.S. unemployment was considerably lower than European. Only recently has the German unemployment level reached 8 percent, still well above ours. Today the highest percent of our working-age population in history is employed.

There are several myths connected with this expansion. The first is that these jobs are dead-end, McDonald's-type hamburger-flipping jobs. That just isn't true. Two-thirds of the new employment is in the highest paid occupations:

managerial, professional, and technical. Only 12 percent are in low-skilled jobs. Eighty-five percent of the new full-time jobs pay more than $20,000 a year.

The second myth is that the United States is deindustrializing. This belief is also untrue. While employment in manufacturing has remained flat, real manufacturing output has grown and, as a percentage of GNP, has remained relatively constant at around 22–23 percent. Recently, real manufacturing output as a percentage of GNP has been at its highest level since 1960.

Manufacturing output is up 46 percent in this expansion, 30 percent since early 1979. Real total output is up more than 20 percent over this period of time. Manufacturing productivity has been growing at a 4.4 percent annual rate—one and a half times higher than the historical average. The assertion that productivity is not growing is untrue for manufacturing. Overall productivity includes services in which productivity has been stagnating. However, manufacturing productivity, the sector that competes with the rest of the world, has been growing very fast. Together with modest wage growth and the decline in the dollar against the yen and European currencies, U.S. manufacturing has become highly competitive in the world market. U.S. labor costs, relative to European and Japanese, are lower than at any time since 1980.

While the economy has expanded strongly, inflation has not resurged. In the early 1980s, when President Reagan first proposed tax cuts, many economists predicted that inflation would be rekindled. During the Carter administration, whenever an expansion occurred, inflation shot up. In 1979, as the economy expanded, prices rose over 13 percent. In 1980, another year of growth, prices rose over 12 percent. Since 1982 inflation has averaged about 4 percent. Some years have been a little bit lower, some years a little bit higher. Unfortunately, inflation appears to be picking up. Last year (1989), prices rose nearly 5 percent, still substantially lower than during the Carter administration.

The government faces two policy problems: the twin deficits. In this volume many of the contributing authors have discussed the fiscal and/or trade deficit.

The fiscal deficit appears on the surface to be too large. However, it has declined by one-third since 1986, when it reached $221 billion. The deficit last year (1989) was approximately $152 billion. Unfortunately, for the last few years, the fiscal deficit seems to have stalled at around $150 to $160 billion.

The importance of this deficit can be exaggerated. David Stockman, Reagan's first director of the Office of Management and Budget, claimed that deficits in 1981 through 1986 were going to ruin the economy.[1] If we continued at the same rate, the United States would either have a deep depression, or high inflation, or both. Martin Feldstein, chairman of the Council of Economic Advisors, made the same kind of prediction in 1984.[2] Since Stockman's and Feldstein's predictions, five to eight years of strong, low-inflationary growth have elapsed. Catastrophe predictions must be taken with a very large dose of salt.

Moreover, the fiscal deficit, when measured carefully, is really not so big or so important. First, most other countries have a single central government budget for all activities. Therefore, for comparison purposes, and in order to know how much governments are borrowing from the savings stream, state and local surpluses should be combined with the federal deficit. State and local surpluses have been about $50 billion in recent years. Adding these surpluses to the federal deficit, which is roughly $150 billion, yields a government deficit of about $100 billion, not $150.

The federal government has over two trillion dollars of debt outstanding in the hands of the public. The interest on that debt in 1989 was nearly $170 billion, more than the entire fiscal deficit. Much of that interest is paid to compensate bond holders for the loss in value that their bonds suffered due to inflation. If the inflation rate is about 5 percent, then 5 percent of $2.2 trillion is $110 billion. In other words, the government is taxing bond holders by about $110 billion a year due to inflation. The government then repays them $110 billion dollars in higher interest. Thus, if inflation is taken into account the government deficit is approximately zero.

Let me make the point another way. If the real debt of the United States is not increasing, is there a deficit? In real terms, there would be no increase in the burden on future taxpayers from the deficit. Moreover, as the GNP grows, the burden as percent of income declines.

The fact is that the nominal federal deficit and the total government deficit are falling, as a percentage of GNP. The federal deficit has fallen from 6.1 percent of GNP in 1983 to 2.9 percent in 1989. Today the total deficit, including state and local surpluses, is around 2 percent of GNP, which makes it lower than the average deficit of Organization for Economic Cooperation and Development countries. Many other countries have larger deficits in relation to their economy than does the United States. The current federal deficit as a percentage of GNP is well below the deficits of many other industrialized countries.

Many in Washington want the public to believe the deficit is important because they have other agendas. The Republicans want to stress the deficit as a lever to reduce government spending. The Democrats stress the deficit in order to build a case for higher taxes; more taxes means that more can be spent. Consequently, Washington politicians are in a conspiracy to emphasize the catastrophic size of the deficit. However, there have been six years of these deficits and the sky has not fallen.

Both Ronald Reagan and George Bush (the latter until 1990) resisted raising taxes for two good reasons. First, higher taxes, especially income taxes, would undoubtedly slow the economy. Such taxes might easily drive the economy into a recession. Moreover, higher taxes would simply mean more domestic spending, and not a reduction in the deficit. With the Gramm-Rudman-Hollings target, an increase in revenue would lead to more spending, with the deficit remaining at the target. Therefore a $20 billion increase in revenue would simply result in a $20 billion increase in domestic spending.

The other major problem that both the Reagan and Bush administrations have had to deal with is the trade deficit. The trade deficit is largely the result of macroeconomic forces, the U.S. savings and investment imbalance. Total national savings are much lower than U.S. investment, partly as a result of the government deficit, which subtracts from national savings. Until the fiscal deficit is eliminated, the United States will be unable to cure its trade deficit.

However, the significance of the trade deficit can be grossly exaggerated. If the imported savings are being invested productively in the United States, they will generate the earnings to pay foreign investors.

Throughout most of the nineteenth century, the United States imported vast amounts of capital. Our railroad system was built with British capital. Foreign investment during the nineteenth century changed the United States from a simple agricultural society to an industrial giant.

Many commentators have expressed alarm about the United States becoming a net debtor nation. Commerce Department numbers indicate that the United States is the world's largest debtor nation; the difference between U.S.-owned assets abroad and foreign-owned assets is about half a trillion dollars. However, these numbers are very shaky and not much confidence should be placed in them.

In 1988, the last year for which there are data, the United States earned more in interest and dividends from its investments abroad than it paid in interest and dividends on foreign investment at home. It is the flow of payments that is important. Properly measured, our investments abroad must still be larger than foreign investments in the United States. The United States may become a debtor nation but it is not one now.

The major problem with the trade deficit is political. A large trade deficit generates protectionist sentiments and provides a rationale for protectionists to argue for greater trade barriers. Protectionism is unduly popular in Washington. The trade bill, passed in 1988 and signed reluctantly by Ronald Reagan, is protectionist. The worst economic performance of Ronald Reagan's administration was the increase in trade barriers. Reagan was under tremendous pressure from Congress to provide protection. Supporters of trade barriers argued that if the administration would not provide help, Congress would do worse. I was never convinced by this argument. When Reagan stood up against protectionism, for example, in vetoing the textile bill twice, he was sustained twice. I believe he could have sustained other vetoes. Nevertheless, while a number of officials in the Reagan administration, including the CEA, urged a veto of the 1988 trade bill, the President decided that he could not sustain a veto and that he could offset the protectionist provisions by careful interpretation.

The trade bill included many sections that will have the ultimate effect of closing our markets. The most blatant, called Super 301, requires that the U.S. trade representative identifies countries that have a practice of unfair trade. The President then has a period of time to negotiate with the offending country to remove the barriers. If the President is unsuccessful, the administration must retaliate or explain why retaliation is not in the national interest. In June, Carla

Hills, the trade representative, identified the three countries of Japan, Brazil, and India. Japan was included because Congress informed the administration that it intended to have Japan identified.

A case can be made that Japan has done more to reduce trade barriers in the 1980s than has the United States or Europe. In fact, U.S. protection has been increasing while Japanese border controls have declined. Nevertheless, the trade representative had to identify Japan. In order that Japan would not stand alone, Carla Hills named Brazil and India as well. Brazil actually has followed a very protectionist policy. These countries have said that they would not negotiate with the Untied States under Super 301. Unless our negotiations can claim success, the Bush administration will have to retaliate against Japan, India, and Brazil, which will be costly to U.S. consumers.

The trade bill also included a provision for examining whether past trade agreements were being fulfilled. The Congress was particularly concerned with agreements dealing with telecommunication. In the early months of the Bush administration, the United States accused Japan of not living up to an agreement on telecommunication. On my last day at the Council of Economic Advisers, I represented the CEA at the White House Economic Policy Council meeting with the President. Carla Hills argued that the Japanese had violated a contract on telecommunications.

I pointed out to the President that most people would not call this a contract. Our officials wrote them letters; they wrote us letters. There was never a piece of paper that both sides signed, and there was never agreement in their letters to what we said in our letters. We have, in fact, said certain things in our letters that they did not live up to, but they have never agreed in writing to live up to them. Is that an agreement? It certainly was not a contract.

Under the threat of sanctions, the Japanese agreed to permit Motorola to provide cellular service throughout Tokyo and its surrounding regions. While this was a good result, the fact is that such successes encourage more threats and more potential retaliations.

The other worrisome aspect of the trade deficit is that the public has become concerned about foreign ownership of assets in the United States. Some states are even prohibiting foreigners from buying farm land. What do they fear? Will a Japanese owner of a farm dig it up and take it back to Tokyo?

Over the next few years, trade issues are probably going to dominate economic policy. Tax policy will not be subject to significant changes. Regulatory policy is likely to become more restrictive rather then less; we've already seen a little of that in terms of requiring greater gas mileage for new cars, and more stringent air pollution standards. The Bush administration wants to appear more environmentally sensitive. Since the budget deficit prevents the government from spending more, regulation will be extended to force the private sector to invest more in pollution control. Notwithstanding Bush's "read my lips" pledge, these regulations are effectively a tax.

In conclusion, it is difficult to be very optimistic about the immediate future.

The United States is liable to become more protectionist and more regulatory. A significant slowdown, even a recession, in the economy is possible while inflation, unfortunately, will not decline. However, even though I am an economist, I cannot read the future, so maybe we will be lucky. Maybe we will just muddle through. In any case, this volume is on Reagan's economic performance and apart from trade policy, I find it difficult to think of how to improve on that.

NOTES

1. See Stockman (1986) and Greider (1981).
2. See Feldstein (March and December 1984).

Part III

Deregulation and the Free-Market Ideology

7

The Reagan Regulatory Regime: Reality vs. Rhetoric

Peter J. Boettke

The Reagan presidency surely promised more than it delivered in terms of regulatory relief. Despite the rhetoric, the Reagan administration did little to turn back the role of the state in economic activity. For those who believe in the efficacy of the free market and the ideals of limited government, the Reagan years represent merely frustration and missed opportunities—the embodiment of the triumph of politics over principle.

I will not in this short chapter repeat the arguments for deregulation of economic activity or the case for limited government. Rather, I wish to summarize briefly the events in economic theory over the past 25 years that provided the intellectual justification for the implementation of such a program of limited government.[1] In addition, I hope to offer an explanation of why such opportunities were not acted on successfully during an administration that as outwardly predisposed to such efforts. If anything, the Reagan years should demonstrate to us the difficulty of shifting the basic organizational structure of any political economy toward a reduced involvement of the state.

THE PRODUCTION AND DISTRIBUTION OF IDEAS IN SOCIETY

Ideas have consequences. History has been, and continues to be, shaped by ideas. John Maynard Keynes perhaps summed it up best when he wrote:

The ideas of economists and political philosophers, both when they are right and when they are wrong, are more powerful than is commonly understood. Indeed the world is ruled by little else. Practical men, who believe themselves to be quite exempt from any intellectual influences, are usually the slaves of some defunct economist. Madmen in authority, who hear voices in the air, are distilling their frenzy from some academic scribbler of a few years back. (1936: 383)

The question we must address, however, is how ideas are produced and distributed in society. Does policy follow ideas or do ideas follow policy? Ideas, I believe, can be fruitfully viewed as the social capital stock in a society and as such can be analyzed from the perspective of capital theory.

It takes time for ideas to be produced and distributed. The production of abstract ideas is a roundabout process of production. F. A. Hayek (1967) has addressed aspects of the distilling of ideas in society in his analysis of the intellectuals and socialism. Hayek focuses his analysis on what could be termed the intellectual pyramid in society, with academic specialists occupying the top, other traders of ideas occupying lower levels, and the public representing the base. This formulation can easily be represented within a capital structure framework.

The production of higher-order ideas, or ideas more remote from final consumption, takes place within the universities and is supported by the charitable foundations or government agencies that invest in this research. These ideas are filtered down, through the academic journals, seminars, books, and lectures, to the "think tanks," which take the latest developments and formulate possible public policy statements from them. Think tanks, such as Brookings, American Enterprise Institute, Heritage Foundation, and CATO, do not create ideas but transform abstract academic ideas into public policy research in a manner similar to the factory that turns iron ore into steel.

The results from these public policy studies are then filtered down to the media through newspaper columns, editorial pages, and radio or television appearances. Through media coverage, then, these ideas will exert influence directly on politicians and the public, who rely almost exclusively on the media for information concerning public policy. The political dissemination of ideas is also aided by public interest lobby groups or citizens' groups. These two groups, the media and citizens' groups, are like a car salesman who is trying to sell a car that was produced by Chrysler, which depended on steel that was made from iron ore. Without the iron ore, though, the salesman would not have much of a car to sell.

Prior to the Reagan administration much "new thinking" had developed on the economic front—higher-quality iron ore was being found. In addition, several think tanks had established themselves throughout the late 1970s and early 1980s to transform this iron ore into workable steel. As Martha Derthick and Paul J. Quirk (1985: 36) argue in their work on the deregulation movement:

We are convinced that except for the development of this academic critique of policy, the reforms we are trying to explain would never have occurred; yet for the reforms to become possible, the academic critique had to cease being merely academic and enter into the stream of policy discussion in official Washington. That this happened is largely accounted for by three circumstances. First, the critique was taken up by precisely those organizations—foundations and policy-oriented research institutions—that specialize in linking social science analysis to public policy formation. Second, economists entered public service in large enough numbers, and in offices sufficiently influential and strategically placed, to constitute an important force for advocacy within the government. And, finally, several elements of the executive branch were disposed to promote pro-competitive policies.

INTELLECTUAL JUSTIFICATION

Over the past 25 years there has been growing dissatisfaction among economists with the standard model of competitive equilibrium and the policy implications derived from that model. While very few economists would go as far as to challenge the idea of market failure itself, it has become standard practice to recognize the possibility of government failure in the attempted solution of the problem.[2] The traditional market failure theory, sometimes referred to as "normative analysis as positive theory" (NPT), viewed government intervention as if it were being introduced by a benevolent dictator.

While the 1960s saw the dominance of this NPT approach in policy, among academic circles the theory was being increasingly challenged, by thinkers like Armen Alchian, James Buchanan, Ronald Coase, Harold Demsetz, G. Warren Nutter, George Stigler, and Gordon Tullock in such journals as *The Journal of Political Economy* and *The Journal of Law and Economics*. The more philosophical works of F. A. Hayek, *Constitution of Liberty* (1960), Ludwig von Mises, *Liberalism* (1962), and Milton Friedman, *Capitalism and Freedom* (1962) should also be mentioned as offering sustained challenges to the prevailing opinion of government intervention.

By the 1970s, with the development of the property rights school, public choice economics, and the economic theory of regulation, along with the debacle of the Nixon administration and the apparent failure of the Keynesian system, a romantic vision of politics was no longer intellectually in vogue (see Buchanan 1989). The public-choice school had provided a theory of government failure that existed side-by-side with the theory of market failure. The development of the economic theory of regulation had provided a cogent explanation of the regulatory behavior we witnessed, pointing out the strategic use of government by business to capture monopoly rents.[3] And the development of rent-seeking theory by public-choice scholars, such as Gordon Tullock and Robert Tollison, complemented the Chicago studies on political economy.[4]

But these ideas were not limited to the journals or scholarly books; they filtered down into popular textbooks such as Alchian and Allen, *Exchange and Production;* Gwartney and Stroup, *Economics: Private and Public Choice;* Heyne, *Economic Way of Thinking;* Ekelund and Tollison, *Economics;* Dolan, *Economics;* and Arnold, *Economics.* It represented a revolution not only in economic thinking, but also in economic education (see DiLorenzo 1987).[5]

These economic ideas, along with an increasing tax burden, high inflation and high unemployment, created the background and atmosphere for the Reagan revolution. Reagan was a self-avowed conservative ideologue who wished to roll back big government.

REALITY VS. RHETORIC

The administration came to power in January 1981 promising "a far-reaching program of regulatory relief." By January 22 a task force on regulatory relief was formed with Vice-President Bush chairing the effort. On January 28 many pending regulations were suspended for 60 days to permit review by the new administration and remaining price controls on oil were eliminated. Regulatory review was to be centralized in the OMB Office of Information and Regulatory Affairs (OIRA). James Miller and Murray Weidenbaum designed the original agenda for deregulation and were appointed to key positions— Miller as head of OIRA and Weidenbaum as head of the CEA.

Yet despite such a well-placed group of committed deregulators, all the Reagan team can claim is that it *slowed* the growth of federal regulatory spending.[6] No overall victory for deregulation can be claimed of the Reagan years. Regulatory expenditure increased more than 21 percent (in real terms) between the 1981 budget and the 1990 budget (see Warren and Chilton 1989). The administration's attempt to rein in the federal regulatory establishment died by 1984 and the growth in federal regulatory program resumed between 1985 and 1990. This can be show in the federal regulatory staffing figures: 119,000 in 1980, down to 101,000 in 1985, but up again to 107,000 in 1990 (ibid.).

The task force in regulatory relief was disbanded in August 1983 as the Reagan momentum toward real change lost out to political expediency. As William Niskanen has argued,

The Reagan program of regulatory relief promised more than it delivered. The failure to achieve a substantial reduction in or reform of federal regulations, building on the considerable momentum established during the Carter administration, was the major missed opportunity of the initial Reagan program. (1988: 115)

The reason for the failure to grasp the opportunity is a confirmation of the very theory that created the opportunity in the first place.[7] The administration proposed few changes in the basic regulatory legislation and it succumbed to political commitments toward those who had supplied votes and campaign contributions, particularly construction, maritime, and trucking unions, among others. As Robert Higgs (1987: 255–56) points out:

After the first few hectic months, when the administration wielded the preponderance of power, politics as usual began to reassert itself. Offended constituencies rallied their troops, who dug in for a long battle or counterattacked. . . . So the heralded Reagan

Revolution fizzled. In part it failed because the administration never had a strong commitment to fundamental change in the first place. . . . Virtually the entire hodgepodge, described by Stockman as a "coast-to-coast patchwork of dependencies, shelters, protections, and redistributions that the nation's politicians had brokered over the decades," remained intact. Political expediency reigned as supreme as ever.

A major problem with the Reagan administration was that the emphasis was placed on people, and not the rules that govern the mechanism.[8] By putting a good team in place, such as Weidenbaum, Miller, Niskanen, and Tollison, it was believed that victory was already assured. The solution, however, does not lie in people but in the rules.[9] Reform is not simply about changing the names of those in charge. There is a categorical difference between "policy within politics" and structural reform. As Buchanan writes:

"Policy within politics" embodies the presumption that the rules, the institutional-constitutional structure from which political decisions emerge, are fixed. By inference, the failure of pre-Reagan politics to have advanced the cause of depoliticization was attributed to the presence of the "wrong" parties and the "wrong" politicians in positions of decision-making authority. . . . In [the public choice] approach, it matters relatively little, if at all, which parties or which politicians succeed or fail in the overt electoral competition. The constitutional economist would have based his expectations for any permanent change only in modifications of the incentive structure. (1989: 4)

A POLITICAL ECONOMY PERSPECTIVE

Does this mean that for those who wish to see a limited government, all is hopeless? Is Washington merely the bastion of rent-seekers? Will principle always lose out to expediency in politics? Have we finally succumbed, as Madison warned 200 years ago, to the rule of factions and special interests? Yes.

But hope does still remain in the realm of ideas. Ideas have consequences. As Keynes (1936: 383) stated, "Indeed the world is ruled by little else." We face the formidable task of reforming the rent-seeking society.[10] Political economy as a discipline has much to offer in that endeavor.

We must recognize, as Buchanan has stressed, that "ideas can, and do, matter, and political leaders can, and do, make a difference. But ideas and politicians exist in both time and space. And institutions that constitute a social order, once entrenched, are not readily displaced, turned off, or turned around" (1986a: 33). Much of the hope for real reform lies in the rediscovery of the relationship and task of social philosophy and political economy (Buchanan 1986c).

As economists we must recognize our limits. Political economy can be fruitfully viewed as divided into two separate fields: pre- and postconstitutional analysis. Preconstitutional analysis is the realm of social philosophy, and political theory broadly understood. At this level of analysis discussion is over the rules of the game and the nature of what constitutes a "good" game; the work of Hobbes, Hume, Smith, Rousseau, Rawls, or Nozick becomes apparent. We cannot help but be normative. The false belief in "scientism" does nothing but hinder the development of our discipline. Our modernist preconceptions must be thrown off if we wish to develop a political economy that is relevant to the problems at hand.[11] The engineering mentality that has dominated economics in the twentieth century has bought increased mathematical sophistication at the price of decreased relevance. We had better recognize this fact, and be willing to discuss such issues as ethics, if we hope to improve our discipline (see Sen 1987).

But technical economics does play a vitally important role in the research program at the level of postconstitutional analysis: analysis within the constituted rules. And here lies the special contribution of economic theory. The weaving back and forth between pre- and postconstitutional analysis is the task of the political economist. We must ask not only abstractly what might be a good game, but also examine very concretely how the game will most likely be played within the existing rules. Changing the players won't produce any lasting effects; changes in the rules will. The problem with the so-called Reagan revolution was that the emphasis was almost completely on the players and not on the rules of the game.

With a renewed appreciation of political economy it seems that all is not necessarily lost for those who hope to reform political and economic systems in a peaceful manner. The intellectual pyramid must translate and disseminate academic developments. The importance of rules over discretion, and specifically, the idea that it is not people but a framework of rules (independent of political parties and individuals) that will promote economic prosperity and protect our liberties must be conveyed in a convincing manner to the general public. If we wish to "change history in the direction of a society that combines liberty of person, prosperity and order," as Buchanan has stated, we must dare to "dream attainable dreams, and to recover the faith that dreams can become realities" (1986b). Political economy has its work cut out for it, but hope does remain for those who wish not merely to interpret the world but to change it.

NOTES

I would like to thank Jack High (George Mason University), Jeff Friedman (University of California, Berkeley), Steven Horwitz (St. Lawrence University), Sherman Folland (Oakland University), and Anandi Sahu (Oakland University) for helpful comments on an earlier draft. Responsibility for remaining errors is my own.

1. The following presentation of developments in economic thinking is admittedly one-sided and, as a result, does not capture fully the evolution of economic thought in the past 25 years. My purpose in this chapter, however, is to explain the rise of a set of ideas favorable to free markets and limited government. One need only look at the candidacy of Barry Goldwater as compared with that of Ronald Reagan to notice that something drastic had indeed changed in the political and intellectual environment be-

tween 1964 and 1980. I am simply trying to sketch an outline of some of the academic developments that changed the climate of opinion during that period.

2. See T. Cowen (1988) for a collection of the relevant papers.

3. I should also mention that the work of the revisionist historians, such as Gabriel Kolko (1963) and James Weinstein (1968), provided convincing evidence of government failure to promote the public interest. Government regulation, rather than promoting the public interest, was instituted by private interest groups to protect their economic profits from competitors. The history of U.S. regulatory initiatives was one of government being "captured" by the very groups it was supposed to be regulating.

4. See Buchanan, Tollison, and Tullock (1980) and Stigler (1988) for collections of the relevant essays.

5. The ideas developed by economists have also reached wider and more popular audiences. Robert Nozick won the national book award in 1974 for his philosophical work, *Anarchy, State and Utopia,* which put the classical liberal case for limited government on the playing field again both in academic and intellectual circles. Moreover, Milton Friedman's 1979 television series and his subsequent book with his wife Rose, *Free to Choose,* popularized the argument for economic and political freedom associated with classical liberalism.

6. William Niskanen (1988: 131) provides some indirect evidence of the slowing:

The annual number of new rules declined about one-fourth and the pages in the *Federal Register*. declined by 39 percent. The growth of real spending by the federal regulatory agencies slowed from 4.5 percent a year from FY 1977 through FY 1981 to 1.4 percent from FY 1981 through FY 1985. The total number of lawyers in active practice, an index of all sorts of problems, tells a similar story, increasing by 7.4 percent a year from 1977 through 1981 and 3 percent a year from 1981 through 1985. The regulatory momentum was clearly slowed, but it was not reversed.

7. The Reagan regulatory reform failure should not be construed as challenging the basic claim of the efficacy of deregulation. The evidence from the ten-year history of airline deregulation suggests that the economic consequences of deregulation are extremely beneficial from the perspective of consumer welfare. See Poole (1989) and Semmens and Kresich (1989) and the references cited therein for a discussion of the benefits of airline deregulation for consumers. For a fascinating discussion of the passage of the Airline Deregulation Act of 1978 see Thomas McCraw (1984).

8. Other reasons for the failure of deregulation initiatives have been suggested by leading public choice scholars. The political incentives for deregulation are mainly absent due to the fact that the supposed efficiency gains are overestimated by economists (see McCormick, Shughart, and Tollison 1984). But, as Peltzman (1989) has pointed out, the coalitional aspects of politics help explain some of the push for deregulation, as long as deregulation benefits some part of the relevant coalition, it remains a viable policy option. The problem lies in organizing the coalition in an effective manner. And the move is not toward a change in the general rules, but toward specific deregulatory acts designed to benefit some well-organized group.

9. Even Adam Smith himself proved to be a model regulator when he served in customs (see Anderson, Shughart, and Tollison 1985).

10. To varying degrees this is the difficulty we are witnessing around the world, from the Eastern bloc to Asia, from Latin America to the Third World.

11. See McCloskey (1985) for a recent criticism of modernism in economics. For the classic critique of scientism in the social sciences see Hayek (1979).

"The Reagan Regulatory Regime": *Comment*

Kenneth D. Boyer

In his chapter "The Reagan Regulatory Regime: Reality vs. Rhetoric," Peter J. Boettke claims that the Reagan administration failed to achieve its deregulatory objectives because it relied too heavily on putting "good people" in positions of authority instead of changing rules of policymaking. Before evaluating this claim, it is important to identify what we mean by "regulation" and "deregulation." Subjecting a company to "economic regulation" has usually meant:

1. Requiring the company offering a service do so to all who request it without discrimination among groups of consumers (so-called "common carriage requirements").
2. Transferring to the government the right to determine prices for services.
3. Limiting entry into a service area to those franchised by the government.

Gas supply, electricity, and telephones have been the classic examples of economic regulation. Such public utilities were granted monopoly franchises within their service areas, in return for which they were able to expect the government regulating agency to set prices that allowed a normal rate of return on invested capital.[1]

In the first part of the twentieth century, the public utility form of regulation was extended to transportation industries and to sectors like banking, stock brokerage, cable television, and other industries that had only some aspects of public utilities. In most of these nonutility instances, suppliers did not receive monopoly franchises. It was these competitively structure-regulated industries that were substantially deregulated in the 1970s and 1980s. One traditional public utility industry—long-distance telephone service—has also been shifted into the ranks of deregulated service suppliers. Deregulation has meant freedom of entry into these industries, freedom from government approval to change prices, and an elimination of common carriage requirements.

The Process of Deregulation

While deregulation has come to be associated with the anti-government policies of the Reagan administration, deregulation is actually the intellectual offspring of the Carter administration and the Democratic Congress between 1976 and 1980. It was Carter's appointees to the Civil Aeronautics Board and Interstate Commerce Commission who changed the traditionally cozy relationship between the regulated industries and the regulatory authorities. When Congress acted on the Airline Deregulation Act in 1978 and the Staggers Act and Motor Carrier Act in 1980, it did little more than ratify administrative changes that had already taken place.

The Reagan administration continued the process begun in the Carter administration. Busses were deregulated, limits on banking were further liberalized, and the remaining price controls on natural gas and oil were eliminated. The most influential act of deregulation, however, was the consent decree in 1982 with the American Telephone and Telegraph Company in a case begun under the Ford administration; that decree paved the way for competition and the lifting of price controls in the long-distance telecommunications market. It is true, as Boettke claims, that the process of deregulation lagged in the Reagan administration as compared with the previous four years. The reason, however, is that most of the instances of industries that were not natural monopolies but subject to economic regulation were already deregulated. There simply were not many more industries to deregulate.

Beginning in 1981, there was a reorientation of political activity in the executive branch away from removing economic regulation to eliminating other forms of government activity. Environmental regulations were attacked, land controls removed, health and safety regulations weakened. Even rules designed to encourage a diversity of views in broadcast media were attacked—all in the name of "deregulation." Deregulation became confused with the Reagan administration's attempt to narrow the scope of the nonmilitary parts of the federal government. In the latter part of the 1980s, this form of deregulation became discredited. As bank failures have become costly to the national treasury, as the public demand for improved environmental quality has increased, as airline hubs have become more and more concentrated, the discussion has turned to reregulation rather than deregulation. Among the calls for reregulation, however, none has called for an imposition of the old form of economic regulation in industries with a competitive structure. The reregulation discussion has centered on changing particular rules for individual industries to enhance their performance.

Why Did Deregulation Succeed?

Prior to deregulation, George Stigler's "capture theory" of regulation and its close cousin, Sam Peltzman's "economic theory of politics," the dominant theories of regulatory motivation, were used to claim that deregulation would be impossible.[2] These theories were based on models in which regulators' motivations were identical with those of politicians, which they assumed to be maximization of political support. According to the economic theory of politics, political support is related to the amount of income that can be redistributed from a large, passive, and ill-organized group (consumers) to a small, well-organized group with similar interests (industry). In their models, it was implausible for regulation to have any outcome other than to benefit the regulated industry at the expense of the general public; the strength of the industries and the inability of the disadvantaged general public to organize a protest precluded the possibility of deregulation.

But deregulation did occur in almost all competitively structured industries subject to public utility regulation at the federal level. The fact that deregulation did occur is powerful evidence against the various theories of regulatory motivation that see regulation as a conspiracy of producers against consumers. But if the conspiracy theory of regulation cannot explain deregulation, what can? Despite several attempts by political scientists, there is no well-established explanation for the success of deregulation in the late 1970s.[3] To the extent that there was an intellectual justification for deregulation, it was that government policy should make the most efficient use of the scarce resources in the economy and that the regulation of nonmonopoly industries was hindering such efficient outcomes. For example, Alfred Kahn gave the following arguments in favor of deregulating telephone service:

The inefficiencies of present telephone pricing policies maintain an unrealistic, inequitable, and inefficient regime in which certain groups of consumers subsidize others in ways unrelated to rational social goals. To correct these inefficiencies, we must move to cost-based, unbundled pricing. The arguments against that kind of pricing, particularly concerns about telephone service for the poor and the desire to maintain universal service, fail to acknowledge that, in the long run, marginal cost pricing is both equitable, since it charges people the costs they impose on society, and efficient, since it decreases total costs and makes it easier to direct subsidies to those who need them most. . . . True, competition poses both practical and political problems. Its beauty, however, is that it forces us to comply with the dictates of economic reality; its consolation is that to the extent we do, there will be improved welfare for most of us and efficient ways of taking care of those who fall behind and genuinely need help.[4]

Using standard economic theory, Kahn argued that deregulation would lead to competition, which would in turn force cost-based pricing and generate the efficiencies associated with such price structures.

To the extent that deregulation was generated by "ideas," they were practical and nonideological in nature; in short, not the sort of ideas that dominated in the first years of the Reagan administration. Those who were influential in advocating deregulation—Alfred Kahn, for example—were not members of the Austrian School, or even the Chicago School. The agenda of deregulation was led in Congress by Senator Kennedy, surely no conservative in the Reagan mold. Deregulation was sold to the public not as an element of a grand scheme for reducing the size of government, but as a means to eliminate waste and to reduce prices for consumers. Deregulation succeeded not because it was part of the conservative agenda, but because it had broad-based support among both conservatives and liberals.

To the extent that deregulation became associated with the conservative agenda during the Reagan years, it diminished political support for the concept. A far more important reason for the decline in the popularity of deregulation, however, was that deregulation did not always work as advertised. The savings and loan debacle of the late 1980s is seen as a failure of bank deregulation. Increasing domination of air traffic at individual cities is another example of deregulation's failure. The public seems to believe that deregulation has worsened safety in the trucking industry as well. With increasing dissatisfaction with the results of deregulation, the discussion turns to reregulation.

Rather than lament lost opportunities for radically shrinking the role of government during the Reagan years, we as economists can assist the ongoing debate about reregulation. Reregulation does not mean a return to the old subjection of competitively structured industries to public utility-type controls. Rather, reregulation refers to specific policies to deal with particular performance defects of individual industries. Our role should be to tell policymakers and the public about the consequences of proposed actions. By understanding how different industries behave, and by studying how governments behave, we should be able to make projections about which policies will achieve performance goals with least cost. If there are actions that the government can take to improve industrial performance, we should not hesitate to say so.

NOTES

1. The classic textbook is Kahn (1970).
2. See Stigler (1971) and Peltzman (1976).
3. See, for example, Derthick and Quirk (1985).
4. See Kahn (1984).

8

Securities Regulation during the Reagan Administration: Corporate Takeovers and the 1987 Stock Market Crash

Jeffry Davis and Kenneth Lehn

Two of the most significant business developments that occurred during the Reagan administration were (1) the advent of hostile takeovers and leveraged buyouts of large U.S. corporations, and (2) the October 1987 stock market crash. Although corporate takeovers have created substantial shareholder value in the 1980s, they also have spawned a great deal of political controversy concerning their economic and social desirability. Similarly, the 1987 stock market crash has provoked considerable controversy over the advent of new financial products (e.g., stock index futures) and trading strategies (e.g., index arbitrage and portfolio insurance). It has also focused the attention of policymakers on possible reforms of U.S. securities markets. This chapter reviews the policy responses of the Reagan administration to the issues raised by corporate takeovers and the stock market crash and argues that the administration's laissez-faire policies reflect sound economic thinking and an appreciation of the academic literature on corporate takeovers and the microstructure of securities markets.

THE CORPORATE TAKEOVER CONTROVERSY

It is well known that during the 1980s both the number and value of corporate takeovers increased significantly. Data from the May/June 1989 issue of *Mergers and Acquisitions* reveal that the number of mergers and acquisitions increased from 10,108 during 1979–83 (an average of 2,022 per year) to 18,389 during 1984–88 (an average of 3,678 per year), an increase of 81.9 percent. Even more striking is the fact that the total value of mergers and acquisitions increased from $249.9 billion during the first five years of this period to $880.3 billion during the last five years of this period, an increase of 252.2 percent.

Among the targets of hostile takeover attempts during this period were dozens of large well-known companies, including CBS, Revlon, Safeway Stores, Goodyear, and TWA.

Although little evidence exists for the reasons for this increase in takeover activity, several possible explanations can be suggested.[1] First, the significant deregulation of numerous industries during both the Carter and Reagan administrations presumably has precipitated some of this takeover activity. Since deregulation changes relative asset values within industries, and since the management skills that are effective in running regulated companies may be inadequate in running deregulated companies, it is not surprising that several deregulated industries (e.g., airlines, oil, natural gas) have been subject to a great deal of takeover activity, both hostile and friendly.

Second, the change in antitrust policy during the Reagan years, represented largely in the administration's merger guidelines, undoubtedly has contributed to this increase in takeover activity. For example, several large oil mergers (e.g., Chevron-Gulf, Mobil-Superior, Texaco-Getty) during the mid-1980s might very well have been challenged by previous administrations because of their size alone. In addition, the *raison d'être* of many large hostile takeovers and leveraged buyouts appears to be the acquirer's desire to restructure the target firm's asset base. Many of the asset sales that follow these so-called "bust-up" takeovers undoubtedly have been facilitated by the less restrictive antitrust policy of the Reagan administration.

Third, the development of novel forms of financing takeovers, including, perhaps most prominently, the use of "junk bonds," has allowed relatively small firms, such as Mesa Petroleum (Boone Pickens's firm) to launch hostile takeovers for companies many times their size. The evolution of junk-bond financing seems to be part of a more general securitization of debt in the 1980s that, presumably, has lowered the relative cost of debt financing. In this sense, the advent of new forms of financing not only has facilitated takeover activity, but has also led to a general restructuring of U.S. corporations.

Whatever the reason, corporate takeovers and restructurings have created substantial wealth gains for stockholders in the 1980s.[2] Several studies have found that, on average, takeover premiums paid to stockholders in target firms range from 30 to 50 percent. Jensen (1988) estimates that shareholders received approximately $346 billion in wealth gains associated with takeovers and restructurings during the 1980s. Much of the political controversy over corporate takeovers in the 1980s concerns the source of these shareholder wealth gains. Do the gains come from improved operating efficiencies and the discipline of inefficient management? Or do the shareholder gains represent wealth that is "simply" redistributed from other claimants on corporate assets, including bondholders, employees, and the U.S. Treasury Department? In addition, are the shareholder gains received in takeovers financed out of reductions in expenditures on valuable research projects?

Evidence on the Takeover Debate

Evidence from the academic literature on corporate takeovers, which played an important role in the development of the Reagan administration's takeover policy, strongly suggests that these transactions promote economic efficiency. In short, there are three potential sources of value in corporate takeovers.

First, combinations of two firms in the same industry can create value by allowing the combined firms to exploit economies of scale. This potential source of value is likely to be important in explaining takeovers in industries with declining growth rates, such as the beer mergers in the early 1980s and the oil mergers in the mid-1980s. In addition to creating value by allowing economies of scale to be realized, combinations of firms' complementary assets may result in downward shifts in cost schedules. For example, combining a firm that has a good product and a weak distribution system with a firm that has a good distribution system may lower the unit costs of distributing the good product over all levels of output. Finally, and perhaps most controversially, takeovers can create value by disciplining managers who operate their firms in ways that do not maximize profits.

Since Berle and Means's classic book *The Modern Corporation and Private Property* (1932), economists and legal scholars generally have recognized that the interests of managers and stockholders in publicly traded corporations potentially may diverge, since these firms are often characterized by diffuse ownership structures and relatively small shareholdings by corporate managers. According to Berle and Means, this potential conflict arises because shareholders in these companies have inadequate incentives to closely monitor the performance of managers.

Although Berle and Means's discussion of these potential agency problems is rich, they ignored numerous institutions that may mitigate these problems, including competitive product and managerial labor markets, endogenous ownership structures, incentive compensation plans, and corporate takeovers. In independent studies, Marris (1963) and Manne (1965) argued that managers who fail to maximize their companies' profits will find their companies' stock trading at prices that are lower than they otherwise could be. This disparity between actual and potential stock prices, they argued, creates financial incentives for disciplinary takeovers that simultaneously increase stockholders' value and promote economic efficiency. One explanation for the dramatic increase in takeover activity in the 1980s is that the relative cost of takeovers, vis-à-vis other ways of disciplining managers, has declined, due perhaps to both relaxed antitrust rules and the evolution of junk-bond financing.

In the takeover controversy, the term "managerial inefficiency" often refers to an excessive consumption of perquisites by top-level managers in large corporations. Undoubtedly, there are examples of takeovers in which managers in the target firms have overindulged in the consumption of these perks. However, it is difficult to believe that a large part of the substantial premiums paid in takeovers derives largely from a reduction in the value of these perks. It seems more reasonable that an important source of value in corporate takeovers is the discipline that these transactions impose on managers who pursue strategies that diminish the value of their firms. Along these lines, Jensen (1986) has argued that takeovers partly discipline managers in firms that generate abundant free cash flow (i.e., cash flow in excess of what is required to finance positive return investment projects). According to Jensen, managers of these firms may prefer to invest excess cash flow in value-reducing projects that expand firm size (e.g., value-reducing acquisitions), rather than pay out the excess cash flow to stockholders in the form of either dividends or stock buybacks.

Some research by Mitchell and Lehn (1990) provides empirical support for the "free cash flow" theory of takeovers. They find evidence consistent with the argument that the motive behind many takeover attempts in the 1980s was the acquirers' desire to undo previous acquisitions made by the target firms. The case of Sir James Goldsmith's hostile takeover attempt of Goodyear Tire and Rubber in 1986 anecdotally illustrates a more general result in the Mitchell and Lehn study. Goldsmith indicated that if his takeover attempt was success-ful, he would sell Goodyear's oil and aerospace assets and concentrate its op-erations in the tire and rubber industry. Interestingly, on the single day that Goodyear announced its first major energy acquisition (Celeron Corporation for $800 million in 1983), its stock price fell approximately 10 percent; over a period of five days before this announcement through 40 days after the an-nouncement, Goodyear's market-adjusted stock price fell almost 25 percent. This stock price reaction presumably reflected the stock market's dissatisfaction with Goodyear's diversification strategy. In part, then, the $1 billion premium offered by Goldsmith would have restored equity value that had been lost when Goodyear management initially embarked on a major acquisition program.

The Mitchell and Lehn study finds that the Goodyear example generalizes to a large sample of firms in the 1980s. Firms that subsequently became takeover targets between July 1982 and July 1988 had been making acquisitions that were systematically diminishing their stock prices, whereas firms that did not become takeover targets during this same period had been making acquisitions that were systematically increasing their stock prices. These results suggest that in addition to benefiting target stockholders, many bust-up takeovers during the 1980s have redeployed assets to more profitable uses, thereby benefiting the economy at large.

Other studies find that leveraged buyouts in the 1980s have increased the operating efficiency and profits of target firms. Lichtenberg and Siegel (1989) found that plant productivity increases significantly following leveraged buy-outs. Smith (1988) found that management buyouts result in increased profits, in part because of a significant reduction in the amount of resources that are tied up in working capital following the buyouts. In particular, she found a significant reduction in both the inventory holding period and receivables collection period following these transactions. Similarly, Kaplan (1988b) found a shortened inventory holding period following management buyouts.

Several studies also shed light on many of the public policy issues concerning corporate takeovers. Numerous studies have examined the effects of highly leveraged takeovers on the bond prices of target firms.[3] Although these studies generally have found losses for bondholders, these losses are small relative to the stockholder gains, suggesting that these transactions involve more than a simple redistribution of wealth from bondholders to stockholders.

Numerous studies have attempted to measure the extent to which takeovers are driven largely by tax reasons, as opposed to efficiency measures. Several tax explanations for takeovers have been provided, including the liberalized depreciation deductions allowed in 1981 tax legislation, which purportedly increased incentives of companies to step up asset values; the interest deductions associated with debt used to finance takeovers; and the tax advantages associated with buyouts financed by employee stock ownership plans (ESOPs).[4] Although most research has failed to find a significant empirical relationship between tax motives and takeovers in general, Schipper and Smith (1988) and Kaplan (1988a) found evidence that a large part of the gains in leveraged buyouts is related to tax advantages. However, the stockholder gains in these transactions exceed the tax savings, suggesting that tax savings alone cannot explain these transactions. Furthermore, Gilson, Scholes, and Wolfson (1988) have questioned the importance of tax savings in takeovers, since most of these tax savings can be achieved short of a takeover.

A popular criticism of takeovers generally, and leveraged buyouts in particular, is that these transactions are causing U.S. firms to reduce their spending on research and development (R&D), purportedly in order to increase their reported earnings and to maintain their stock prices at sufficiently high levels to deter takeover attempts. The overwhelming evidence in support of the efficient market hypothesis suggests the futility of this argument. If managers reduce spending on valuable research and development projects, their companies' stock prices will fall, not rise, and hence the likelihood of a takeover attempt should increase, not decrease. Contrary to the critics' argument, evidence shows that target firms of takeovers in the 1980s were spending less, not more, on research and development as compared with other firms in their respective industries, during a period preceding the reception of their bids.[5]

In a related view, critics of leveraged buyouts often argue that the substantial debt incurred in these transactions causes companies to curtail drastically expenditures on research and development following these transactions. However, most leveraged buyouts have not occurred in industries that are research-intensive. Research reveals that the industries with the greatest activity during the 1980s, normalized by industry size, are textiles, apparel, grocery stores, and furniture stores—four industries that typically do not spend much on research and development. In addition, Smith (1988) found that five of 58 companies that were taken private in management buyouts during 1977–86 had research and development expenditures that were large enough to be reported in their 10K filings before the buyouts. Similarly, research finds that of 329 going private transactions during 1980–88, 254 companies (77 percent) reported no spending on research and development during the year preceding their transactions. Hence, it appears that, typically, target firms of going private transactions have little or no R&D to curtail.

Relatively little evidence exists on the employment effects of takeovers. Kaplan (1988b) found that, on average, and controlling for subsequent divestitures, employment is relatively unaffected in leveraged buyouts. Currently, the Securities and Exchange Commission (SEC) is conducting a study of this issue; preliminary results suggest that the employment effects of leveraged buyouts are relatively small. Parenthetically, it is worth mentioning that with the significant increase in takeover activity during the 1980s there has been a concomitant significant reduction in the U.S. unemployment rate. Although this is not meant to suggest that takeovers have caused the unemployment rate to decline, this observation is generally inconsistent with the argument that these transactions have created widespread layoffs of employees throughout the nation.

Policy Proposals to Curtail Takeovers

Notwithstanding an abundance of academic literature that generally is inconsistent with the popular criticisms of takeovers, numerous policy proposals have been advanced, at both the federal and state levels, to curtail takeover activity significantly. These proposals have ranged from amendments to federal securities laws that would regulate the tactics of targets and bidders, to amendments to antitrust, banking, tax, energy, transportation, and communication laws. Despite dozens of legislative proposals to restrict takeovers, no significant antitakeover legislation was passed during the Reagan administration, at least in part, presumably, because of the administration's strong opposition to these proposals.

The cornerstone of the administration's policy toward takeovers was its recognition that these transactions facilitated the reallocation of capital to higher-valued uses, and hence contributed to economic efficiency. Perhaps the best summary of the administration's policy on takeovers is contained in the 1985 *Economic Report of the President,* which contains a chapter entitled "The Market for Corporate Control." As an indication of the influence that academic research had on the drafting of the administration's position, this chapter adopts an "efficient markets" perspective and makes liberal references to academic evidence on numerous topics. For example, in the concluding paragraph of this chapter, the *Economic Report* states that:

Publicly traded corporations account for a substantial portion of the Nation's wealth and productive capacity, and it is important that the management of these firms not be insulated from competition in the market for corporate control. The available evidence is that the operation of this market has generated net benefits for the economy. The evidence also suggests that abusive practices in the market for corporate control are limited largely to tactics employed by target managements who, in opposing takeover bids, defeat or deter tender offers at the expense of their stockholders and the economy.

In addition to opposing federal antitakeover legislation on "purely" economic grounds, the Reagan administration also opposed it on federalist grounds. Specifically, the administration argued that corporate law traditionally has been the domain of state rather than federal regulation. The *Economic Report* cites economic evidence in defense of its federalist position, stating that "because the evidence is that deference to the States in matters of internal corporate governance is beneficial, there is sound economic rationale for continued reliance on the principle of federalism in the market for corporate control."

In 1987 the U.S. Supreme Court, in *CTS v. Dynamics Corp. of America,* upheld an Indiana State takeover law, which has led most other major states, including Delaware, to pass new laws that further restrict takeovers for companies chartered in their respective jurisdictions. Evidence on state takeover laws generally indicates that these laws impede the takeover market and adversely affect stock prices of companies chartered in these states.[6] The *CTS v. Dynamics Corp.* decision, and the flurry of state takeover laws that it precipitated, created a quandary for the Reagan administration. It was apparent that if the administration continued to rely on state corporation law to govern takeover issues, a costlier market for corporate control would exist. On the other hand, if a more fluid market for corporate control was desired, the administration would have to abandon, at least in part, its federalist principles.

THE OCTOBER 1987 STOCK MARKET CRASH

The stock market crash of October 1987 provided a very strong test of the Reagan administration's attitude toward the regulation of securities markets. In exceeding the price decline of the great crash of 1929, the 1987 crash could well have been used as an opportunity to increase dramatically the power of the federal government to control the operation of Wall Street. That this did not occur (yet) is perhaps as surprising as the crash itself, but, of course, the administration's response to the crash is consistent with its avowed respect for free markets.

The initial response of the Reagan administration was to create a Presidential Task Force on Market Mechanisms (the Brady Commission), with a mandate to find out what happened and why and to make recommendations to solve any identified problems. Within three months the Brady Commission filed its report, which called for (1) a single agency to coordinate the regulatory decisions across market segments; (2) unified clearing systems; (3) consistent margins across market segments; (4) "circuit breaker" mechanisms; and (5) improved regulatory information systems.[7] The Brady Commission dutifully carried out its assigned task, but its report apparently was not received with enthusiasm at the White House. Instead of endorsing the recommendations and forwarding them to Congress for legislation, the President established a new group to restudy the matter and to pursue means of improving market mechanisms.

This second group, the Presidential Working Group on Financial Markets (Interagency Working Group), submitted its report to the President in May 1988, but did not subsequently disband.[8] The group consists of the secretary of the Treasury, the chairman of the board of Governors of the Federal Reserve System, the chairman of the Securities and Exchange Commission, and the chairman of the Commodities Futures Trading Commission (or their respective designees).

Although the report of the Brady Commission was somewhat supplanted by the Interagency Working Group's report, it was nevertheless influential, if only because it established the agenda for the Interagency Working Group and, indeed, for most subsequent debate over the need for regulatory changes. Although each of these five recommendations raises interesting issues, the two of particular interest to economists and with the most direct effects on the functioning of the securities markets are those dealing with margins and circuit breakers.

Margins

The Brady Commission called for consistent margins across market segments. Since margins on futures contracts were (and are) much smaller than margins on stocks, this recommendation generally was viewed as a call for increased margins on stock index futures contracts. Interestingly, the Brady Commission explicitly recognized two separate functions of margins: (1) to serve as a performance bond and (2) to control leverage. With regard to the first function, the Brady Commission declared futures margins to be adequate, but not with regard to the second function. In particular, the Brady Commission saw speculation by professional market participants to have been a contributor to the crash and the low futures margins to have been a significant contributor to that speculation. Accordingly, the Commission saw increased futures margins, though not necessarily increased to the level of stock margins, as a means to control speculation and thus to reduce the risk of another crash.

The Interagency Working Group recognized only the first function as a legitimate function of margins. This group (or, more accurately, three of its four members) disagreed with the Brady Commission view that higher margins would reduce volatility.[9] They viewed the evidence as insufficient to support the excess speculation theory underlying the Brady prescription.

The Federal Reserve Board concluded in its 1984 examination of stock margins that the experience in that arena offered no evidence that its margin regulation reduced stock price volatility.[10] Prior academic studies (in particular, Officer 1973) also were unable to find any causal connection between margins and stock price volatility. Subsequent to the report of the Interagency Working Group, however, Hardouvelis (1988a and 1988b) reported finding such a connection.

The primary reason for the difference between the findings of Officer (1973) and the findings of Hardouvelis (1988a and 1988b) appears to be the difference in the way they specified their respective models. Officer's model sought to measure the effect of changes in margin levels on stock price volatility. Hardouvelis, however, specified a model focused on the effects of margin levels on stock price volatility. This difference is particularly important given that the margin level has been changed only 22 times since margin regulation was begun in 1934. Officer's model, by restricting itself to the infrequent changes, greatly restricts its degrees of freedom but minimizes the danger that the influence of margins will be confused with that of other factors. In contrast, Hardouvelis's model has an abundance of degrees of freedom, or so it appears from the reported results. The apparent gain in degrees of freedom, however, comes at the expense of confidence in the claimed findings.

Lacking confidence in the findings reported by Hardouvelis, we are left with no empirical support for the belief that margins are effective in limiting destabilizing speculation. It may be that margin requirements do serve to inhibit speculation, but the proof has yet to be produced. The problem is that too little is known about the determinants of volatility. Until we learn more about the other determinants, we cannot confidently assert that margin regulation is an effective tool, except to serve as a performance bond, as recognized by the Interagency Working Group.

Circuit Breakers

In the view of the Brady Commission, increased futures margins are needed to prevent excessive speculation, but, apparently, even with the "right" margin levels, there remains a need for the provision of emergency measures to be taken in emergency situations. Thus the Brady Commission urged the adoption of "circuit breaker mechanisms."

Circuit breaker mechanisms are essentially any rules or procedures that produce trading halts. Of course, such mechanisms already existed in both the stock markets and the futures markets. In the stock markets there are procedures for halting trading in an individual stock when there is an order imbalance, that is, when the flow of incoming orders to buy (or to sell) greatly exceeds the orders to sell (or to buy) and the dictated equilibrium price suggests the need for a much larger change from the last price than can be achieved in an orderly fashion (i.e., in increments of approximately one-eighth of a dollar). The futures markets also have their own circuit breaker mechanisms, known as price limit rules. According to these rules the price of a futures contract cannot change by more than a preestablished limit; thus trading is not allowed beyond the limit price.

The Brady Commission recommended adding to this arsenal of circuit breakers a new and much broader form of circuit breaker. The coordinated circuit breaker mechanism envisioned by the Brady Commission would, when triggered, halt trading across all market segments. The Interagency Working Group agreed on this point, but stated its preference that the mechanisms be adopted through rulemaking by the self-regulatory organizations.

Interestingly, the Brady Commission singled out for criticism the nonfunctioning of the New York Stock Exchange's (NYSE's) automated stock order system (the Designated Order Turnaround, or DOT, system) as contributing to the huge futures discount that developed during the crash. Ironically, when the NYSE, subsequent to the crash, proposed a rule calling for the suspension of the DOT system for index arbitrage trades whenever the Dow Jones Industrials Index moved more than 50 points, it referred to its rule as a circuit breaker. It was the view of the NYSE that index arbitrage served to transmit to the stock market (either directly, in the form of orders to sell baskets of stocks, or indirectly, in the form of a market "overhang" effect) the instability of index futures prices, thus causing or contributing to the crash.

That the London market, for example, which has only a very small futures market, suffered a similar crash suggests that index futures had little to do with the events of October 19 and 20, 1987, and that the huge demand for liquidity was not a product of any new trading mechanisms. But it might still be argued that London was overwhelmed by the international demand for liquidity, the roots of which can be traced to the U.S. market, and particularly the index futures market.

The huge discounts from the cash market observed in the futures market during the crash could not have persisted until arbitrage was virtually impossible. If the observed discounts were real, then an arbitrageur could profitably exploit them and, in the process, eliminate them. The fact that the discounts persisted can only mean that arbitrage could not be conducted. It is not likely that the futures leg of the potential arbitrage was the source of the difficulty; a buyer of futures would have been more than welcome. The obstacle must have existed in the stock market, where there was no shortage of anxious sellers, where the sheer volume of trading made it difficult to do the stock leg, and where the short-sale rule may have stood in the way.

The data on index arbitrage support this analysis. As late as 1:00 PM on October 19 the Standard and Poor's (S & P) 500 futures discount was only three points. It was after 1:00 PM that the discount grew dramatically, reaching 20 points at 1:30 PM. It remained large throughout the remainder of October 19 and all through October 20. This period of time is remarkable for its paucity of index arbitrage trading. Thus we find seemingly irresistible incentives for index arbitrage coinciding with remarkable abstinence on the part of the arbitrageurs. The discount, as large as it was, was not large enough to compensate an arbitrageur for assuming the risk of buying the future and attempting to cover in the stock market. The discount, then, should be viewed as demonstrating not the illiquidity of the futures market vis-à-vis the stock market, but rather the cost of immediate liquidity in the market for portfolios (or baskets) of stocks.

A seller of a portfolio of stocks on October 19 or 20 could sell futures contracts and incur a highly visible cost in the form of a discount from the cash market. Or sellers could try to sell a basket of individual stocks, in which case they would incur a not-so-visible cost in the form of assuming the risk that their individual stock sales would take place (if they could get them executed) at prices considerably less than the current quotes might suggest. Some portfolio sellers turned to the futures market, others traded in the stock market, and some used both. None, however, avoided the high cost of liquidity, whether it was visible or not so visible. It seems reasonable, therefore, to consider the futures discount to be not only a measure of the visible cost of liquidity in the futures market, but also the best estimate of the not-so-visible cost of liquidity in the stock market. If viewed in this way, the discount does not stand as an indictment of either marketplace.

The huge discounts, then, were not a product of the futures market that was transmitted to the stock market. However, a recognition of this fact does not resolve what continues to be the key issue: Did the existence of the index futures market create a net imbalance that flowed to the stock market, or would that imbalance have existed without the futures market? We probably can never answer this question, but we may not need to know the answer to devise responsible policy.

If the imbalance would have been just as large or larger without the futures market, then proposals that would make futures trading more costly or that would somehow restrict it are misplaced. If, however, the futures market contributed to the net imbalance, then we need to know why before we can recommend "solutions."

The best argument that the futures market contributed to the overwhelming demand for liquidity during the crash rests on the misperceptions of portfolio insurers. The argument is that portfolio insurers, enamored with the low transaction costs in the futures market, built a strategy that implicitly assumed those costs would continue to be low even if all of them attempted to follow the strategy simultaneously. (In this regard, of course, portfolio insurance is no different from the much older strategy of using stop-loss orders.) The argument further contends that, based on this false sense of security, portfolio insurers either continued to bid up stock prices beyond sustainable levels or failed to liquidate gradually, as they might otherwise have done. Finally, according to this argument, a tremendous demand for liquidity was allowed to build up, only to be released by any severe market downturn. And when that downturn came, the flood of selling overwhelmed the futures market and then spread to the stock market.

If this is in fact what happened, it would appear that most, if not all, of the remedy lies in the unavoidable education from the experience. No one could still believe that the cost of liquidity is insensitive to the demand for it. This does not mean that everyone will abandon portfolio insurance. Undoubtedly, it will survive in some form or another. There will always be a market for a "foolproof" scheme to defeat the risks inherent in investing. It seems reasonable, however, to believe that the events of October 1987 have altered the liquidity cost assumptions of those who continue to use portfolio insurance.

In any event, all of the marketplaces now have in place the type of circuit breaker mechanisms recommended by both the Brady Commission and the Interagency Working Group. As the Interagency Working Group expressed it, the circuit breakers were designed to be triggered by events so dramatic that they would otherwise trigger *"ad hoc* and destabilizing market closings."* The intent, then, was simply to substitute orderly, planned closings for chaotic, unplanned ones.

CONCLUSION

The Reagan administration's policy responses to the issues raised by corporate takeovers and the stock market crash were, as expected, restrained. In spite of dozens of legislative proposals emanating from Congress to "do something" about the "takeover frenzy," the Reagan administration withheld its support for any interventionist proposals. As for market "reform" proposals following the stock market crash, the Reagan administration resisted demands for sweeping changes in market mechanisms, and instead opted for a minimal regulatory response.

NOTES

The Securities and Exchange Commission, as a matter of policy, disclaims responsibility for any private publication or statement by any of its employees. The views expressed herein are those of the authors and do not necessarily reflect the view of the Commission or the authors' colleagues on the staff of the Commission.

1. These explanations, and others, also are suggested in Jarrell, Brickley, and Netter (1988).

2. For a review of the evidence on stockholder gains in takeovers, see Jarrell, Brickley, and Netter (1988) and Jensen and Ruback (1983).

3. See, for example, Travlos and Millon (1987), Lehn and Poulsen (1988), and Marais, Schipper, and Smith (1988).

4. For discussions of possible tax advantages associated with mergers and acquisitions, see Macris (1988) and Breen (1987).

5. Securities and Exchange Commission (1985).

6. See Ryngaert and Netter (1988) and Schumann (1988).

7. See Presidential Task Force on Market Mechanisms (1988).

8. See Working Group on Financial Markets (1988).

9. Chairman Ruder of the Securities and Exchange Commission disagreed on this point with the other members of the Working Group.

10. Board of Governors of the Federal Reserve System (1984).

"Securities Regulation during the Reagan Administration": *Comment*

Robert T. Kleiman

I found the chapter by Jeffry Davis and Kenneth Lehn to be very stimulating, and I am in agreement with their major conclusions regarding the current merger wave and the role of market mechanisms in the stock market crash of 1987. There are, however, some areas that their analysis does not address, and these will be the subject of my remarks.

As noted by Davis and Lehn, analyses utilizing the event study methodology uniformly indicate statistically significant positive abnormal returns to the target firms in merger and acquisition activity. However, the abnormal returns experienced by acquiring firms are subject to a great deal of debate. Using short event windows, merger studies employing the cumulative abnormal return methodology do not indicate significant shareholder wealth effects in either direction. When the relevant event window is extended to one to three years after the merger announcement, acquiring firms are found to experience negative abnormal returns. In seven one-year studies examined by Jensen and Ruback (1983), the net of market returns averaged −5.5 percent. Similarly, over the three-year period examined by Maggenheim and Mueller (1987), the abnormal returns were measures at −16 percent using the most conservative measurement technique. As noted by Jensen and Ruback, "these post-merger negative abnormal returns are unsettling because they are inconsistent with market efficiency and suggest that changes in stock price during takeovers overestimate the efficiency gains from mergers."

Other studies also call into question the success of acquiring firms' merger and acquisition activities. Ravenscraft and Scherer (1987) carried out an analysis of postmerger profitability using detailed line-of-business data collected by the Federal Trade Commission. If a change in corporate control replaces inefficient management, posttakeover profitability should rise in comparison to pre-merger profitability, conditions in the acquired firm's industry held constant. Ravenscraft and Scherer analyzed posttakeover profitability by computing profitability indices for the acquired lines of businesses. Those lines subject to tender offer-related acquisitions were 23 percent less profitable on average than comparable lines not involved in takeovers. Porter (1987) disclosed that 33 companies, "many of which have reputations for good management," on average divested over half of their acquisitions. Furthermore, the track record is even worse for unrelated acquisitions: The average divestment rate is almost 75 percent. Although both of the aforementioned studies cover time periods predating the current merger wave, similar results may also apply to merger and acquisition activity during the Reagan years.

Some of the increases in the shareholder value of the target firm may also have resulted from wealth transfers from other stakeholders of the firm. Using recent examples from the airline industry, Shleifer and Summers (1987) argue that some of the gains accruing to the target firm's shareholders come from cutbacks in wages and benefits and from employee layoffs. There may also be wealth transfers from the firm's bondholders. Although Marais, Schipper, and Smith (1988) do not find evidence of bondholder losses over the period surrounding leveraged buyout announcements, they do find wholesale downgradings of the publicly traded bonds of firms undertaking going-private transactions. This suggests that these bondholders may suffer negative wealth effects when returns are measured over longer time periods.

With regard to the October 1987 stock market crash, Davis and Lehn concentrate on the role of margin requirements and circuit breakers in preventing a recurrence. As noted by the authors, the causes and consequences of stock market volatility are not well known, and therefore it is difficult to formulate an appropriate policy response.[1]

In the aftermath of the crash, there have been a number of studies that examined the causes of the unprecedented market downturn. The list of explanations for the crash runs the entire gamut with no consensus among the various studies. The Brady Commission concludes that a limited number of institutional investors using portfolio insurance played a major role in the crash. This, in turn, has led to suggestions that margin requirements on stock index futures be increased. However, studies by the Commodity Futures Trading Commission and the Chicago Mercantile Exchange attribute the decline to a massive revision in investors' perceptions of the fundamental determinants of stock prices.

Roll (1988) examined institutional characteristics of the stock markets in 23 countries with respect to the extent of the price decline. He found no evidence to support the view that institutional arrangements in the United States were related to the stock market crash. His results also indicated no relationship between the relative stock price decline in the 23 markets and margins, price limits, futures trading, or options trading. Thus the existence of an active market for stock index futures trading does not appear to have been the major cause of the crash. However, it is difficult to accept the view that the stock market volatility occurring during the crash was the result of changes in fundamental values. The extent of the price decline was well in excess of that justified on the basis of new information reaching the financial markets, and thus is inconsistent with the efficient-markets hypothesis. Given the lack of conclusive evidence regarding the causes of the crash, the Reagan administration acted in a restrained manner and avoided sweeping changes in market mechanisms.

NOTE

1. For example, Schwert (1987) found that the volatility of U.S. stock prices was not closely related to the volatility of other macroeconomic variables.

Part IV

Monetary Policy and the Federal Reserve

9

Interest Rates in the Reagan Years

*Patric H. Hendershott
and Joe Peek*

The Reagan administration entered office in 1981 with one of the clearest and most ambitious agendas in recent times. The new administration advanced five economic and budgetary goals to rebuild the United States economically and militarily: (1) reduce inflation; (2) deregulate the economy; (3) cut taxes; (4) increase military spending; and (5) reduce nondefense spending sufficiently to balance the budget. Deregulation and the military build-up were begun under the Carter administration; major commitments to reduce inflation and to cut taxes and nondefense spending were new.[1]

In its first term, the Reagan administration successfully achieved the first four goals. However, while nondefense spending was cut, the reduction was insufficient to offset the tax reductions, leaving a substantial structural deficit. In its second term, some progress was made toward reducing this deficit, but the progress was achieved largely by scaling back defense, not nondefense, outlays. In addition, tax reform was passed, but this was a tax shift (household taxes lowered, business taxes raised), and not an overall cut. Nonetheless, both personal and corporate marginal tax rates were cut.

Achieving, or not achieving, these economic and budgetary goals likely had a significant impact on interest rates. Six specific hypotheses are investigated in this chapter:

1. The cut in the inflation rate from 10 to 4 percent lowered nominal interest rates generally by reducing the inflation premium in them.
2. The increased structural deficits raised real interest rates generally (Feldstein 1985).
3. The severity of the tight money policy, which led to the inflation reduction, was unprecedented and caused equally unprecedented high real interest rates (Clarida and Friedman 1983; Blanchard and Summers 1984).

4. The process by which inflation was cut—the switch of the Federal Reserve from interest rate to money supply targets—increased the volatility of nominal interest rates and thus raised real rates on securities with borrower call or prepayment options, such as long-term fixed-rate mortgages (Hendershott and Buser 1984).

5. The deregulation of thrift institutions raised rates on fixed-rate mortgages relative to those on Treasuries.

6. The cut in personal and corporate marginal tax rates and "tax reforms" raised yields on tax-exempt securities relative to those on Treasuries.

The first three hypotheses relate to interest rates generally and are best addressed by examining yields on noncallable Treasury securities. The second three pertain to the relationship between yields on Treasury and other securities and thus require analyses of other yields.

Our investigation is divided into three parts, the first dealing with Treasury securities (six-month and ten-year maturities), the second with fixed-rate mortgages, and the third with tax-exempt securities (one and five years). In each part we begin by examining how interest rates (or interest rate relationships) have changed in the 1980s relative to the 1970s and then discuss the role of Reagan policies in these changes. The first two parts draw heavily on Hendershott and Peek (1989) and Hendershott and Van Order (1989). We generally find support for all the hypotheses except those relating to the impact of monetary and fiscal policies on real interest rates. These impacts have been overstated.

TREASURY RATES

Expected Inflation, Nominal Rates, and Real Rates

The top two series in Figure 9.1 are the yields on six-month and ten-year Treasury securities, both computed on a bond-equivalent basis, for the 1970s and 1980s. April and October values of the yields are plotted. The bottom two series are the expected inflation rates from the Livingston survey and the Hoey survey on corresponding dates; the latter survey did not begin until September 1978 and was not collected continuously until the 1980s.[2] The long rise in nominal rates up to 1981 is clear, as is the decline since then. The rise and fall correspond to a rise and fall in expected inflation, although the correspondence is far from perfect. The figure suggests about a one-for-one relationship between interest rates and expected inflation, and empirical estimation supports this view.

The term structure of interest rates appears to be related to the term structure of inflation rates. Twice the term structure became inverted (the six-month rate exceeded the ten-year rate), briefly in 1973–74 and for an extended period between 1978 and 1981. Both episodes correspond to a sharp but temporary surge in inflation. If the temporary nature of this shock was perceived, short-

Figure 9.1
Six-Month and Ten-Year Nominal Treasury Rates and Six-Month and Ten-Year
Expected Inflation Rates

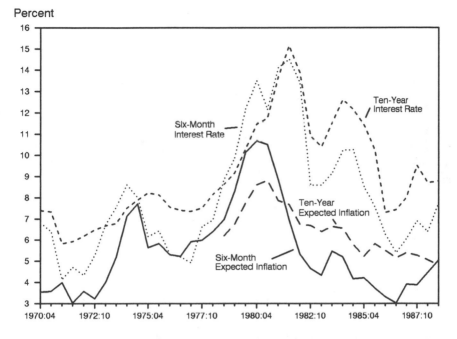

term expected inflation would likely have exceeded longer-term expected inflation. We have a long-run expected inflation rate only for the second inversion.
During this inversion, the short-term expected inflation rate did in fact exceed
the long-term rate, and when the short-term expected inflation rate fell below
the long-term rate, the inversion ceased.

Figure 9.2 plots the pretax real six-month and ten-year Treasury rates and
the aftertax real six-month rate. The tax rate is a weighted average marginal
tax rate paid by households on interest income.[3] To put these real rates in
perspective, we have plotted them for the longer 1964–88 period. Here, the
high pretax real rates in the early 1980s, especially relative to the mid-1970s,
are obvious. The real six-month Treasury rate averaged 5.5 percent in the 1981–
84 period, a level previously observed only in the 1926–30 period, as opposed
to only 0.2 percent in the mid-1974 to mid-1978 span. Real ten-year Treasury
rates appear to have jumped similarly in the early 1980s. Furthermore, real
short- and long-term Treasury rates have been similar in magnitude in the 1980s;
that is, the long-term premium has not systematically exceeded the short-term
premium.

Also noteworthy is the decline in real interest rates since 1984. The real six-
month bill rate in the 1986–88 period was slightly below its average in the
previous quarter-century. This little-recognized fact is particularly remarkable

Figure 9.2
Ex Ante Pretax and After-Tax Real Interest Rates

Percent

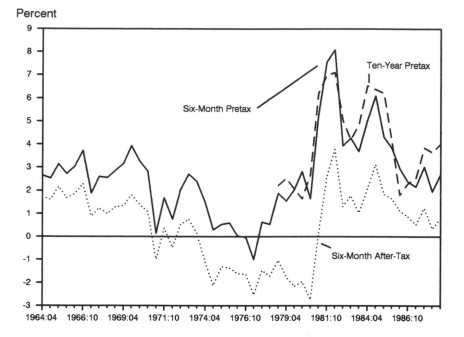

because real activity has been so strong in recent years and real bill rates have historically exhibited a strong procyclical pattern (Hendershott 1986b).

Movements in the aftertax real bill rate are also interesting. According to this measure, the interest rate puzzle hasn't been the high rates in the 1980s so much as the low rates in the 1970s; the aftertax real rate never exceeded −1 percent for the entire 1974–80 period. The early 1980s values are quite comparable to those observed throughout the 1960s, and more recent values are roughly half those in the 1960s. In any event, explaining the jump in real interest rates in the 1980s, either before or after tax, requires an explanation of the reasons that interest rates were so low in the mid-1970s. (Wilcox 1983 attributes these low rates to the first OPEC shock.)

Reagan Policies and Real Rates

How did fiscal and monetary policy affect the pattern of real rates in the 1980s? Figure 9.3 contains the real interest rate and two fiscal policy variables: the structural federal deficit as a fraction of middle-expansion trend GNP, and the average marginal tax rate used to measure aftertax real interest rates.[4] The deficit would appear to be negatively correlated with real rates in the 1970s and early 1980s. More specifically, the structural deficit had hardly begun to

Figure 9.3
**Six-Month Pretax Real Treasury Bill Rate, Marginal Tax Rate, and Cyclically
Adjusted Deficit**

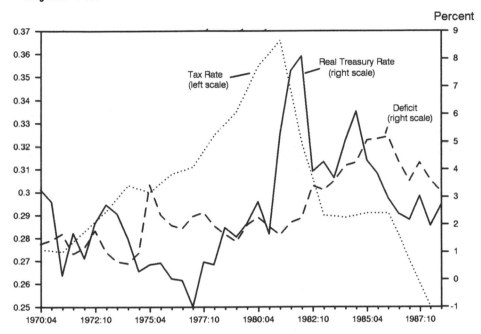

rise when the real rate peaked in the 1980s, and the real rate was back down
to a normal level before the deficit reversed course. While the deficit might be
badly mismeasured, any reasonable measure must have risen between 1981 and
1983, just when the real rate was declining.[5] The tax rate series is positively
correlated with the real rate during the 1977–88 period, as we would expect
(the pretax rate rises in response to an increase in the tax rate in order to
maintain the aftertax rate at a given level).

Our multivariate analysis (Hendershott and Peek 1989) suggests a small positive impact (less than a quarter percentage point) of the 1980s structural deficits on yields. However, the cut in marginal tax rates has an even larger negative impact. Thus fiscal policy, broadly defined, tended to lower, not raise,
Treasury rates during the Reagan years.

Figure 9.4 plots the real six-month rate against our estimate of the impact of
monetary policy on the six-month rate. (Monetary policy is attributed to Reagan, despite the Federal Reserve's ''independence,'' because of his strong support of the Federal Reserve.) Our estimate is obtained by first constructing a
proxy for monetary policy and then using this proxy as a regressor in an equation explaining the aftertax bill rate. We developed this proxy because custom-
ary money measures are of doubtful validity when effective deposit rate ceilings are changed and/or new ''money-like'' financial claims are introduced.

Figure 9.4
Pretax Real Six-Month Treasury Bill Rate and Monetary Policy Impact

Percent

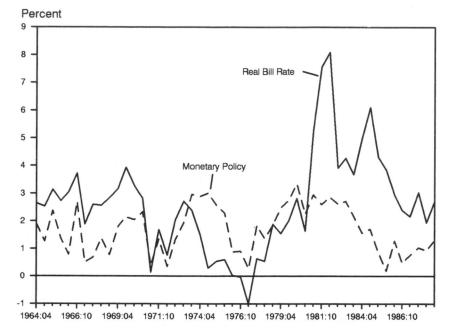

Our proxy is based on the behavior of the six-month bill rate, which the Federal Reserve can control over short periods, relative to that of the five-year Treasury bond rate, over which the Federal Reserve has decidedly less control. More specifically, we explain the term structure of interest rates with the term structure of expected inflation, the business cycle, and traditional monetary policy variables. We then attribute the residual (plus the traditional monetary policy variable's contribution) to monetary policy.

A number of observations follow from Figure 9.4. First, the decline in the real rate from 2.5 percent in late 1973 to −1 percent in early 1977 and the rebound to 2.5 percent in 1980 are almost fully accounted for by monetary policy. Second, while changes in monetary policy explain both the rebound in real rates to normal levels in the 1978–80 period and much of the decline since 1984, by our estimates monetary policy does not account for the jump in real rates between 1978–80 and 1981–84. In summary, monetary policy was not noticeably tighter in the early 1980s than in the 1973–84 period, although the period of tightness, mid-1979 to mid-1983, lasted much longer. As a result, the quarter-century upward trend in inflation was finally broken. Similarly, the recent period of ease has been longer than any in the last quarter-century and has contributed to the longest peacetime expansion on record.

Our principal conclusion is that the emphasis on the high real interest rates in the early 1980s has been overstated. The key to understanding real interest rates in the last quarter-century is the extraordinarily low interest rates in much of the 1970s owing to the two OPEC oil shocks, which lowered investment demand and increased world saving by transferring wealth from the high-consuming developed countries to OPEC. Figure 9.4 clearly indicates lower real rates relative to the contribution of monetary policy in the 1974–80 period than existed either before or after. Monetary policy was tight for a long stretch in the early 1980s, but only tight enough to cause real interest rates to be about a percentage point and a half above normal. Fiscal policy, however, had little impact, with decreasing marginal tax rates more than offsetting the increase in structural deficits. Finally, some evidence suggests that foreign policy—Reagan's "evil empire" posture in his first term—contributed marginally (about a half percentage point) to the high real rates by increasing the fear of nuclear war and thus reducing the private propensity to save.

THE YIELD ON FIXED-RATE MORTGAGES

Volatility and Yields on Fixed-Rate Mortgages

A fixed-rate mortgage differs from a Treasury security with equal duration because homeowners can call or prepay the mortgage while the Treasury cannot prepay its debt. For equal coupon securities, investors will prefer the Treasury; if market interest rates decline, investors in Treasuries will continue to receive their now above-market coupons, while investors in mortgages will find their funds repaid and themselves forced to invest in the now lower market coupons. To compensate for the possibility of borrowers prepaying when rates decline, investors in fixed-rate mortgages must receive a higher coupon than investors in Treasuries. The size of this coupon differential will depend on the probability that interest rates will decline sufficiently to trigger prepayment. This probability, in turn, will be greater the more volatile interest rates become and the greater the expectation that interest rates will decline.

Figure 9.5 plots the ex post volatility of interest rates and the spread between the conventional new issue mortgage rate and the seven-year Treasury rate (comparable duration Treasury).[6] The spread oscillated between about one and two percentage points in the 1970s before the switch to a more volatile interest-rate monetary policy in late 1979. From this point, the spread continued upward until it peaked at over three percentage points in 1981 and 1982. After dipping below two percentage points in early 1984, the spread again rose to nearly three percentage points in late 1986 before finally declining to about two percentage points.

That increased interest rate volatility explains some of the increase in the mortgage-Treasury rate spread is obvious from the figure. Volatility jumped in late 1979 at the same time as the spread did, and remained high through the peak of the spread in late 1982. That is, much of the relative increase in the mortgage rate in 1981–82 simply reflected a more valuable prepayment or call

Figure 9.5
Mortgage Rate–Treasury Rate Spread and Interest Rate Volatility

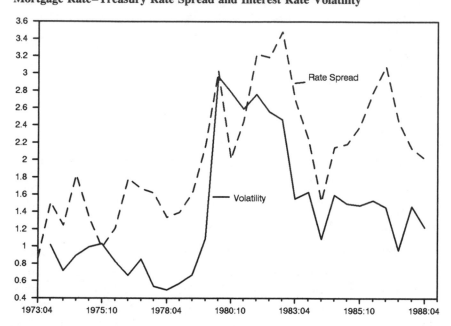

option. However, more than the rising call value contributed to the relatively high mortgage rates in the early 1980s.

The Savings and Loans, the Agencies, and the Mortgage Rate

Figure 9.6 plots both the actual conventional mortgage coupon rate and an estimate of what the rate should have been, given seven-year Treasury rates and the value of the homeowner's call option (Hendershott and Van Order (1989) label this the "perfect-market" coupon rate). As can be seen, the actual rate was about a half percentage point too low during most of the 1970s, but then was about a half point too high in the 1982–86 period, giving a total increase of a full percentage point. Since early 1987, the actual rate has been equal to the perfect market rate. In the 1970s, mortgage lending was largely tied to the thrifts. Portfolio restrictions on savings and loans (no corporate loans, bonds, or equities) encouraged their investment in residential mortgages, and these investments were especially profitable to thrifts owing to special tax advantages. Thrifts that invested a large fraction of their assets in housing-related loans or liquid assets could transfer a large fraction of their pretax income to loan loss reserves, thereby avoiding taxes. Between 1962 and 1969, this fraction was 60 percent; between 1969 and 1979, the fraction was gradually reduced to 40 percent. The Tax Reform Act of 1986 then lowered the fraction to

Figure 9.6
Effective Mortgage Commitment Rate, Actual and Perfect Market

Percent

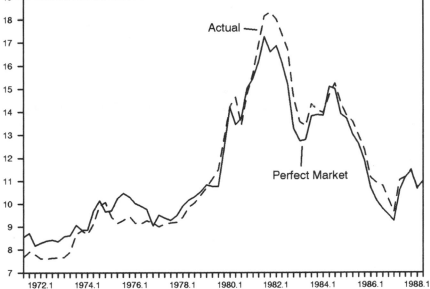

8 percent. The incentive for mortgage investment provided by the extraordinary transfers to loan loss reserves was substantial in the 1960s and 1970s. Savings and loans would have accepted a half to three-quarters of a percentage point lower pretax return on tax-preferred housing-related assets than on comparable nonpreferred assets.

Thrifts have shifted sharply out of fixed-rate home mortgages (FRMs) in the 1980s. Most strikingly, the share of savings and loan total assets in home mortgages and agency securities (largely Fannie Mae and Freddie Mac pass-throughs) fell from 72 to 57 percent during the 1982–87 period. Because savings and loans have aggressively added adjustable-rate mortgages (ARMs) to their portfolios, the shift from FRMs was far greater than 15 percent of the portfolio. These portfolio shifts were in response to the reduced profitability of savings and loans (first due to high interest rates and a maturity mismatch, and then due to disinflation and credit losses), the expansion of savings and loan asset powers, and a regulatory-enhanced aversion to interest rate risk. The reduced profitability eroded the tax incentive for residential mortgage investment, while the expansion of powers and regulatory risk aversion encouraged thrifts to invest more widely (the latter also encouraged switching from FRMs to ARMs). The net result was a rise in the mortgage rate from a half percentage point below the perfect-market rate to a half point above.

The half percentage point premium in the early 1980s provided the incentive for the securitization of conventional FRMs by Fannie Mae and Freddie Mac. The premium covered both the start-up cost of the securitizers and the liquidity premium demanded by investors. And securitize Fannie and Freddie did: Roughly half of newly issued conventional fixed-rate mortgages originated in 1986 and 1987 were sold directly to Fannie and Freddie to be packaged into mortgage pools. As the volume of mortgage pools grew, bid/ask spreads were bid down (and thus the liquidity premium fell), and the marginal costs of the securitizers declined. As a result, the yields on conventional loans have fallen back in line with capital market rates.

Nonetheless, conventional FRM rates are still about a half percentage point higher, relative to Treasury rates, than they were in the 1970s. Attributing this half-point increase to Reagan policies seems inappropriate, however. The deterioration of the thrifts' relative position as profitable investors can be traced to policy errors, such as the regulatory prevention of adjustable-rate mortgages and the imposition of deposit rate ceilings, that date back to the 1960s.

YIELDS ON TAX-EXEMPT SECURITIES

Determinants of Tax-Exempt Yields

Because investors are interested in aftertax returns, the tax-exempt status of a security will result in its pretax yield being bid down relative to pretax yields on fully taxable securities. Tax-exempt yields, then, will be only a fraction of taxable yields, the fraction being greater the less heavily taxed are returns on taxable securities. The relationship between yields on default-free exempts (r_{ex}) and taxables (r_{tx}) will depend on the state of the economy as well as tax rates. A deteriorating economy, for example, could lead to greater probability of bankruptcy (larger debt contracting costs) and thus reduced issues of fully taxable debt. Also, the deterioration could stimulate a flight to quality or greater demand for Treasury debt. In both cases, fully taxable rates would fall relative to tax-exempt yields. We thus express the ratio of exempt to taxable rates as

$$r_{ex} / r_{tx} = \theta(t_c, t_p, \rho)$$

where t_c is the corporate tax rate, t_p is an index representing the marginal personal tax rate schedule, and ρ is a risk adjustment that varies with the state of the economy.

Figure 9.7 plots the ratio of one-year exempt to one-year taxable yields (r_{ex}/r_{tx}), $1-t_p$, and a proxy for cyclical swings in the economy (GAP). The latter is measured as 100 times the difference between middle-expansion trend GNP and actual GNP, all divided by trend GNP. The corporate tax rate is not plotted because it varied so little during this period. The personal tax rate is the average marginal personal tax rate on interest income earned (see note 3). The broad decrease and then increase in $1-t_p$ reflects both the bracket creep of the

Figure 9.7
Ratio of One-Year Exempt to One-Year Taxable Yields, One Minus Marginal Tax Rate, and Percentage GNP Gap

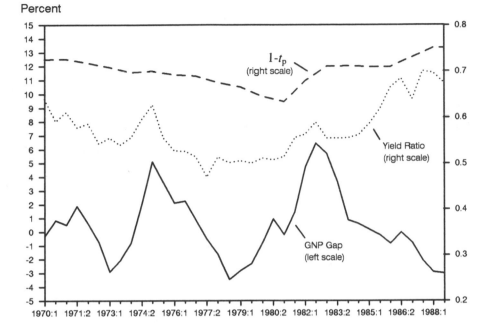

1970s and the 1980s Reagan tax cuts. Figure 9.8 plots the same ratio for five-year securities. Here the personal tax rate is a five-year forward-looking rate (the single tax rate applied to all future cash flows that gives the same aftertax rate of return as the stream of aftertax payments based on the average marginal personal tax rates that actually evolved). The general correlation of the rate ratios with the $1\text{-}t_p$'s and GAP seems clear.[7]

Closer inspection of the Figures suggests two further points. First, the cyclical impact of GAP seems to be limited to positive values; when GAP is negative in the 1972–73, 1978–80, and 1986–88 periods, the rate ratios cease to follow its movements. This is consistent with a risk adjustment that develops when the economy falls below trend but is fully eliminated when the economy gets back to trend. Also, the one-period future, rather than current, value of GAP seems to influence the rate ratio. Second, both the one-year and five-year rate ratios are too high after about 1984 relative to the pattern existing over the 1970–84 period. More specifically, the rate ratios are far closer to the $1\text{-}t_p$'s than they were during comparable periods in which the economy was above trend (1972–73 and 1978–80).

An alternative or additional proxy for the risk adjustment is the spread between the six-month commercial paper and Treasury bill rates divided by the

Figure 9.8
Ratio of Five-Year Exempt to Five-Year Taxable Yields, One Minus Marginal
Tax Rate, and Percentage GNP Gap

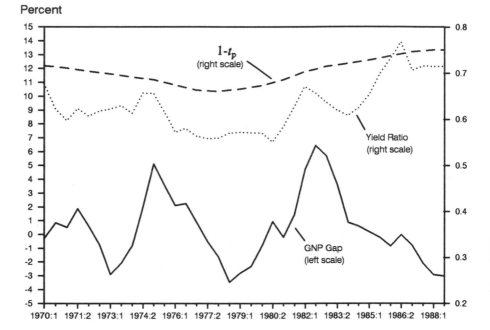

Percent

bill rate (PREM).[8] As Buser and Hess (1986) note, the corporate-Treasury yield spread is a contemporaneous proxy for expected bankruptcy. This variable moves somewhat like GAP, but falls far more abruptly in 1975 and rises much less in the 1980–82 period.

Computing the Impact of Reagan Policies

We have estimated some simple regression equations for the 1970–84 period and extrapolated them through 1988. The equations confirm both the importance of our variables and the unusually high rate ratios in the late 1980s. Representative equations are:

One-year: $r_{ex}/r_{tx} = -.179 + 1.012\,(1-t_p) + .0080\ \text{GAPZ} + .159\ \text{PREM}$
$$(.107)\quad(0.155)\qquad\quad(.0022)\qquad\qquad(.057)$$
$$\bar{R}^2 = .709,\ \text{SEE} = .022,\ \text{DW} = 1.69$$

Five-year: $r_{ex}/r_{tx} = -.111 + 1.008\,(1-t_p) + .0084\ \text{GAPZ} + .093\ \text{PREM}$
$$(.125)\quad(0.183)\qquad\quad(.0019)\qquad\qquad(.050)$$
$$\bar{R}^2 = .724,\ \text{SEE} = .019,\ \text{DW} = 1.32$$

Figure 9.9
**Ratio of One-Year Exempt to One-Year Taxable Yields: Actual and
Fitted/Forecasted**

where GAPZ is zero when GAP_{+1} is negative and equals GAP_{+1} otherwise;
coefficient standard errors are in parentheses. Note the similarity of the tax rate
and GAP coefficients in the two equations and the closeness of that on $1 - t_p$
to unity.

Plots of the actual and fitted/forecasted rate-ratio values are presented in Figures 9.9 and 9.10. The one- and five-year rate ratios appear to be roughly 0.08
and 0.06 too high, respectively, in 1986–88. That is, the tax-exempt rates are
roughly 50 basis points too high.

The rise in the rate ratios far above those predicted in 1985–88 is likely due
to the anticipation and enactment of the 1986 Tax Reform Act. The 1986 Act
cut corporate tax rates from 0.46 to 0.34 (the impact of the personal rate cut is
already included in the forecasted rate ratio), disallowed all bank interest expense allocable to newly acquired tax-exempt bonds, enacted an alternative
minimum tax with tax-exempt interest included in the base, and substantially
restricted future issues of business industrial revenue and household mortgage
revenue bonds (since the end of 1985, the quantity of these bonds outstanding
has declined by 10 percent). The rate cut, the disallowance of bank interest
expense, and the alternative minimum tax should all reduce commercial bank
demand for tax-exempts (Neubig and Sullivan 1987). In fact, commercial bank
holdings of tax-exempts declined from $231 billion at the end of 1985 to $152

Figure 9.10
Ratio of Five-Year Exempt to Five-Year Taxable Yields: Actual and Fitted/Forecasted

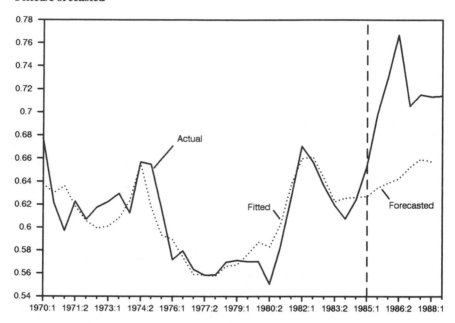

billion at the end of 1988. The increase in the rate-ratios in 1985 reflected a surge in tax-exempt issues in anticipation of the Tax Reform Act. Tax-exempt debt outstanding rose by $139 billion in 1985 ($98 billion in the fourth quarter alone), as compared with $51–54 billion in 1983 and 1984.[9]

What do we conclude about the impact of Reagan policies on tax-exempt yields? In effect, we can attribute all of the 0.17 increase in the rate-ratios since 1980 to Reagan policies, first the 1981 rate cuts and later the 1986 Act. At a 7.5 percent taxable rate, this amounts to a one and a quarter percentage point increase in tax-exempt yields. Of course, if the Reagan tax cuts themselves lowered taxable rates by nearly a percentage point, as we are prepared to argue, then the net increase in tax-exempt yields is only about three-quarters of a percentage point.

SUMMARY

During the first Reagan term, the battle to lower inflation acted to maintain the high real interest rates carried over from the Carter years and, while the increase in structural deficits did not raise real rates much, an aggressive foreign policy increased them by half a percentage point by heightening fears of nuclear war and thus reducing private saving. These factors, strongly reinforced by the unwinding of the second OPEC shock, raised real interest rates to levels not seen since the late 1920s. Moreover, the increased volatility of interest rates during this protracted battle with inflation raised yields on callable fixed-rate mortgages by over a percentage point relative to the already inflated yields on noncallable Treasuries.

By the end of Reagan's second term, inflation, marginal tax rates, nuclear fears, and interest rate volatility were all down. As a result, nominal Treasury rates plunged, and yields on callable securities such as fixed-rate mortgages receded to more normal levels relative to noncallable Treasuries. Real Treasury rates since 1986 are below their average values for the previous quarter-century. Yields on tax-exempt securities are one and a quarter percentage points higher relative to Treasuries than in the pre-Reagan years, and yields on fixed-rate mortgages are up by a half percentage point. These constitute a (possibly intended) reduction in the previous financial subsidies to state, local, and household capital formation, respectively.

NOTES

Comments by James Wilcox are gratefully acknowledged. The views expressed here are those of the authors and not of the organizations with which they are associated.

1. While the period of tight money began well before Reagan took office, his support of that policy allowed it to continue until inflation was substantially reduced. Numerous previous administrations had begun attacks on inflation, but all had backed off before inflation was permanently lowered.

2. The interest rate series are the April and October monthly averages of daily secondary market six-month Treasury bill rates (converted from a discount basis to a bond-equivalent yield) and the ten-year constant maturity Treasury bond yield, both from the *Federal Reserve Bulletin*. The April and October observations were selected to correspond with the approximate dates at which respondents to the semiannual Livingston survey form their expectations. The Livingston six-month expected inflation rate series was provided by the Federal Reserve Bank of Philadelphia. The ten-year expected inflation rate series is from the Decision-Makers Survey conducted by Richard B. Hoey at Drexel Burnham Lambert, Inc. This series is not available for every April and October; when necessary, it has been interpolated from the data for nearby months.

3. The ex ante six-month pretax real interest rate is calculated as the six-month Treasury bill rate less the six-month Livingston expected inflation series. The ex ante ten-year pretax real rate is from the Decision-Makers Survey. Missing April and October observations have been interpolated from the data for nearby months. The aftertax real rate is calculated as the aftertax nominal rate less expected inflation. The tax rate on interest income is an average marginal tax rate constructed from the data contained in annual editions of *Statistics of Income, Individual Income Tax Returns* as a weighted average of the statutory marginal personal income tax rate for each adjusted gross income class. The weight for each class is equal to its share of the total interest received by all income classes.

4. Both the real interest rate and the tax rate were described in note 3. The deficit measure is the cyclically adjusted federal budget deficit as a percentage of middle-

expansion trend GNP and is based on the series constructed by the Bureau of Economic Analysis. Our measure is an average of this series for the quarter beginning in April (or October) and the subsequent quarter to correspond to the time span covered by the six-month Treasury bill rate.

5. An inflation-adjusted measure of the deficit would exhibit an even sharper increase between 1981 and 1983 because the inflation rate fell. However, any particular deficit measure will suffer from a number of problems. On general measurement issues, see, for example, Eisner (1989) and Kotlikoff (1986).

6. The seven-year Treasury rate is the constant maturity series from the *Federal Reserve Bulletin*. The mortgage rate and the volatility measure are both based on data from Hendershott and Van Order (1989). The mortgage rate is the conventional commitment mortgage coupon rate adjusted for points, where that adjustment is equal to

$$(\text{Points} - 1)/(4.2 + .106 \text{ slope} - .69 \text{ vol})$$

where slope is the difference between the seven-year and six-month Treasury rates and volatility (vol) is one-half the cumulative absolute change in the seven-year Treasury rate over the previous 20 weeks. We plot semiannual averages of weekly data.

7. The five-year rate-ratio exceeds the one-year ratio by about 0.05 on average. This could reflect the value of the tax-trading option (let capital gains run but take capital losses) of the longer-term securities (Hendershott 1985: 158–60).

8. The commercial paper rate is for firms with bond ratings of Aa or equivalent and is obtained from the *Federal Reserve Bulletin*.

9. Part of the 1985 surge was matched by an increase in commercial bank demand—an increase of $57 billion in 1985 ($49 billion in the fourth quarter) as compared with $11 billion in 1984—as banks stocked up in anticipation of the 1986 Act.

10

Monetary Policy in the 1980s: Admirable Objectives and Failed Realizations

Robert H. Rasche

The Reagan administration assumed office with a precisely articulated objective for monetary policy during the decade of the 1980s. In the Reagan Economic Plan of February 1981, the role of the Federal Reserve System was to restore price stability by the end of the administration. In particular:

To achieve the goals of the Administration's economic program, consistent monetary policy must be applied. Thus, it is expected that the rate of money and credit growth will be brought down to levels consistent with noninflationary expansion of the economy. . . .

With money and credit growth undergoing steady, gradual reduction over a period of years, it will be possible to reduce inflation substantially and permanently. In this regard, the Administration supports the announced objective of the Federal Reserve to continue to seek gradual reduction in the growth of money and credit aggregates during the years ahead. . . .

Better monetary control is not consistent with the management of interest rates in the short run. But, with monetary policy focusing on long-term objectives, the resultant restraint on money and credit growth would interact with the tax and expenditure proposals to lower inflation as well as interest rates. . . .

To that end, the economic scenario assumes that the growth rates of money and credit are steadily reduced from the 1980 levels to one-half those levels by 1986. (Reagan 1981: 22–23)

It appears fair to conclude that the broad objective for monetary policy in the 1981 White Paper on economic policy was not achieved. This failure is conceded in the retrospective on economic policy contained in the January 1989 *Economic Report of the President:* "Thus far in the current expansion, the

Federal Reserve has successfully kept inflation from rising. Still, inflation remains above the Administration's goal of a zero average rate'' (p. 270).

This study examines alternative hypotheses concerning the failure to achieve
this policy objective. In the next section the history of monetary policy and
inflation during the Reagan administration is reviewed. In the third section several hypotheses are presented about the reasons for the failure to achieve price
stability in the 1980s. In the fourth section the available evidence is reviewed
for consistency with the various hypotheses. In the final section the conclusions
of the analysis are summarized.

MONETARY POLICY AND INFLATION IN THE 1980s

The history of monetary policy and inflation during the Reagan years is relatively uncontroversial, although this is not true of the implementation of monetary policy. At the time the administration took office, the Federal Reserve
had already initiated an effort to bring the inflation rate down from the record
rates of 1979–80. This policy continued throughout 1981 and probably into
1982. Depending on exactly how one chooses to measure inflation rates, and
how much adjustment is made for one-time changes in the price level associated with the 1979 and 1980 oil price shocks, the case can be made that the
Federal Reserve achieved the administration's interim goal of cutting the inflation rate in half by 1986 at least three to four years ahead of schedule—by the
end of 1982.[1] For example, the CPI index excluding food and energy, which
rose at a rate of 12.2 percent from December 1979 through December 1980,
only increased by 4.5 percent from December 1981 through December 1982
(Economic Report of the President, January 1989, Table B-61).

Of course, this rapid reduction in the inflation rate was accompanied by the
severe recession of 1981–82. Sometime between the summer and fall of 1982,
ostensibly because of a breakdown in the traditional relationship between M1
and nominal measures of economic activity, the Fed completely abandoned the
"New Operating Procedures" of 1979 and reverted to an implementation of
monetary policy closely akin to the federal funds approach of the 1970s, and
even more closely related to the "Free Reserves" concept of monetary policy
of the late 1950s and early 1960s. While I know of no rationalization for this
change in policy implementation other then the alleged breakdown in the reli-
ability of narrowly defined monetary aggregates, the sharpness and severity of
the recession undoubtedly influenced Federal Reserve thinking at that time.

Regardless of the underlying reasons for the 1982 change in the approach to
monetary policy, the subsequent outcome in terms of inflation and real economic growth is quite clear. The current expansion of real economic activity
began, and the inflation rate was effectively stabilized at 4 percent per annum
for the next five years.[2] The three-year period from the fall of 1982 until the
fall of 1985 perhaps should be characterized as the inflation stabilization period
of monetary policy during the Reagan administration.

Fall 1985 represents another watershed in Federal Reserve behavior. It is argued below that the change at this time was not initiated by the Federal Reserve, but came about in response to a change in the view within the administration toward the appropriate role of monetary policy. Subsequent to this point, the growth rates of the various monetary aggregates accelerated sharply and there is strong evidence of a controversy within the Federal Reserve over the primary role of monetary policy, with significant support for the view that the Fed should be concerned with fostering continued real economic expansion. This phase of monetary policy in the Reagan years appears to have prevailed through the remaining months of the Volcker era.

Finally, subsequent to the confirmation of Alan Greenspan as chairman of the Fed in 1987, and certainly throughout 1988, the emphasis in monetary policy returned to the 1981–82 concern about and preoccupation with restraining inflation. In spite of Chairman Greenspan's (1989) stated view that "maximum sustainable economic growth over time is the Federal Reserve's ultimate objective" and that "the primary role of monetary policy in pursuit of this goal is to foster price stability," the conduct of monetary policy in the recent past appears to be strongly influenced by the concern with short-run inflation and the employment outlook.

ALTERNATIVE HYPOTHESES ON THE FAILURE TO ACHIEVE PRICE STABILITY IN THE 1980s

There are two popular alternative "explanations" for the failure to achieve price stability during the Reagan administration. Both are invoked in the *1989 Annual Report of the Council of Economic Advisers:*

The Federal Reserve has faced two main challenges in formulating monetary policy during the current expansion. One was conducting monetary policy without a reliable relationship between the monetary aggregates and economic activity. The short-run relationship between various monetary aggregates and income and interest rates, which began to break down in the mid-1970s, became further distorted by a combination of financial deregulation, disinflation, and possibly other unknown factors. Monetary policy actions tended to react more to developments in the real economy than to deviations of the monetary aggregates from their announced targets. (pp. 269–70)

At least two additional hypotheses can be added to this list. The first is that the administration's objective was frustrated by the independence of the Fed. Monetary policy is not the direct responsibility of the executive branch of the U.S. government, and in principle the Federal Reserve can establish and implement its own objectives for monetary policy and inflation.

Finally, consideration must be given to the possibility that the original administration "game plan" was abandoned sometime during the course of the decade, and that a set of different objectives for monetary policy emerged and was implemented by the Federal Reserve. Some evidence on these four alternatives is discussed in the following section.

EVIDENCE FOR ALTERNATIVE HYPOTHESES ON THE FAILURE TO ACHIEVE PRICE STABILITY

Financial Deregulation

The process of financial innovation in the United States can be traced back at least 25 years. This innovation process culminated in 1980 with the passage of the Depository Institutions Deregulation and Monetary Control Act of 1980, which was followed by the Garn–St. Germain Depository Institutions Act of 1982.[3] Three aspects of these acts are directly relevant to the conduct of monetary policy in the 1980s. First, the 1980 Act provided for the gradual phase-out of all interest rate ceilings and allowed depository institutions, regardless of geographical location, to offer an interest-bearing checkable account to households starting in January 1981. Second, the 1980 Act extended the reserve requirement authority of the Federal Reserve to all depository institutions that offered transactions accounts (checkable accounts) regardless of their charter or membership status in the Federal Reserve System. Third, subsequent to the 1982 Act, depository institutions were able to offer short-term time deposits (Money Market Deposit Accounts) and checkable deposits (Super NOW accounts) without legal restriction on interest rates, so long as other regulatory restrictions, such as the minimum number of withdrawals or minimum average balance requirements, were observed. Other aspects of the regulatory changes of the early 1980s are less significant for monetary policy in the United States.

One aspect of the argument that financial deregulation handicapped the successful pursuit of a disinflationary monetary policy during the 1980s is that the deregulation implemented under these acts generated substantial portfolio shifts that contributed to a breakdown of a reliable relationship between monetary aggregates and economic activity. There certainly were major portfolio shifts in the first few months of 1981. The best available evidence is that the adjustments to the nationwide NOW account availability were accomplished in a matter of a few months, and research into the magnitude of these portfolio shifts provided accurate evidence no later than May 1981.[4] The available evidence is consistent with the conclusion that these portfolio shifts had no effect on the growth rates of the monetary aggregates after the middle of 1981. Thus, while the NOW account problem may have caused difficulties in interpreting the direction of monetary policy for a short time during the first half of 1981, it cannot be held directly responsible for the inability of monetary policy to achieve price stability by the end of the decade.

A second aspect to the argument that financial deregulation made life difficult or impossible for the Federal Reserve during the 1980s is that the availability of interest-bearing checkable deposits fundamentally changed the aggregate demand for money function.

The debate about the way in which the spread of checkable deposits that carried explicit interest would influence the demand function for narrowly defined money in the United States started in the late 1970s. The initial investigations of this question did not reach a strong conclusion. A Federal Reserve Staff study (Board of Governors of the Federal Reserve System, 1977) concluded that:

Payment of interest on demand deposits may somewhat increase the speed with which the economy responds to monetary policy to the extent that explicit rates are adjusted more promptly than implicit returns have been to changing market interest rates. A more flexible adjustment of explicit rates would reduce the extent to which changes in the velocity of money would offset changes in the money supply.

My interpretation of the inference about the size of the offsetting response of velocity to changes in the money stock is that the interest elasticity of velocity was presumed to be lower with explicit interest payments than with implicit interest payments, although other interpretations are possible. Subsequent investigations reached more explicit conclusions, until by the mid-1980s

The profession's consensus view is that permission to pay market-determined rates on transactions deposits will reduce the opportunity cost of holding money. If money demand retains the same interest elasticity with respect to this opportunity cost, it will be less elastic with respect to changes in the level of interest rates paid on money substitutes. The traditional LM function will become less interest elastic. (Cargill and Garcia 1985:114)

This consensus is reflected by a number of contributors to a Federal Reserve Bank of San Francisco Conference on "Interest Rate Deregulation and Monetary Policy," held in 1982. In the keynote address at that conference, Axilrod (1982) noted:

Institutions over time may also be sluggish in adjusting the price of transactions accounts to market rate changes. Even so, the interest-elasticity of M1 demand will still probably be reduced, and possibly also made less certain than it now is because decisions about offering rates on the part of depository institutions represent an additional uncertainty to the ever-present doubts about the public's attitude to money as income and interest rates change. (p. 8)

In his presentation at the same conference, Davis (1982) writes:

In any case, the interest elasticity of demand for a comprehensive transactions money measure including the new instruments clearly would decline as a larger and larger fraction of the funds included in this total paid "own rates" that move more or less in tandem with short-term market rates. (p. 27)

This opinion was also supported in the contribution by Judd and Scaddings (1982):

The issue under consideration is how will the demand for M1 behave when its own yield begins to vary more flexibly with market rates? The answer should be *qualitatively* the same for M1 and M2. Deregulation should cause an upward level effect on the demand for *both* M1 and M2. The elasticity of both M1 and M2 with respect to market rates should be lower than before deregulation. (p. 96)

The sole dissent recorded at that conference from the prevailing view that interest rate deregulation would *reduce* the interest elasticity of the demand for transactions deposits was drawn by Howard and Johnson (1982) from an analysis of the Canadian experience under financial innovation, and reached exactly the opposite conclusion: "In fact, in Canada the growth of bank accounts paying market rates of interest actually increased rather than decreased the interest sensitivity of the demand for M1 as currently defined" (p. 170).

The surprising aspect of this history is that it appears to be forgotten (or at least ignored) during the 1980s. Since the introduction of NOW accounts the prevailing view about the interest elasticity of money demand in the United States is directly opposite that conjectured during the 1970s. The recent literature suggests that the interest elasticity of the aggregate demand for narrowly defined monetary aggregates has *increased* since the introduction of interest-bearing transactions deposits.[5] This view has prevailed in spite of the evidence that the explicit rates paid on transactions deposits respond very sluggishly to changes in market rates of interest.[6] In the absence of explicit interest payments on transactions deposits that are highly sensitive to changes in market interest rates, it is not clear that the current situation is substantially different from the environment in which the only available interest on such deposits was available in implicit form. The empirical evidence on this issue is quite mixed. The case can be made that the changes that have occurred in the aggregate demand function for narrowly defined monetary aggregates in the 1980s do not involve changes in the interest elasticities. The general nature of such changes is discussed below. In the absence of such elasticity changes and/or continuing portfolio shifts, there does not appear to be any strong case for the hypothesis that financial deregulation provided a major source of difficulty for a successful implementation of noninflationary monetary policy during the 1980s.

General Instability of the Relationship between Monetary Aggregates and Economic Activity in the 1980s

Considerable evidence has been presented since the mid-1970s in favor of the hypothesis that the demand function for M1 in the United States is very unstable. All of this evidence is in terms of the breakdown of some short-run specification, either a demand for money function or a "St. Louis"–type "reduced form" equation. The difficulties with these specifications appear either as severely biased postsample forecasts or as coefficient instability across subsamples. Sometimes the alleged instability is attributed to financial deregulation as discussed above, sometimes it is attributed to financial innovations within an existing regulatory environment, but most frequently a general nonspecific allegation is made to the effect that the old relationships have changed (Friedman 1988a, 1988b). From this the conclusion is reached that the Federal Reserve faced the challenge of "conducting monetary policy without a reliable relationship between the monetary aggregates and economic activity" *(Economic Report of the President,* January 1989, p. 270).

There is strong evidence that the relationship between the narrowly defined monetary aggregates and economic activity was different during the 1980s from that which prevailed in the previous post-accord period. However, it does not appear appropriate to make the leap from this statement to the conclusion that this poses a significant difficulty for the implementation of noninflationary monetary policy over the course of eight to ten years.

The differences in the behavior of several monetary aggregates relative to measures of nominal economic activity in the 1980s as compared with the previous 30 years have been well documented for several years, although the nature and significance of these changes apparently is not widely understood. The change can be easily and accurately characterized in terms of a random walk model of velocity. Prior to 1982, the velocities of narrowly defined monetary aggregates are well described in terms of a random walk model with a positive "drift." For M1 this drift is approximately 3 percent per annum. For the monetary base velocity the drift is somewhat smaller. Since 1981, the same velocities are well described in terms of the same random walk model, but without significant drift. More importantly, there is no evidence in support of the conclusion that the variance of this random walk process has increased in the 1980s over the variance of the process in the earlier period. Equally significant, there is no evidence that the random walk model is subject to continuing change during the 1980s.

The best available evidence is that an abrupt one-time shift in the drift parameter of this model occurred sometime during the latter part of 1981. The dating cannot be determined precisely because of the NOW account changes at the beginning of 1981, but the change began and was completed within 1981. The evidence for this characterization is consistent across a wide selection of narrowly defined monetary aggregates. The discrete nature of this change in the statistical process is not consistent with the financial innovation and deregulation hypotheses that have been advanced in recent years.[7]

Furthermore, there is strong evidence that, in spite of these changes in the drift of the velocity of narrowly defined monetary aggregates, there exists a well-defined long-run demand function relating the (log) level of real balances in the United States to the (log) level of real income and the (log) level of a nominal interest rate. This evidence suggests that the income elasticity of this long-run relationship is not significantly different from unity (so the concept of velocity of such aggregates has long-run economic content) and that the interest elasticity of this relationship is on the order of -0.5 to -0.6 (for M1; smaller in absolute value for the Monetary Base), depending on whether long-term or short-term nominal interest rates are specified. This relationship is extremely robust to changes in sample periods throughout the 1953–87 period (Hoffman and Rasche 1991). The relationship exists even though the velocities of narrowly defined monetary aggregates cannot be distinguished from random walks, because the velocity measures and interest rates are cointegrated (Engle and Granger 1987). There is no statistical inconsistency between the existence of a long-run money demand relationship and a time series process for velocity that cannot be distinguished from a random walk. Neither is there an inconsistency between a change in the drift parameter in the statistical characterization of velocity and stability of the money demand function. These two features of the data are reconciled if cross-equation restrictions hold between the parameters of the univariate time series model of velocity and the univariate time series model of interest rates. Our preliminary analyses suggest that such cross-equation restrictions cannot be rejected.

This kind of evidence is very important for our understanding of the problems in implementing disinflationary monetary policy in the 1980s and in the future. The particular type of change in the relationship between the narrowly defined monetary aggregates and nominal measures of economic activity is the image of a change in the time series character of nominal interest rates. I have suggested elsewhere that the one hypothesis consistent with these data is that in 1981 there was an abrupt change in inflationary expectations.

Assume that in the 1960s and 1970s the expected inflation rate was approximately a random walk with a positive drift. Further assume that after severe monetary contraction in 1980–81 the expected rate of inflation process changed, and since then is approximately a random walk without drift. Such an assumption is consistent with the time series behavior of actual inflation, but it is difficult, if not impossible, to test directly with the limited independent information that is available on inflation expectations. Under many hypotheses about the behavior of real interest rates, such a shift in the constant parameter of the inflation expectations model produces a corresponding shift in the constant parameter in a time series model of the change in the nominal interest rate. Given the available evidence on the stability of the long-run demand for real balances, such a change in the time series representation of nominal rates must be reflected in a change in the constant parameter of the random walk representation of velocity.

The hypothesis that the change in the relationship between monetary aggregates and nominal income measures resulted from a change in inflation expectations has been advanced by a number of economists throughout the 1980s,

Milton Friedman in particular. Until recently I have been skeptical of this argument because I could not reconcile it with the statistical patterns in the data. While the above story must be tested rigorously, I now believe that it can be tentatively regarded as the most plausible explanation of the observed change in the relationship between the monetary aggregates and nominal income that occurred in 1981.

This interpretation suggests that there are "Lucas effects" associated with the implementation of a credible disinflationary monetary policy. Under this hypothesis, when agents come to believe that the monetary policy regime has switched from one that permits accelerating inflation to one of stable or decelerating inflation, then the monetary authorities should expect a change in the average growth rate of velocity of narrowly defined monetary aggregates. If this average growth rate declines, then it will not be necessary to slow the growth of the monetary aggregates as much as would appear from an examination of the historical data generated by the accelerating inflation policy regime in order to accomplish the objective of a constant or declining rate of inflation. For example, using the data from the 1960s and 1970s it was generally believed that to stabilize the inflation rate at 4 percent per annum, the Fed would have to achieve a long-run growth rate of the monetary base of the order of 4 percent per annum to allow for the historical drift of base velocity of around 2 percent. If agents come to believe that inflation is stabilized, and this in turn eliminates the drift of base velocity, then reducing the long-run growth rate of the monetary base to only 6 percent per annum will accomplish the objective of a stable inflation at 4 percent.

With respect to the monetary policy in the 1980s, two things should be noted. First, the "Lucas effect" described above is not the result of financial innovation or deregulation. Under the hypothesis that I have advanced, it will be observed even if deregulation and innovation are absent. Second, it is not appropriate to blame this regime change effect for the fact that inflation did not fall substantially below 4 percent in the 1980s. By the end of the period of inflation stabilization, in late 1985 or early 1986, the characteristics of the change in the behavior of the various velocities were clear to many analysts, even if the reasons for the change are only now being discovered. At that time the average growth rates of the monetary aggregates had not been lowered to anywhere near the rates consistent with price stability, even under the new parameter values for velocity growth.

Independence of the Federal Reserve

The initial statement from the Reagan administration on economic policy recognized the independence of the Federal Reserve System, and appears carefully worded to avoid the appearance of an attempt by the executive branch to dictate policy to the Fed.

Nevertheless, during the course of the administration the opportunity emerged to influence the course of Federal Reserve policy closely. Turnover among Federal Reserve Board members during the 1980s was extremely rapid. By February 1986, the administration had the opportunity to submit and have confirmed four Federal Reserve Board members: Preston Martin, Martha Seger, Manuel Johnson, and Wayne Angell. By the end of the administration the entire membership of the Board had turned over. A considerable number of retirements among the regional Federal Reserve Bank presidents also occurred during these years.

Thus the Reagan administration had ample opportunity to construct a Federal Reserve System that would implement the stated monetary policy objective. However, it is difficult to make the case that any such "packing" of the Federal Reserve Board took place during these years. None of the Reagan nominees is strongly associated with the "slow and steady money growth" advisers to the administration. Several appointees are associated (at least in the press) with the "supply-side" advisers within the administration. As a whole, there does not seem to be any specific strongly held monetary policy philosophy or ideology among the current membership of the Board.

Perhaps the only striking example of a concerted action by the Reagan nominees occurred in March 1986. It was widely reported that there was a "colonels' revolt" against Chairman Volcker at that time over whether the discount rate should be lowered. The alleged rebels were Vice Chairman Martin and Board members Seger, Johnson, and Angell, all Reagan nominees. The popular interpretation is that this was an "uprising" of the "pro-growth" group within the Board against the "anti-inflation" position of Chairman Volcker. Rumors circulated that Chairman Volcker would resign. Shortly thereafter the discount rate was lowered. Chairman Volcker did not resign, although Vice Chairman Martin did leave the Federal Reserve within a matter of months.

It is unlikely that we will ever determine whether the internal controversy over changing the discount rate at that time was anywhere as intense as it was pictured in the press. For purposes of this discussion the important point is that the Reagan nominees were able to promote their views on appropriate monetary policy actions at least by the early part of 1986. Thus the hypothesis that the administration's initial monetary policy objectives were frustrated by the inability to overcome the independence of the Federal Reserve Board is not supported. An alternative to this hypothesis is that the administration submitted nominees who were believed to be sympathetic to the stated monetary policy objective, but who proved their independence after confirmation. This would require strong evidence that the policy positions of these individuals after confirmation are consistently different from their views prior to or during the confirmation proceedings. I have been unable to find such supporting evidence, but a more detailed search might be more productive.

Revised Objectives for Monetary Policy

If we reject the hypotheses that financial deregulation and innovation provided ongoing problems that made achievement of price stability in the 1980s impossible, and we accept the hypothesis that the Reagan administration had tremendous opportunities to construct a Federal Reserve Board sympathetic to the stated monetary policy objective, why has inflation proved so persistent? I believe the most plausible hypothesis is that the administration abandoned the original policy objective of price stability. It is possible to argue that this occurred relatively early, for example, after the international debt crisis in the summer of 1982. My own interpretation of the monetary history of these years is that September 1985 represents a clear break with the initial monetary policy objective by the administration.[8] The Plaza agreements at that time appear as a clear statement of a policy to accelerate the decline of the U.S. dollar against major international currencies. There is support for this hypothesis in the official administration analyses of monetary policy actions in 1985–86:

Monetary policy actions in 1985 were generally accommodative over the year as interest rates fell, the dollar depreciated, and money growth was rapid. The Federal Reserve's accommodative actions were apparently motivated by a perceived need to foster stronger real growth. *(Economic Report of the President,* February 1986, p. 66)

As the economy expanded more slowly than expected during the year and inflation continued to be moderate, the Federal Reserve allowed M1 growth to exceed its predefined target range and relied more heavily on a broader range of economic data. Further depreciation of the dollar in 1986 was apparently not interpreted as a signal of the need for slower monetary growth, probably because real dollar depreciation was widely regarded as desirable to improve U.S. international competitiveness, and because the lower dollar had little visible effect on the inflation rate. In the context of moderate real growth, very low inflation, and falling inflation expectations and given the uncertainty about the behavior of velocity, the de-emphasis of M1 in favor of other variables to gauge the conduct of monetary policy appears to have been an appropriate judgement. *(Economic Report of the President,* January 1987, p. 55)

With a continuation of slower than expected economic growth, moderate inflation, and serious stress in some sectors of the economy, the dangers of a monetary restriction of economic activity are real and important. *(Economic Report of the President,* January 1987, p. 56)

All of these statements are consistent with the abandonment of a long-run price stability objective for monetary policy, in favor of efforts to use monetary policy to influence real economic growth and/or the dollar exchange rate in the short run.

Judging from the public record, the Federal Reserve did not lead in this policy initiative; indeed, the speculation at the time of the Plaza meeting was that Chairman Volcker reluctantly agreed to conform to this revised policy objective. Nevertheless, in the following year and a half to two years, growth rates of the various monetary aggregates accelerated, and within six months the discount rate dispute discussed above erupted among the Federal Reserve Board members.

CONCLUSIONS

Monetary policy during the Reagan administration did not achieve the initial administration objective of price stability by the end of the decade. Apologists argue that success was precluded by events that were outside of the control of either the administration or the Federal Reserve. The available evidence does not provide significant support for these arguments. It is likely that price stability was not achieved during the 1980s because monetary policy was utilized for other objectives, in particular attempts in the short run to influence real economic growth and the exchange rate. These latter objectives are not necessarily consistent with the long-run price stability objective. This was recognized at the time by the Council of Economic Advisers:

Efforts to tailor monetary policy to contemporaneous economic conditions run the risk of being destabilizing. Because of lags and inaccuracies in reported contemporaneous economic data, and the length and variability of the lags in the effect of monetary policy, policy action aimed at a currently perceived problem will not affect the economy until well after the problem has appeared and perhaps disappeared. A policy of targeting real economic activity increases the probability that policy itself becomes destabilizing as economic developments emerge that are unanticipated or inaccurately forecast. *(Economic Report of the President,* February 1986, p. 66)

Nevertheless, such objectives achieved priority.

NOTES

The opinions expressed here are those of the author and not those of the National Bureau of Economic Research.

1. This apparently was also the view of the Reagan administration:

It is difficult to characterize the deceleration in money growth in 1981–82 as either gradual or predictable. The Administration's recommendation assumed a gradual reduction in money growth to 3 percent in 1986. In fact, more than half of the deceleration in money growth that the Administration had envisioned occurring over 6 years occurred during 1981. *(Economic Report of the President,* February 1986, p. 36)

2. On a December to December basis, the CPI excluding food and energy only fluctuated in the range of 3.8 to 4.8 percent during the 1982–87 period.

3. An excellent analysis of the regulatory changes affecting United States financial markets can be found in Cargill and Garcia (1985).

4. The research staff of the Board of Governors estimated and published the magnitude of such portfolio shifts in terms of a "shift adjustment" to the M1 monetary

aggregate. For a discussion of this adjustment see Bennett (1982). For an independent test of the accuracy of these estimates as measures of the effect of these portfolio shifts on the components of the monetary base multiplier, see Rasche and Johannes (1987).

5. Contrasting interpretations of the 1980s can be found in Poole (1988) and Hoffman and Rasche (1989).

6. For evidence on the reaction of explicit rates of interest on transactions deposits to changes in market rates of interest, see Moore, Porter, and Small (1990).

7. See Rasche (1987: 9–88) for a review of a large number of such hypotheses.

8. The Council of Economic Advisers cites two distinct break points in monetary policy implementation during the first Reagan term: Fall 1982 and late 1984 *(Economic Report of the President,* February 1986, pp. 56–57).

"Interest Rates in the Reagan Years" and "Monetary Policy in the 1980s": *Comment*

Anandi P. Sahu and
Ronald L. Tracy

The performance of monetary policy under the Reagan administration was of great significance as both the nominal interest and inflation rates were at double-digit levels when Reagan came to power. The two chapters by Hendershott and Peek, and Rasche evaluate the performance of Reagan monetary policy from slightly different perspectives. While the Hendershott and Peek study examines the ability of Reagan monetary policy to lower nominal interest rates (and its inability to reduce real interest rates), the Rasche chapter evaluates the success of Reagan monetary policy in terms of the objectives articulated at the time the Reagan administration assumed office. The two chapters also arrive at somewhat different conclusions regarding the success of monetary policy during the Reagan years.

HENDERSHOTT AND PEEK

Hendershott and Peek empirically examine whether Reagan's economic and budgetary goals had a significant impact on interest rates. They investigate these effects in the framework of analyzing the importance of diverse economic factors. In particular, they examine the following factors: the lower inflation rate, the increased budget deficits, the tight money supply of the early 1980s, the switch in Fed operating procedures, financial deregulation, and the reduction in marginal tax rates. These six hypotheses are analyzed using yields on Treasury securities, fixed-rate mortgages, and tax-exempt securities. They examine the behavior of both nominal and real interest rates.

The Hendershott and Peek study suggests that the rise and fall in nominal interest rates closely corresponds to the rise and fall in inflation and expected inflation. To the extent that the Reagan Administration can claim credit for the sharp reduction in the inflation rate, it can take credit for lower nominal interest rates.

They argue, based on their previous study (Hendershott and Peek 1989), that the Reagan fiscal policy, broadly defined to include changes in tax rates and structural deficits, lowers real rates, instead of raising them. The evidence in the literature regarding the effect of fiscal policy (especially the effects of the federal budget deficit) on the real interest rate is quite muddled. Hendershott and Peek's findings try to resolve these inconsistencies. Since, however, there are problems in measuring both "structural" deficits and the "expected" inflation rate, those that disagree with their findings will probably not be convinced.

With respect to the effects of Reagan monetary policy on the real interest rate, Hendershott and Peek conclude that monetary policy could not be held responsible for the rise in interest rates during 1981–84. This is contrary to the popular view. Their chapter itself does not provide any hard evidence to support their claim or discuss the statistical significance of the effects of the Reagan fiscal and monetary policies. They argue that the emphasis on the high real interest rates in the early 1980s has been overdone, as people had become used to the extraordinarily low real rates during much of the 1970s.

Hendershott and Peek do provide convincing evidence that the volatility of interest rates did affect mortgage rates. Also, regulatory reforms and profit squeeze led thrifts to shift out of fixed-rate home mortgages in the 1980s, contributing to the rise in the mortgage rate.

According to this study, the Reagan marginal tax cuts put an upward pressure on interest rates, as measured by the ratio of tax-exempt to taxable yields. This conclusion is supported by estimated simple regressions. This finding, however, is inconsistent with their statements in the early part of the chapter, in which they argue that the tax rate series is positively correlated with the real rate.

Taken as a whole, Hendershott and Peek do not find evidence of adverse effects of monetary and fiscal policies on real interest rates. They do, however, suggest that changes in inflation (and expected inflation), interest rate volatility, thrift deregulation, and the reduction in marginal tax rates put an upward pressure on nominal interest rates. The main problem that one may face in using the Hendershott and Peek study in evaluating the Reagan economic legacy is that the latter four factors were also components of the broader Reagan policy. Thus, a more comprehensive study should discuss the net effect of all Reagan policies as well as effects attributable to monetary policy, fiscal policy, and factors beyond the control of policymakers.

RASCHE

As pointed out earlier, the Rasche chapter examines the success of Reagan monetary policy on the basis of its own stated objectives. The goal of the Reagan administration was to lower the inflation rate from the double-digit levels to a zero average rate. Despite the continued expansion, the inflation rate was substantially reduced. The inflation rate, as measured by the CPI index, excluding food and energy components, was at 12.2 percent during 1979–80 (December to December). It fell to 4.5 percent during 1981–82 and as Rasche himself points out, on a December-to-December basis, the CPI index, excluding food and energy components, only fluctuated in the range of 3.8 to 4.8 percent during the 1982–87 period. This performance on the inflation front is adjudged by Rasche as the failure of Reagan monetary policy to realize the admirable objective of a zero average inflation rate.

Rasche then examines alternative explanations of the failure of Reagan's monetary policy to achieve price stability. The two popular explanations he examines were offered in the *1989 Annual Report of the Council of Economic Advisors:* the absence of a reliable relationship between the monetary aggregates and economic activity, and a breakdown in the short-term relationship between various monetary aggregates and income and interest rates. He adds two additional hypotheses to this list: the "independence" of the Fed, and the possibility that the administration's original "game plan" was abandoned sometime during the course of the decade. After examining these hypotheses, Rasche concludes that the failure was not due to events outside the control of the administration or the Federal Reserve, as argued by "apologists." He contends that "it is likely that price stability was not achieved during the 1980s because monetary policy was utilized for other objectives, in particular attempts in the short run to influence real economic growth and the exchange rate."

While it is difficult to deny that the conduct of monetary policy during the Reagan administration as well as in the recent past is geared mainly to stabilize short-run inflation and unemployment rates, it is also difficult to accept the view that being able to stabilize inflation only at about 4 percent implies a dismal policy failure. One cannot dispute Rasche's argument that Reagan monetary policy failed to achieve a zero average inflation rate. However, one must ask if a zero rate of inflation is either a realistic or a desirable goal. A 5 percent inflation in one year followed by a 5 percent disinflation would produce a zero average inflation rate. Will this inflation behavior be considered more desirable than, say, a 3 percent stable inflation rate? While moderately rising prices are good, a zero inflation may be unrealistic. Average zero inflation, if generated through deflation and instability, is definitely undesirable. One must admit, nevertheless, the current inflation rate of about 5 percent is somewhat high. If the monetary policy can stabilize inflation in the 2–3 percent range without sacrificing employment, economists should celebrate!

11

Monetary Policy in the Reagan Era

Martha Seger

I am supposed to discuss monetary policy in the Reagan era. However, it is a little difficult to do this in an objective way since at least for part of the Reagan term I have been a part of the policymaking apparatus. During the first four years of the Reagan administration, I was, of course, watching, while during the last four and half years I was a part of it. Hence, I hope I will have at least a little bit of objectivity.

The unprecedented economic expansion we experienced since 1982 followed some major reorientation in economic policies at the outset of the Reagan administration. Monetary policy was a key element in that reorientation. Although it did not always follow the stable and gradual path envisioned by the administration, its conduct, nevertheless, complemented the various economic policies that contributed to the outbreak of prosperity in the 1980s.

BACKGROUND

It is helpful to examine the economic background at the time the Reagan administration came into office in 1981. The U.S. economy was experiencing unprecedented inflation caused by various supply disturbances and monetary policies of the past. Economic growth was sluggish despite a rapidly expanding labor force. The unemployment rate was quite high and manufacturing productivity performance was lackluster. There was a general sense of unease in the business community due to excessive regulatory burden. The stock market performance was unexciting, to say the least, while rising interest rates kept buying markets subdued. At the same time, confidence in the dollar had eroded significantly. It was against this disturbing economic backdrop that Ronald Reagan was voted into office. His economic program encompassed several elements, but its unifying principle was its rededication to incentives—incentives to innovate, save, invest, produce, and work. The rededication appeared on several fronts under the rubric of supply-side economics.

First, very heavy emphasis was placed on reducing the role of government through tax reform. Reduction in individual and corporate marginal tax rates, and other distortionary effects of taxation were a major part of the Reagan agenda. The objective here was twofold: first, to elicit a larger production work effort, and second, to control the lifeline of government. More revenues for government spending could only be possible through an expansion of the tax base.

The second task of containing government was to contain growth in spending. Expansion of entitlement programs and other nondefense government transfer programs was to be brought under control. At the same time, a redirection of emphasis on the social welfare spending away from the federal government and more toward the states was to be accomplished. In the other camps, substantial increases in defense expenditures were envisaged as part of the administration's national security agenda.

The third element in the program was deregulation. After almost two decades of unwise and counterproductive regulation of the private sector, deleterious effects on economic activity and export became visible. At the same time, regulation of specific industries served to inhibit competition and foster inefficiency. To combat these effects, the Reagan administration undertook to deregulate specific industries and to lighten the regulatory burden on businesses in general. Various regulatory agencies were now disposed toward a more rational approach to regulation.

Finally, price stability was once again to be a paramount objective of monetary policy. By the end of the 1970s, the political consensus had formed around the necessity to gear monetary policy toward controlling inflation. A noninflationary environment was seen as the path to sustainable and stable economic growth. The distortionary effects of inflation on the price signals, which are essential for efficient allocation of resources, were recognized. Fostering price stability was intended to promote investment by reducing the uncertainty and by promoting greater stability in financial and foreign exchange markets.

Reflecting the consensus on containing inflation, the Fed moved in October 1979 to alter its operating procedures so as to achieve more stringent control of the rate of growth of the money supply. Prior to this change, through most of the 1970s, interest rates served as the primary instrument of monetary policy. This effectively produced a policy that emphasized interest rate stability to a degree inconsistent with the role of price stability. Interest rate target ranges were not adjusted frequently or sufficiently enough to yield money supply growth consistent with low inflation. Moreover, monetary policy became actually procyclical so that money supply growth increased during expansion and decreased during recession. Consequent ratcheting-up of inflation and inflationary expectations necessitated a more direct and stricter control of the money supply. Hence a change in the operating procedure was instituted.

THE 1981–82 RECESSION

I think one cannot overemphasize the significance of the endorsement of the Reagan administration of a monetary policy more firmly committed to combating inflation. While consensus had emerged on the primacy of the price stability objective, the medicine to be swallowed to achieve it required strong political will and support. The sequence of events during 1981 and 1982 is well known.

The Fed's new operating procedures meant strict adherence to nonborrowed reserves targets and a tolerance of the implied variability of interest rates. The results were: a sharp run-up of interest rates to a stratospheric level, a severe contraction of economic activity, very high unemployment rates, and near-depression conditions in some parts of the country. Unfortunately, the list is long.

In a nutshell, the worst postwar recession was upon us. These were not conditions that weak administrations could withstand politically. However, for the Reagan administration, the President's popularity and persuasiveness helped ease the political pressure. The change in the Fed's operating procedures was predicated on the traditional belief in a strong relationship between the money supply and the nominal GNP. The philosophy of a stable relationship, of course, implies that an increase in the money supply leads to a proportional increase in the nominal GNP. The precise distribution of this increase between output and prices depends on the degree of resource utilization in the economy and the way in which inflationary expectations are formed as well as the time horizon under consideration. This was a long-term proposition under stable money demand conditions. Its reasoning is the basis for the connection between excessive money growth and inflation. For much of the postwar period, the evidence seemed to support the fundamental implications of this reasoning. However, since the early 1980s this relationship has become much looser, primarily because of the erratic behavior of interest rates.

Ironically, the change in money stock-oriented operating procedure coincided with the significant institutional changes that contributed to the reduced relevance of monetary aggregates for stabilizing prices. Deregulation, the application of advanced automation and communication systems in the provision of financial services, and a proliferation of new financial instruments blurred the distinction between transactions and other types of money balances. In retrospect, therefore, the outcome of the new operating procedures in the wake of financial innovation and deregulation was a policy that turned out to be tighter than was actually intended. However, a sympathetic administration allowed it to persist longer than it might have otherwise.

Once the loss of stability in the relationship between monetary growth and economic activity was recognized, it became necessary for the Fed to adopt a more flexible approach to monetary policy while still appearing to adhere to its commitment to price stability. Thus, starting in late 1982, the Fed began to pursue a more eclectic approach which proved, I would argue, rather effective. Broader aggregates were given weight in policy decisions and deliberations. Increasing attention was given to other indicators such as commodity prices, interest rates (especially the yield curve), and exchange rates. Such flexibility was also necessitated by the greater uncertainty resulting from the rapid structural change and various imbalances. The range of policy objectives therefore widened, with exchange rate stability and financial and credit market conditions at times receiving greater emphasis.

THE HISTORIC ECONOMIC EXPANSION

The 1982 recession, accompanied by a significant reduction in inflation, paved the way for what was to be a historic period of economic expansion and prosperity. By most broad measures, the performance of the economy since then has been impressive. Since 1983, real growth has averaged 4.2 percent, inflation as measured by CPI has averaged 3.5 percent, and the unemployment rate has been cut in half. Not only is this record remarkable by our own historical standards, it also compares very favorably with that of other countries. We have enjoyed a remarkable degree of price stability. At the producer level, excluding the bulk of food and energy components, prices have risen moderately and unit labor costs have increased even less than the broader measures of inflation. While international competition, global excess capacity, and slack in labor markets contributed to this stability, monetary policy also remained vigilant. Thus in 1984, as the rate of economic expansion appeared strong, monetary policy turned restrictive until concerns arose about an impending slowdown toward the end of the year.

For most of 1987 monetary policy again leaned in the direction of restraint to counter potential inflationary pressures from the depreciating dollar and the rise in oil prices. The gradual tightening was interrupted by the stock market crash in October 1987. In its aftermath, the Federal Reserve provided sufficient liquidity to restore confidence in the financial markets and to ensure the viability of financial systems. As confidence was restored and fears of adverse effects on economic activity receded, the Fed absorbed this excess liquidity.

In the spring of 1988, as concerns about impending inflationary pressures mounted, monetary policy was again tightened. It is noteworthy that as events unfolded during these weeks, monetary policy carried an unusually heavy burden. The gradual winding of the Reagan monetary expansion envisioned at the outset of the Reagan era was not to come about until the final years of his administration. The shock treatment in the early years quickly wrung out the inflationary impetus. However, velocity disturbances, financial shocks, and exchange rate considerations precluded the adoption of a gradual approach in subsequent years. During these years monetary policy had to respond to developments and crises of great economic concern, and thereby deviated from the stable monetary growth blueprint of the Reagan monetary advisers.

Two additional factors complicated the conduct of monetary policy in the Reagan years. First was the large fiscal deficit that resulted from a combination of spending increases, tax rate cuts, the effects of the severe 1981 recession on both revenues and spending, and rising interest rates. Clearly, by closing the fiscal option, the massive budget deficits restricted the Fed's room to maneuver and led to higher interest rates then, I think, would have otherwise prevailed. Second, the greater globalization of the world financial market probably further loosened the connection between money supply and economic activity, making it difficult to gauge the effect of monetary policy actions on economic growth.

Despite these complications, since 1986 monetary policy has been on a stable path and has achieved price stability. Since then M2 growth has averaged about 4.5 percent and M3 growth about 5.5 percent. Each year the target ranges for monetary growth have been lowered to underscore the Federal Reserve's long-term commitment to price stability. In fact, the more recent figures put M2 growth below its target range.

CONCLUSION

The experience of the 1980s indicates that the Fed enjoyed considerable support of the Reagan administration in pursuing policies designed to break inflation. While Reagan's advisers may have preferred to pursue a more gradual and smoother transition to lower inflation, their support for the Fed's stringent policy in the early 1980s was essential to the success of monetary policy in bringing down inflation. Without this support, the outcome of the nonborrowed reserve target approach of the Fed may have concluded sooner.

Several lessons can be drawn from the evolution of monetary policy in the Reagan era. First, price stability should be a paramount objective of monetary policy and inflationary pressures must be checked early, as they emerge. The cost of controlling inflation is compounded the longer inflation is allowed to persist. Moreover, once inflation takes hold, the critical will required to bear the cost becomes difficult to muster because of the resulting inflation-dependent constituency.

Second, effective monetary policy requires cooperation, mutual respect, and trust between an administration and the Fed. This is especially necessary when policy actions might be politically unpopular. But at the same time, independence of the monetary authority certainly must be preserved. The experience of the 1960s and 1970s and that of many other nations around the world suggest that if this independence is compromised, monetary authorities are unable to carry out their primary task—to foster economic growth in the environment of price stability. Support and mutual respect still implies support for this in-dependence.

Third, flexibility and discretion in monetary policy is desirable, despite fear. This is particularly true if the environment in which this policy operates is characterized by rapid change. It is, at the same time, imperative that monetary authorities use this flexibility judiciously in the achievement of their ultimate objectives.

While history is often rewritten, the verdict so far on monetary policy during the Reagan era has, I believe, been favorable. I am obviously biased, but I am also optimistic that this legacy will prevail for a very long time.

NOTE

Views expressed in this chapter are solely those of the author and do not necessarily reflect the views of the Federal Reserve Board.

Part V

International Trade

12

Trade Policy of the Reagan Years

Alan V. Deardorff

The Reagan administration was founded on a commitment to free-market principles, in the international arena as well as domestically. However, there is wide agreement that in practice the Reagan years were marked by much less withdrawal from government intervention in trade than in domestic economic affairs. On the contrary, some have condemned the Reagan administration as the most protectionist since Herbert Hoover, an astonishing criticism given the ideological stance that was consistently maintained. In this chapter I will review the record of the Reagan years as it relates to trade and trade policy, and I will attempt to discern whether this condemnation of that record is justified.

Disappointment in the trade policies of the Reagan years is widely felt. Given the free-market orientation of the administration's ideology, one might have expected to witness a marked movement in the direction of freer trade.[1] Instead, the best that even the Reagan administration itself can say about its trade policies is that "the record of the 1980s has largely paralleled that of the 1970s."[2] After having participated in the Reagan administration for a time, William Niskanen (1988: 137) viewed the record more critically:

Trade policy in the Reagan administration is best described as a strategic retreat. The consistent goal of the president was free trade, both in the United States and abroad. In response to domestic political pressure, however, the administration imposed more restraints on trade than any administration since Hoover.

And this view is evidently shared abroad, as, for example, where the *Economist* (January 21, 1989: 75) notes that "Mr. Reagan claimed to be a free trader, but he has been the most protectionist president for decades."

Charles Pearson (1989: 2) has provided the most recent and detailed critical evaluation of the Reagan trade record, which he finds wanting, both by the standard of free trade and by the less demanding standard of liberal trade:

When measured against the criterion of a laissez faire, or free trade, policy the Reagan record falls short. . . . Yet even when measured against the less demanding criteria of liberal trade—resisting new import restrictions, nondiscrimination among trade partners, a broad (traditional) view of reciprocity, minimal subsidization or restriction of exports, and a reluctance to use trade policy to promote foreign policy objectives—the Reagan record also falls short, and, arguably, shorter than that of all other postwar Presidents.

The practice of U.S. trade policy in the past eight years has been characterized by frequent rhetorical bows toward liberal trade and some actions that promote liberal trade, but it also displayed a ready acceptance of departures based on "political" or pragmatic considerations, not on principle. In this respect the Reagan administration is indistinguishable from its predecessors in the postwar era.

Readers who wish to see in detail the bases for these conclusions should read Pearson's excellent treatment directly. I will provide more of an overview of the issues and some broad indicators of the stance of trade and trade policy during the Reagan years.

I begin with a brief review of some of the major trade policy events of the Reagan years. These are listed on p. 189.[3]

The list reveals what others also have mentioned as the two distinctive threads of the trade policy of the era: continued and increased trade restrictions, and discriminatory reductions in trade restrictions. With only two exceptions, the items listed fall into one or the other of these two categories.

The two exceptions are important, however, and should be mentioned first. One was the attempt in 1982, at the first General Agreement on Tariffs and Trade (GATT) ministerial meeting in nine years, first, to extend liberalized trade to agriculture and services, and second, to inaugurate a new round of multilateral trade negotiations. These attempts failed and the meeting ended without any major breakthroughs, in part because of the worldwide recession but also in part because the United States "backed off from [the second] goal even before the meeting began."[4]

The other exception was the successful inauguration of the Uruguay Round of Multilateral Trade Negotiations in 1987. Here the Reagan administration did take charge, not only in getting the negotiations underway, but also in forming the agenda. The Uruguay Round negotiations are currently proceeding in a number of areas, including not only agriculture and services, but also such new areas as intellectual property rights and trade-related investment measures.[5]

With the exception of these two ventures into the realm of multilateral trade liberalization, all of the events listed represent either increased barriers to trade or discriminatory reductions in barriers. Thus the United States either renegotiated existing barriers or negotiated new ones in textiles, autos, and sugar in 1981, in steel in 1982 and 1984, in machine tools and textiles in 1986, and in

Major Trade Policy Events of the Reagan Years

Year	Event	Description
1981	Renewal of MFA	The second renewal of the Multi-Fiber Arrangement (MFA III) was negotiated, continuing a trend toward tightening its restrictions that had begun with MFA II.
1981	Auto VER	The United States negotiated with Japan to limit automobile exports to the United States.
1981	Sugar Quotas	The existing system of sugar price supports was facilitated by a system of quotas.
1982	GATT Ministerial	A GATT Ministerial Meeting was held in Geneva but failed to make any major breakthrough, and did not succeed in launching a new round of trade negotiations.
1982	Steel VER with Europe	The United States negotiated a comprehensive quota on steel imports from each country in Europe. Further restrictions and agreements regarding steel followed.
1983	Caribbean Basin Initiative	The United States extended preferential access to countries in the Caribbean Basin.
1984	Steel VER	An ITC recommendation for quotas on steel was rejected, and instead VERs were negotiated with all major suppliers except Canada.
1984	Trade and Tariff Act of 1984	Renewed Generalized System of Preferences. Reduced tariffs on about 100 products. Strengthened authority to retaliate against unfair trade practices. Broadened criteria for injury in escape clause cases. Provided authority to establish bilateral free trade areas.
1985	U.S.-Israel FTA	A free trade agreement was negotiated between Israel and the United States.
1986	Machine tool VER	Negotiated voluntary export restraints on machine tool imports from four countries.
1986	Renewal of MFA	The third renewal of the Multi-Fiber Arrangement (MFA IV) was negotiated, extending it for five years. At the United States' insistence, the restrictions on textile trade were extended and tightened.
1986	Semiconductor Accord	Japan agreed to stop dumping chips in third-country markets and to increase the U.S. share of the Japanese chip market.
1986	GATT Ministerial	Approval of agenda to launch the Uruguay Round of Multilateral Trade Negotiations.
1987	Semiconductor Sanctions	The United States imposed sanctions against certain imports from Japan in response to violations of the 1986 accord.
1987	Uruguay Round	The Uruguay Round of Multilateral Trade Negotiations was begun.
1988	U.S.-Canada FTA	Negotiations (begun in 1986) for a free trade agreement between the United States and Canada were completed.
1988	Omnibus Trade and Competitiveness Act	Provided authority for Uruguay Round trade negotiations. Shifted authority for some aspects of trade policy to the U.S. Trade Representative. Made retaliation against some unfair trade practices mandatory.

semiconductors in 1987. At the same time, the United States eliminated trade restrictions, but only with particular trading partners, in the Caribbean Basin Initiative in 1983, the U.S.–Israel Free Trade Agreement in 1985, and the U.S.–Canada Free Trade Agreement (FTA) in 1988. Given the special place that had previously been accorded to the most favored nation principle of non-discrimination in the GATT for the preceding 35 years, the departure from this principle in the negotiation of these free trade agreements has been cause for concern.

However, the U.S. position is that these free trade agreements will serve as stimuli to multilateral liberalization. The hope is that countries that are left out of such bilateral arrangements will recognize the advantages of being included, and thus will be more amenable to participation in multilateral reductions in trade barriers. This could be especially useful if the bilateral arrangements are also able to lead the way into currently uncharted territories of liberalization, such as the new topics being discussed in the Uruguay Round. The success of the U.S.–Canada FTA in dealing with some of these issues indeed suggests that this may be the case. However, until the Uruguay Round is completed successfully, it will be impossible to know whether the short-term adverse effects of discrimination are outweighed by the long-run benefits of the stimulus these agreements may provide to progress on the multilateral front.

Finally, I should mention one other theme of the trade policies of the Reagan years that does not stand out as clearly in the listing of events above but that is nonetheless distinctive of the period. U.S. trade policies have been used actively in an effort to induce our trading partners to open their markets and thus to expand trade, not just by increasing U.S. imports but also by pressing for increases in exports, both of the United States and of other countries as well.

One example of these attempts to open up foreign markets was the Semiconductor Accord of 1986. Under this agreement, the United States persuaded Japan to stop its alleged dumping in third country markets, and also to increase the U.S. share of the Japanese domestic market for computer chips. This second half of the agreement, then, was intended to remove what were perceived to be barriers to the U.S. penetration of the Japanese market and, if successful, would have demonstrated the ability of U.S. trade policy to negotiate the opening of foreign markets. Unfortunately, as it turned out the increased share of the Japanese market was not achieved, and the United States proceeded in 1987 to impose sanctions against a variety of imports from Japan. There has still not been much progress in this area, and it remains the case that this policy, which was intended to expand trade, has had the effect of contracting it.

TRADE VOLUMES

As a first step in assessing the trade policies of the Reagan years, I look at trade itself. There are obviously a great many factors that can influence the

Figure 12.1
U.S. Trade as Percent of GNP

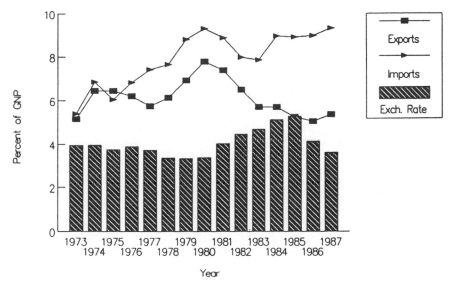

volume of trade other than the stance of trade policy, and it would therefore be inappropriate to conclude that trade policies have been, say, restrictive just because trade has not grown. Nonetheless, the volume of trade surely provides the first piece of evidence that one must look at, since it constitutes the backdrop against which other indicators of trade policy should be viewed.

Figures 12.1 and 12.2 therefore depict the volume of exports and imports of the United States for the years 1973 through 1987. Figure 12.1 shows total trade, while Figure 12.2 shows trade only in manufactures. The vertical distance between the curves in each case is the corresponding trade balance. Because both exports and imports might reasonably be expected to expand and contract with the level of overall economic activity, and in order to abstract from the considerable changes in prices that occurred over the period, the figures present all of these values as percentages of U.S. GNP. It appears from Figure 12.1 that, as fractions of GNP, total exports have grown only slightly if at all, while imports have grown considerably over the last 15 years. Consequently, the trade balance, which has been in deficit over most of this period, has worsened steadily. From Figure 12.1 it is also evident that while total exports and imports both grew during the 1970s, the level of exports then fell off in the 1980s while the level of imports remained approximately constant. Thus the Reagan years have been marked by a decline in total exports and roughly constant total imports. This is hardly the record one might expect of a regime of liberal trade.

Of course, the performance of exports and imports in the 1980s has been very much associated with the behavior of the U.S. exchange rate. The consid-

Figure 12.2
Manufacturing Trade as Percent of GNP

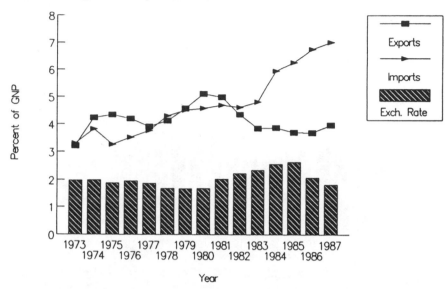

erable appreciation of the dollar in the early 1980s was notorious for stimulating U.S. imports and depressing exports, while the subsequent depreciation was expected to have the opposite effects. An index of the effective value (trade weighted) of the U.S. dollar is therefore also reported in Figures 12.1 and 12.2 to assist in interpreting what occurred.

From Figure 12.1 it appears that while the effect of the dollar appreciation in retarding exports is evident, its presumed effect in expanding imports is not. Total imports reached their peak in 1980, before the appreciation had begun, and remained approximately level thereafter. Thus if the appreciation did have its presumed effect in stimulating imports, then there must have been something else happening that offset this effect. This supports the hypothesis that other trade policies may have been becoming more restrictive.

I should point out, however, that merchandise imports did behave somewhat differently from total imports. As is shown in Figure 12.2, imports of manufactures grew from about 5 percent of GNP in 1980 to 7 percent of GNP in 1987. Much of this increase can indeed be attributed to the rising dollar. Evidently, then, the failure of total imports to grow over this period was due to a substantial decline in nonmanufacturing imports. This was indeed what happened. While space does not permit a report on the sectoral performance of U.S. trade, primary product imports did in fact decline substantially from 1980 to 1987, and virtually all of that decline occurred in the fuels sector. Thus the message given by the performance of total trade in Figure 12.1 may be misleading, and a more accurate picture may be given in Figure 12.2, where the message is much more neutral. Manufacturing exports fell and imports rose after 1980 in a manner that can reasonably be attributed to the appreciation of the dollar.

FORMAL TRADE BARRIERS

I turn now to an investigation of the formal trade barriers that the United States has maintained against imports. While one might expect that an investigation of the openness of U.S. trade policy would be primarily concerned with such formal barriers, it turns out that they are not very useful indicators. The reason is that tariffs, on the one hand, have played only a rather minor role in trade policy in recent years, while other barriers to trade are singularly difficult to get information about. Nonetheless, an examination of U.S. trade policies would be incomplete without at least looking at the information that does exist.

Tariffs

Tariff levels were bound by the signatories of the General Agreement on Tariffs and Trade (GATT) at the time of its formation. Since then tariffs in all GATT members have been reduced substantially, mostly through a succession of rounds of trade negotiations. The levels of U.S. tariffs are therefore almost entirely reflective of these negotiations. Because the last completed negotiation, the Tokyo Round, was concluded in 1979, the behavior of tariffs in the 1980s reflects decisions that were made in the preceding decade. They are relevant for understanding the trade policies of the 1980s only to the extent that any previously negotiated changes in tariffs may have posed difficulties of adjustment during the 1980s as the negotiated reductions were put in place.

Table 12.1 reports the levels of pre– and post–Tokyo round tariffs for the United States and for an import-weighted average of 17 other major industrialized countries. Since the Tokyo Round tariff reductions were phased in over the eight years beginning in 1980, these figures accurately reflect the performance of tariffs over the Reagan years.

As can be seen, tariffs have been highly uneven across sectors, even at the rather aggregated level of the mostly three-digit International Standard Industrial Classification (ISIC) industries reported in the table. Even before the Tokyo round, sectoral tariff levels in the United States ranged from a low of 0.5 percent in Paper and Paper Products, to a high of 27.8 percent in Wearing Apparel. The range of tariff levels reported for the other industrialized countries was somewhat smaller, although this is undoubtedly because of the averaging across countries. The average tariff levels in these other countries were noticeably higher than those in the United States.

A result of the Tokyo Round was the reduction of tariffs in virtually all sectors and countries.[6] The U.S. average tariff fell from 4.5 percent to 3.1 percent while that of the other industrialized countries fell from 7.1 to 5.5 percent. However, the pattern of tariffs across industries remained roughly as

Table 12.1

Percentage Tariff Levels and Percent of Trade Covered by Nontariff Barriers in the United States and Other Industrialized Countries[a] (selected years)

Industry	ISIC	Percentage Tariff Levels				Percent of Trade Covered by Nontariff Barriers			
		Pre-Tokyo Round (1979)		Post-Tokyo Round (1988)		1973		1983	
		U.S.	Other Industrialized	U.S.	Other Industrialized	U.S.	Other Industrialized	U.S.	Other Industrialized
Agr., For., & Fishing[b]	1	2.2	8.9	1.8	9.2	1.4	43.9	2.9	18.4
Food, Bev., & Tobacco	310	6.3	13.6	4.7	12.3	45.4	19.6	31.1	63.2
Textiles	321	14.4	10.6	9.2	8.4	41.3	28.1	43.5	38.1
Wearing Apparel	322	27.8	18.7	22.7	15.5	66.1	41.2	4.1	56.9
Leather Products	323	5.6	4.3	4.2	3.0	0.0	1.3	0.0	12.5
Footwear	324	8.8	14.4	8.8	13.3	51.2	29.1	25.2	10.8
Wood Products	331	3.6	2.6	1.7	2.5	0.0	0.0	59.3	6.6
Furniture & Fixtures	332	8.1	10.3	4.1	7.4	0.0	0.0	0.0	7.9
Paper & Paper Products	341	0.5	7.3	0.2	5.3	60.6	0.8	0.6	8.9
Printing & Publishing	342	1.1	3.1	0.7	1.7	0.0	4.4	4.6	2.0
Chemicals	35A	3.8	9.8	2.4	7.0	56.2	4.6	1.6	7.5
Petrol. & Rel. Prod.	35B	1.4	1.5	1.4	1.4	0.0	45.1	39.1	15.4
Rubber Products	355	3.6	6.4	2.5	4.4	0.0	4.0	3.5	8.5
Nonmetallic Min. Prod.	36A	9.1	5.3	5.3	3.8	0.0	9.8	4.0	10.3
Glass & Glass Products	362	10.7	10.4	6.2	8.1	0.0	0.0	5.1	2.3
Iron & Steel	371	4.7	5.9	3.6	4.4	10.0	7.7	9.8	25.0
Nonferrous Metals	372	1.2	2.2	0.7	1.9	0.0	8.5	0.5	4.2
Metal Products	381	7.5	9.3	4.8	6.2	0.0	3.1	13.9	4.2
Nonelectric Machinery	382	5.0	7.0	3.3	4.8	0.0	2.2	1.9	4.4
Electric Machinery	383	6.6	10.5	4.4	7.8	8.3	6.7	4.0	13.1
Transportation Equip.	384	3.3	8.9	2.5	7.5	1.8	13.4	5.7	28.2
Miscellaneous Manufac.	38A	7.8	7.7	4.2	4.9	0.5	3.4	5.4	9.1
Total Traded		**4.5**	**7.1**	**3.1**	**5.5**	**22.3**	**18.6**	**19.3**	**18.7**

[a] Other industrialized countries are: Australia, Austria, Canada, Finland, Japan, New Zealand, Norway, Sweden, Switzerland, and the European Economic Community (Belgium-Luxembourg, Denmark, France, Germany, Ireland, Italy, Netherlands, and the United Kingdom)

[b] NTB Coverage for agriculture excludes the European Economic Community due to lack of data on the Common Agricultural Policy.

Sources: Tariffs based on data supplied by the Office of the U.S. Trade Representative. NTB coverage from a World Bank Tape.

before, and there does not seem to have been any tendency to make very large reductions in tariffs of individual sectors, either in the United States or elsewhere. It does not seem likely, therefore, that the Tokyo Round tariff cuts were large enough to have caused noticeable dislocation in individual industries that would have created a need for other policies to assist in the adjustment.[7] On the contrary, one can conclude that tariffs were largely irrelevant to the performance of trade policy in the Reagan years.

Nontariff Barriers

In view of the low levels of tariffs in the industrialized countries, it is generally accepted that other trade-restricting measures, so-called nontariff barriers or NTBs, today constitute the more important impediments to trade.[8] These can in principle include any and all policies other than tariffs that can impact on trade, but the main forms of NTBs that get attention are import quotas and voluntary export restraints (VERs). Unfortunately, even these fairly well-defined forms of NTB are notoriously difficult to quantify, while other forms of NTB are often difficult even to document.[9]

Therefore, most investigators of NTBs have had to make do with an admittedly very poor and often misleading measure of the presence of NTBs: the percentage of trade that appears to be covered by them. The accuracy of this measure is itself suspect since, on the one hand, the presence of many NTBs is difficult to ascertain, and, on the other hand, other NTBs that are known to be present, such as quotas, may well be redundant and hence have no effects on trade. Furthermore, even if measured accurately, this means of quantifying NTBs can be misleading. The more restrictive a particular NTB may be, and hence the smaller the volume of trade that it permits, the smaller will be the percentage of trade that it appears to cover. In the extreme, a complete import prohibition would not show up at all in such a measure of trade coverage.

Nonetheless, there does not exist any other generally available method for measuring NTBs, and I therefore report in Table 12.1 some limited information of this sort about NTBs in the United States and elsewhere. Unfortunately, the only data available are for the years 1973 and 1983, which do a rather poor job of characterizing the behavior of NTBs in the Reagan years.

What appears from the Table is, first, that the overall trade coverage of NTBs did not change much over that ten-year stretch. The trade coverage by NTBs in the United States did fall, but only slightly, from 22.3 percent to 19.3 percent. Given the inaccuracy of the measure being used, that is hardly a significant change. Furthermore, by this measure the coverage by NTBs in the other industrialized countries actually rose a tiny bit.[10] Therefore, by this measure it does not appear that nontariff barriers either increased or decreased significantly during the second half of the 1970s and early 1980s.

There do appear, however, to have been noticeable changes in NTBs in a few particular sectors. The trade coverage by U.S. NTBs declined substantially, for example, in the food, apparel, footwear, and printing and publishing industries, while it increased substantially in wood products, metal products, and transportation equipment. Thus there is evidence, if not of protectionism, at least of activism in the use of nontariff trade barriers.

It is unfortunate that these data, poor as they are, do not extend through the remainder of the Reagan years. One can only speculate on what these trade coverage measures would look like today. I listed in the first section a number of NTBs that were instituted after 1983, including the expansion of the coverage of the VER on steel, the VER on machine tools, and the semiconductor accord. Also, in its 1986 renewal the multifiber arrangement was extended and tightened. At the same time, I am not aware of any important NTBs that have been removed since 1983, except for the lapsing of the VER on automobiles from Japan, a restriction which has nonetheless been extended by Japan voluntarily. Therefore, it appears that when data comparable to those in Table 12.1 do become available for a more recent year, they will probably show an expansion, and not a contraction, of the trade coverage of NTBs during the Reagan years.

ADMINISTERED PROTECTION

It is sometimes argued (notably by Canada) that the most pernicious barriers to U.S. imports are not the formal barriers that exist for long periods of time, but rather the administrative and legal arrangements that we have for interfering with trade on a short-term basis whenever another country exports to us too successfully. These arrangements are sometimes concocted informally (as in the VERs on autos and steel discussed above), but most of them arise during the often very active administration of U.S. trade law. It may therefore be instructive to examine the record of trade actions under U.S. law to see whether this avenue for protection has been used more frequently and/or more successfully during the Reagan years.

Table 12.2 reports the numbers of successful cases filed under each of five sections of the Trade Acts of 1974 and 1979. These numbers are taken from a computerized inventory of trade actions that has been assembled and maintained by my colleague, John H. Jackson. For the purpose of the table I have sorted the completed cases by the latest date for which any action was taken, excluding dates of any court challenges, and I have omitted any cases that were still pending. Cases are classified as successful only if all relevant agencies made affirmative determinations and if some form of import relief was thereafter provided. For sections of the law in which there is presidential discretion, then, the successful cases include only those for which the President did provide some relief.[11] The tabulation includes filings under the escape clause[12] (section 201 of the 1974 Trade Act) and the two major statutes involving unfair trade[13] (sections 301 and 337) from 1975 onward. It also includes filings of countervailing duty cases[14] and anti-dumping duty cases[15] (sections 701 and

Table 12.2
Number of Successful Trade Actions Filed, 1975–88

Trade Action (Section)	\<Year\> 1975	1976	1977	1978	1979	1980	1981	1982	1983	1984	1985	1986	1987	1988	\<Subtotals\> 1975–1980	1981–1988	Total
ESCAPE CLAUSE (201)																	
Cases Filed	3	12	11	10	2	5	2	1	2	5	2	4			43	16	59
Successful	0	1	2	3	1	2	0	0	2	1	0	0			9	3	12
% Successful	0	8	18	30	50	40	0	0	100	20	0	0			21	19	20
UNFAIR TRADE (301)																	
Cases Filed	1	2	3	1	1	8	2	8	1	7	4	4	3	6	16	35	51
Successful	0	2	3	0	1	7	1	1	0	5	3	4	3	3	13	20	33
% Successful	0	100	100	0	100	88	50	13	0	71	75	100	100	50	81	57	65
UNFAIR TRADE (337)																	
Cases Filed	2	18	10	9	22	16	19	20	22	37	40	17	21	16	77	192	269
Successful	2	2	3	2	9	5	5	5	3	9	10	3	3	3	23	41	64
% Successful	100	11	30	22	41	31	26	25	14	24	25	18	14	19	30	21	24
COUNTERVAILING DUTIES (701)																	
Cases Filed						67	17	100	20	12	36	16	14	2	67	217	284
Successful						1	1	6	14	5	7	7	7	1	1	48	49
% Successful						1	6	6	70	42	19	44	50	50	1	22	17
ANTI-DUMPING (731)																	
Cases Filed						31	13	53	41	37	78	65	52	12	31	351	382
Successful						6	5	4	17	16	11	30	31	7	6	121	127
% Successful						19	38	8	41	43	14	46	60	58	19	34	33
TOTAL																	
Cases Filed	6	32	24	20	25	127	53	182	86	98	160	106	90	36	234	811	1045
Successful	2	5	8	5	11	21	12	16	36	36	31	44	44	14	52	233	285
% Successful	33	16	33	25	44	17	23	9	42	37	19	42	49	39	22	29	27

Source: From a trade action database maintained by John H. Jackson.

731 of the 1979 Trade Act) only since 1980, due to the fact that these sections of the law were substantially modified in the 1979 Act.

The numbers convey a mixed message. Certainly the flow of cases has been much greater during the 1980s than before. This increase is exaggerated in the table by the fact that pre-1980 filings of countervailing duty and anti-dumping cases are excluded. However, the revision of the law in 1979 had the effect of shifting many of what would have been escape clause actions to these latter two categories, so that the total is not as misleading as it may at first appear.

The percentage of successful cases overall has also gone up. As indicated in the lower right of the table, of the cases filed during the Reagan years, 29 percent were successful, while only 22 percent were successful during the 1975–80 period.

However, much of this shift is also accounted for by the shift to the use of the countervailing duty and anti-dumping statutes. The percentage of successful cases under each of the first three statutes actually fell during the Reagan years. Thus one could argue that the administration has in fact been more stringent in deciding and acting on trade cases of particular types, and that it has only been the changing composition of the cases themselves that has caused the success rate to increase.

Neither can one necessarily ascribe any increase in either the number or the success of cases filed to the actions of the administration. In 1979 Congress changed the requirements for getting trade relief under the law, with the intent of making that relief easier to obtain. Judging from the numbers in Table 12.2, those changes in the law were quite successful in achieving their objective.

Whoever may deserve the credit or the blame for these results, the fact remains that during the 1980s petitioners had a better than one in three chance of getting relief from trade competition by filing under the U.S. trade laws. Considering the low cost to the petitioner of such a filing in comparison with the benefit that may accrue if protection is granted, these odds must provide quite an incentive to make use of the system. I would conclude that objections to the U.S. system of administered protection are well founded.

FEAR OF TRADE INTERVENTION

Often international trade can be hampered as much by traders' fears of future trade intervention as by actual trade actions that have already occurred. To the extent that procedures for such trade actions are written formally into law, this is the concern about administered protection that was just discussed. But a protectionist environment can also give rise to pressures to create new forms of protection, and traders are well aware that securing a share of the U.S. market is no guarantee that access to that market will be continued. On the contrary, import-competing firms are often adept at using the political process to promote special measures of trade protection that are in their own interests. And knowledge that this may happen, even though the exact mechanism of that protection may not be known in advance, must influence the decision of a foreign exporter as to whether or not to attempt to penetrate the market. Therefore, it is important in evaluating the trade policies of the Reagan years also to consider what the political atmosphere was as it pertained to trade, and whether trade may have been deterred by fears of new protection.

Unfortunately, I know of no feasible way to get a handle on the possible protectionist atmosphere that may have prevailed. Precisely because the focus is actions that did not occur, but were only feared, there probably can be no objective measure of what those fears were.

However, there were at least two "nonevents" of the 1980s that suggest that protectionist sentiments may have been at a high ebb. The first was the push for domestic content legislation in the automobile industry in the early 1980s. This was ultimately defeated, but the same sentiments that propelled that legislation certainly contributed to the decision to impose a VER on Japanese exports. Furthermore, it appears that the fear of such legislation, along with the VER itself, has been an important factor in leading Japanese auto companies to invest in production facilities in the United States.

The second nonevent was the Gephardt amendment. This amendment to the Omnibus Trade Act of 1988 was ultimately defeated, but not before it had propelled Gephardt into the political limelight. The perception that a country's bilateral trade surplus with the United States may ultimately lead the U.S. to restrict imports from that country has surely not faded away completely, judging from the efforts that a number of exporting countries have taken to try to restrict their exports to the United States. If governments continue to be concerned about a future protectionist response to these trade imbalances, then surely the firms within those countries that contemplate exporting must share these concerns and take them into account in their decisions.

As the background of the Gephardt amendment suggests, one of the major causes of protectionist feelings in the 1980s has been the aggregate trade deficit. The trade deficit has fostered the perception that foreign exporters were somehow "beating us" at the game of trade, as well as the rationalization that they were beating us by playing unfairly. The trade deficit itself was accompanied, in the first half of the decade, by the tremendous appreciation of the dollar that priced many U.S. goods out of world markets, and this too made the pressures of import competition more acute and added to the clamor for protection. After 1985, as shown in Figure 12.1, the dollar did decline, and this made it easier for U.S. firms to compete and should have eased the pressure for protection. But the fact that the aggregate trade deficit did not improve with this depreciation, at least initially, may have strengthened the hand of the protectionists even more; they could argue that foreign companies and governments were somehow not allowing market forces to work.

This is not the place to explain or criticize the policies that may have led to the heightened U.S. trade deficit, or to these two large movements in the value of the dollar. These are issues better left to others who will evaluate the macroeconomic policies of the Reagan years. Suffice it to say that the trade balance and the exchange rate are both reflections of macroeconomic policies, not of trade policies at the micro level.

However, while the causes of the deficit and the exchange rate movements are macroeconomic, their effects certainly extend into the determination of the level of trade. The role of the exchange rate itself in determining exports and imports has already been discussed. But what is important here is the additional effect that both the deficit and the exchange rate may have in contributing to a protectionist environment. And this environment is in turn a deterrent to trade.

CONCLUSION: ASSESSING RESPONSIBILITY

I do not believe that there is any very clear-cut conclusion to be drawn from the evidence presented in this chapter. At each stage, the evidence I have found has been at best weak, and often contradictory. The volume of total trade, for example, seemed to stagnate during the Reagan years, while the volume of manufacturing trade did not. Trade barriers in the form of tariffs declined over the period, but solely as a result of the Tokyo Round that had been negotiated in the 1970s. Trade barriers in other forms do not seem to have increased in their trade coverage, at least as of 1983, although they did change their sectoral incidence and it does seem likely that the coverage may have increased after 1983. Filings under the various sections of the U.S. trade acts, whereby industries can seek relief from foreign competition for various reasons, did increase substantially after 1980. However, the increase also reflected a shift away from use of the escape clause and the unfair trade statutes, and toward the countervailing duty and anti-dumping statutes that had been revised by Congress in 1979. Therefore, the increase in filings seems to reflect that change in law, and not necessarily any policy of the Reagan years. This conclusion is supported by the fact that there was no particular increase in the success rate of petitions under the statutes that had not been revised. Finally, there is anecdotal evidence that the 1980s saw an increase in protectionist pressures, and therefore perhaps in the fears of protection by potential foreign exporters.

Therefore, in answer to the question of how well the Reagan administration performed in the area of trade policy, I can only say that the evidence is mixed. As an enthusiastic advocate of free trade myself, I would certainly not say that the record of the Reagan years was the answer to my prayers. However, I find it difficult to see the basis for the view quoted in the introduction that Reagan was the most protectionist president since Hoover. I am forced, however reluctantly, to agree more or less with the administration's self-evaluation: Reagan's record was largely similar to that of previous administrations.

Like previous administrations, the Reagan administration did take the lead— with eventual though not immediate success—in initiating a new round of multilateral trade negotiations, and this round promises to expand the province of liberal trade. At the same time, the administration gave in more frequently than one might have preferred to pressures for protection in particular sectors. The most distinctive contributions to liberalizing trade that were made by the Reagan administration took the form of bilateral agreements that, while they are almost certainly beneficial, are not an unmixed blessing because of their discriminatory nature. At the same time, a number of the administration's trade actions that were most deplored by advocates of liberal trade, such as the semiconductor pact with Japan, were taken with the avowed purpose of opening foreign markets. Thus, again, the trade policies of the Reagan years were a contradictory lot, but this is hardly a novelty among recent administrations in the United States.

There remains the question of assessing who should bear responsibility for this mixed bag of trade policies. It is tempting for his critics to say that the President himself should bear full responsibility for both the good and the bad, since it is his job to lead Congress and the public (and some would say even the world) onto the high road of liberal trade. It must be equally tempting for members of the Reagan administration to seek credit for those policies that did succeed in opening markets, while blaming the Democratic Congress, the self-interested public, or underhanded foreigners for creating situations that forced the administration to choose among the lesser of various protectionist evils.

It is not hard to muster sympathy for the latter view. Robert Baldwin (1982), who probably would not share this view, has aptly described the formation of trade policy as being the result of an interaction between a supply of protection and a demand for protection. In this view, the administration has the power to supply protection to those who request it, but is reluctant to use that power except when the pressure on it is very strong. It is various private interests within the economy, typically, import-competing industries, that are the principal demanders of protection. They make their demands known through lobbyists and through their elected representatives in Congress who act as market intermediaries, supplying protection that they have in turn demanded from the administration. Demanders of protection pay a price for it in the form of political action, while the suppliers of protection benefit from that political action in furthering other political objectives such as reelection.

In this view, then, the equilibrium level of protection is the outcome of the interaction between both supply and demand, and changes in protection cannot be automatically attributed to either one alone. An increase in protection, for example, could be the result of an outward shift of the demand for protection, and hence be the "fault" of the protectionist forces that impinge on the administration. Or it could be the result of an outward shift in supply of protection, and hence the "fault" of an administration that has gone soft in resisting otherwise unchanged protectionist pressures.

Thus, even if we grant that protection did increase during the Reagan years (which, as I have argued, is not necessarily the case), we could still absolve the Reagan administration of responsibility for that increase by noting that the 1980s were marked by protectionist pressures that were unprecedented in the postwar period. That these pressures did exist, I think there can be no doubt.

However, I would conclude by pointing out that Baldwin's neat analogy of trade policy formation to price formation in the analysis of a market can also suggest extending that analysis to a general equilibrium system. In a general equilibrium it is not enough to explain a change just by noting a shift in supply or demand; one must also examine why the shift took place and how it may have reflected other shifts in other markets.

In the context of the Reagan trade policy, this suggests that one ask why there may have been a shift to greater demands for protection during the 1980s. And I have already alluded to the answer to that: The increased aggregate trade deficit and the accompanying changes in the value of the dollar caused tremendous pressure on many of the industries in tradable sectors of the U.S. economy, and they responded to that pressure by seeking protection.

Thus, while I would not suggest that the Reagan administration was more accommodating to protectionist interests than previous administrations had been, I would not hold the Reagan administration blameless as to the increased demands for protection that occurred. For these were the indirect byproduct of other policies that contributed to the U.S. trade deficit and the appreciation of the dollar. These latter policies are rightly the subject of other contributions to this volume. But it is worth noting in closing that less damage may have been done to the liberal trading system of the world by some of the more egregious protectionist acts of the Reagan administration, such as the proliferation of VERs, than by the macroeconomic policies of the Reagan administration that were not, on their face, intended to affect trade at all.

NOTES

I would like to thank Robert M. Stern and John H. Jackson for their helpful advice in the research leading to this chapter. I have also benefited greatly from conversations with Wouter DePloey and Jon Haveman. Laurence Telson provided excellent research assistance, without which I would have been lost. Finally, I would like to thank the Ford Foundation for providing partial support during the writing of this chapter.

1. However, the official policy of the administration was not unambiguously in favor of free trade, but rather espoused a possibly contradictory mix of free trade and "fair trade." The "Administration Statement on International Trade Policy" of September 1985 began with the statement: "A policy of free and fair trade is in the best interest of the citizens of the United States and the world" (USTR 1985).

2. Council of Economic Advisors (1989: 160).

3. This list was compiled from information in Aho and Aronson (1985), Cline (1987), Niskanen (1988), Tarr (1989), Thompson (1989), and various issues of the *Wall Street Journal*.

4. Aho and Aronson (1985: 20).

5. See Baldwin and Richardson (1988) for extensive discussion of the Uruguay Round.

6. The Tokyo Round also had a number of other important results, many involving nontariff barriers. See Deardorff and Stern (1983).

7. This conclusion has been confirmed by Deardorff and Stern (1983) and others who have used computable general equilibrium models to evaluate the employment and other adjustment effects of the Tokyo Round.

8. See Deardorff (1987) for other reasons why nontariff barriers are used.

9. See Deardorff and Stern (1985) for a discussion of these difficulties.

10. Because the source for these data did not happen to include the Common Agricultural Policy of the European Community in 1973, but did include it in 1983, I have excluded European agriculture completely from the calculation.

11. If a case was decided negatively by the agencies but nonetheless led to some form of relief by the President, as was the case with autos in 1981, then the case has been counted as unsuccessful. This biases the number of successful cases downward somewhat, although such cases are unusual.

12. The escape clause is the U.S. implementation of the safeguard clause, Article 19 of the GATT. It permits firms and workers in industries that are injured by imports to seek temporary protection from those imports. There is no presumption in an escape clause action that the foreign importers are behaving unfairly.

13. Section 301 is a broad statute that permits industries to seek government action when foreign governments engage in unfair trade practices, usually against U.S. exports. Section 337 is a much more specific statute, usually used to deal with foreign infringement of U.S. patent and other intellectual property rights.

14. Countervailing duties are the tools permitted by the GATT for retaliating against foreign government subsidies that affect trade. Industries that can establish that they are competing with subsidized imports can seek tariff protection equal to the subsidy under Section 701.

15. Dumping is defined as exporting for a price that is either below the home market price or below cost. Industries can file for protection from dumping, in the form of an anti-dumping duty equal to such price differentials, under Section 731.

13

The Reagan Trade Deficit:
A Bilateral Analysis

Steven Husted

When President Reagan took office in January 1981, the U.S. current account was roughly in balance (see Figure 13.1). In 1980 there had been a small surplus of about $1.8 billion, not much different from the average annual deficit of $440 million over the previous decade. In 1981 the surplus grew to almost $7 billion, the largest (nominal) surplus since 1975. Then, beginning in 1982, the current account swung sharply into deficit, reaching over $107 billion in 1984—roughly 3 percent of U.S. gross national product (GNP)—climbing to $154 billion (or 3.4 percent of GNP) in 1987, before falling to $135 billion (2.7 percent of GNP) in 1988. The U.S. merchandise trade balance, which had been in deficit since 1976 and stood at − $25 billion in 1980, followed a roughly similar pattern, with the deficit peaking at $160 billion in 1987 before falling to $127 billion in 1988. Real net exports deteriorated even more dramatically during this period, moving from a surplus of almost $60 billion in 1980 to a deficit of $130 billion in 1986.[1]

This spectacular and unprecedented behavior of U.S. external balances has generated considerable interest among economists. Countless articles and monographs have been written to explain the recent trade performance of the United States and predict its future course.[2] Many empirical studies agree with standard Mundell-Fleming analysis that the overall deficit can be attributed to macroeconomic causes, especially the Reagan tax cuts and resulting fiscal deficits of the early 1980s.[3] Other factors clearly played a role. These include tight monetary policies of the Federal Reserve, which exacerbated the rise in real interest rates brought on by the fiscal expansion, and the (possibly related) debt crisis of the developing countries that brought on capital flight to and import controls on goods from the United States. In addition, high real interest rates, robust economic growth, and strong and stable political leadership in the United

Figure 13.1
U.S. External Balances: 1960–88

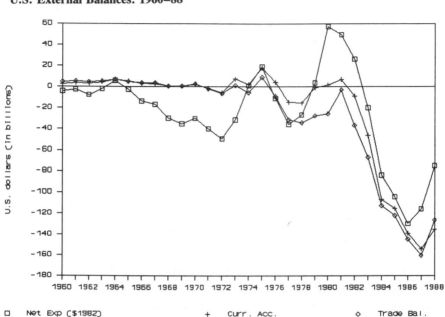

States during the 1980s combined to produce a strong dollar, which encouraged imports and discouraged exports.

One aspect of the recent era that has been relatively ignored in the literature is the behavior of various bilateral trade flows.[4] This omission is somewhat curious because, as will be detailed below, not all of the bilateral imbalances have behaved alike. Moreover, bilateral trade imbalances have become a major focus of trade policy. While acknowledging that unfair foreign practices probably have not been very significant in determining the U.S. trade deficit, Congress nonetheless clearly has had the deficit in mind as it has sought to focus negotiating attention under the authority of Section 301 (and most recently, Super 301) on countries with significant bilateral surpluses. In fact, the celebrated Gephardt amendment found in earlier, unpassed trade legislation had gone so far as to define a formula for "excessive and unwarranted" trade surpluses with the United States.

Consequently, I propose to analyze the overall trade performance of the United States immediately before and during the Reagan era by studying each of the major U.S. bilateral trading relations. Attention will be devoted to comparing various individual experiences and to searching for a common explanation to recent patterns of behavior. To preview one of the chapter's major findings, the behavior of bilateral trade flows is explained well by simple models of import flows combined with very real international differences in aggregate demand growth and movements in prices of tradeables. These price movements, in turn, are driven largely by movements in nominal exchange rates.

TRENDS IN U.S. BILATERAL TRADE FLOWS

Overall Performance

From the end of World War II until about 1970, U.S. trade flows (measured on an NIPA, or national income and product accounts, basis) grew at a rate roughly equal with that of the U.S. economy. The ratio of exports plus imports to GNP held steady at slightly over 9 percent. Between 1970 and 1980, as elsewhere in the world, in the United States international trade accounted for an increasingly larger share of economic activity, with the ratio of trade to GNP almost doubling from 10.8 to 20.8 percent. During this period, the nominal values of U.S. merchandise exports and imports doubled twice. In real terms, exports doubled and imports rose by 50 percent.

This rise in international activity was accompanied by some change in the direction of trade flows. Table 13.1 highlights these patterns. Perhaps the most dramatic change between 1970 and 1980 was the sharp expansion of U.S. trade shares accounted for by the developing countries at the expense of the individual countries. During that period, the share of U.S. exports sold to the industrial countries fell from about 66 percent to 57 percent, with most of this deterioration occurring between 1970 and 1975. In 1970 developing countries accounted for 30 percent of U.S. exports. By 1980 their share had risen to almost 40 percent. Most of the increase in export share was accounted for by expanded exports to Latin America (especially Mexico) and to the Middle East.

The changes in export patterns described above are easily explained by the two OPEC oil price shocks of the 1970s. This is readily confirmed by examining what happened to U.S. import shares by region. Between 1970 and 1980 the share of U.S. imports (in nominal terms) from the Middle East, for instance, rose 700 percent. The value of imports from Mexico rose from $1.3 billion in 1970 to $12.8 billion in 1980, exceeding the value of imports from either Germany or the United Kingdom. And while trade with Africa had been minor and roughly in balance in 1970, by 1980 the largest U.S. bilateral trade deficit was with the African continent—mostly with Libya and Nigeria.

In terms of trade imbalances, the United States had small trade surpluses in 1970 (and in 1975), despite the shift in trade brought on by the first OPEC oil shock. By 1976, however, the U.S. trade balance had slipped into deficit of more than $30 billion, virtually all with the developing countries. This deficit remained roughly constant at that level through 1980. The fact that the U.S. trade balance and bilateral shares did not show more volatility during this period is quite remarkable given the events of the times: the collapse of the Bretton Woods system of fixed exchange rates; a major world recession in 1974–75 brought on at least in part by the first OPEC oil shock; large-scale growth

Table 13.1
U.S. Merchandise Trade Flows and Shares by Region, 1970–88 (in $ millions)

	Exports 1970	Imports 1970	Exports 1975	Imports 1975	Exports 1980	Imports 1980	Exports 1985	Imports 1985	Exports 1987	Imports 1987	Exports 1988	Imports 1988
Industrial Countries	28517	30448	61688	58184	125512	126262	130224	228158	161404	261438	206640	282559
Canada	9084	11779	21744	22752	35395	42001	47251	69427	59814	71510	73116	84078
Japan	4652	6240	9563	12336	20790	32961	22631	72380	28249	88074	37241	89819
EC6	8423	7023	17703	13109	39286	26625	31958	49507	39627	59498	48185	60469
Germany	2740	3324	5194	5750	10960	12370	9050	21232	11748	28028	14085	26333
U.K.	2537	2332	4527	4047	12694	10184	11273	15573	14114	17998	18129	17757
Eastern Bloc	287	227	2597	657	3138	1242	3215	2114	2200	2118	3773	2158
Developing Countries	12978	11098	41137	42402	86801	118125	71672	123050	81691	149666	109492	161713
Lat. America	6538	5056	16623	18724	38718	38758	31019	49096	34979	49094	43687	51338
Mexico	1704	1299	5141	3112	15145	12774	13635	19392	14582	20520	20660	23272
Asia	3826	3460	8040	6989	21784	20298	24530	56860	31994	77606	59745	100925
NICs	1810	2065	3564	3884	10404	11442	16918	41880	23547	61283	34020	63247
Middle East	1498	396	8574	6136	13773	18833	9709	6600	8502	11602	n.a.	n.a.
Africa	810	802	3965	7760	6521	27721	6183	10363	5002	11281	5542	9331
Total	43224	42429	107592	103389	220706	252997	213146	361626	252866	424082	319905	446430

208

	Exports 1970	Imports 1970	Exports 1975	Imports 1975	Exports 1980	Imports 1980	Exports 1985	Imports 1985	Exports 1987	Imports 1987	Exports 1988	Imports 1988
Industrial Countries	65.97%	71.76%	57.34%	56.28%	56.78%	49.91%	61.10%	63.09%	63.83%	61.65%	64.59%	63.29%
Canada	21.02%	27.76%	20.21%	22.01%	16.04%	16.60%	22.17%	19.20%	23.65%	16.86%	22.86%	18.83%
Japan	10.76%	14.71%	8.89%	11.93%	9.42%	13.03%	10.62%	20.02%	11.17%	20.77%	11.64%	20.12%
EC6	19.49%	16.55%	16.45%	12.68%	17.80%	10.52%	14.99%	13.69%	15.67%	14.03%	15.06%	13.55%
Germany	6.34%	7.83%	4.83%	5.56%	4.97%	4.89%	4.25%	5.87%	4.65%	6.61%	4.40%	5.90%
U.K.	5.87%	5.50%	4.21%	3.91%	5.75%	4.03%	5.29%	4.31%	5.58%	4.24%	5.67%	3.98%
Eastern Bloc	0.66%	0.54%	2.41%	0.64%	1.42%	0.49%	1.51%	0.58%	0.87%	0.50%	1.18%	0.48%
Developing Countries	30.02%	26.16%	38.23%	41.01%	39.33%	46.69%	33.63%	34.03%	32.31%	35.29%	34.23%	36.22%
Lat. America	15.13%	11.92%	15.45%	18.11%	17.54%	15.32%	14.55%	13.58%	13.83%	11.58%	13.66%	11.50%
Mexico	3.94%	3.06%	4.78%	3.01%	6.86%	5.05%	6.40%	5.36%	5.77%	4.84%	6.46%	5.21%
Asia	8.85%	8.15%	7.47%	6.76%	9.87%	8.02%	11.51%	15.72%	12.65%	18.30%	18.68%	22.61%
NICs	4.19%	4.87%	3.31%	3.76%	4.71%	4.52%	7.94%	11.58%	9.31%	14.45%	10.63%	14.17%
Middle East	3.47%	0.93%	7.97%	5.93%	6.24%	7.44%	4.56%	1.83%	3.36%	2.74%	n.a.	n.a.
Africa	1.87%	1.89%	3.69%	7.51%	2.95%	10.96%	2.90%	2.87%	1.98%	2.66%	1.73%	2.09%

Sources: 1970–1987, IMF, Direction of Trade Yearbooks; 1988, U.S. Department of Commerce, Survey of Current Business.

in the debts of non-oil-producing developing countries; strong real growth in the United States between 1976 and 1980; and bouts of high inflation both in the United States and around the world.

As in the 1970s, the 1980s saw a variety of major economic shocks. Chief among these were the large real appreciation of the dollar between 1979 and 1985 and its subsequent and equally large real depreciation; the rapid growth in real output in the United States beginning in late 1982, which was both large by historical comparison and with that of major trading partners; the emerging debt crisis in the developing countries of Latin America, Eastern Europe and Africa; and the liberalization of capital markets, especially in Asia. Finally, the 1980s witnessed the U.S. government double its national debt in less than eight years and the U.S. economy move from the world's largest net creditor country to the world's largest net debtor.

Consider again the values in Table 13.1. The first trend to note is the growth in the overall trade deficit, especially between 1980 and 1987. The most startling feature of the overall totals is the complete lack of growth in U.S. merchandise exports. In fact, between 1980 and 1985 total U.S. merchandise exports fell in nominal terms by $7 billion (3 percent). At the same time, merchandise imports rose over 40 percent from their 1980 level. And even though all of the actual decline in U.S. export sales can be attributed to lost sales in the developing countries (exports declined by $15 billion, most notably to Latin America), most of the growth in the deficit came through a rise in the trade imbalance with the industrialized countries. Since 1985 the picture has changed to some extent, with the value of exports rising almost 60 percent and import growth slowing.

The values in the table also seem to suggest that some of the older trade patterns are reemerging. The shares that the industrial countries account for in U.S. exports and imports have risen well above 60 percent. The proportions of U.S. exports going to Canada and Japan are almost identical to those observed in 1970. One major difference between recent experience and the early 1970s is the phenomenal growth in the role played by Asia—especially the newly industrializing countries (NICs). Another difference is the decline in Latin America's trade shares, although Mexico has largely retained the share it reached in the late 1970s.

There appears to be a growing consensus that the U.S. external imbalances of the 1980s were brought on by a combination of strong currency and strong relative demand growth.[5] It has now been over three years since the U.S. dollar began to depreciate from the peak it achieved in early 1985. Growth in the United States, while still relatively strong, has diminished, especially in terms of domestic demand. The trade balance has begun to narrow, in real terms in 1987 and in nominal terms in 1988. As noted above, bilateral trade patterns consistent with an era of near equality between exports and imports have begun to reappear. Yet the imbalances are still large. They persist because there was a period of time during the 1980s in which export growth stagnated or declined, while import growth continued. The aim of the remainder of this section and a good deal of the statistical analysis in the next section is to discuss and explain these events, with a primary focus on bilateral trade flows.

Bilateral Performance

Canada

Canada is the United States' largest trading partner. In 1988 U.S. merchandise exports to Canada totalled $73 billion (23 percent of total merchandise exports), while imports stood at $84 billion (19 percent of total merchandise imports). The emergence of a significant trade deficit with Canada is a relatively new phenomenon. In fact, U.S. trade flows to and from Canada tracked each other very closely up through 1981. Despite a fourfold increase in the values of both flows over the 15-year period 1967–81, the bilateral trade imbalance never exceeded $2.5 billion. In 1982, however, a deficit of $9.2 billion emerged when U.S. exports to Canada fell by $6 billion. In 1983 the deficit remained approximately constant, before increasing by 50 percent in 1984 and widening still further in 1985. Since then the deficit has begun to shrink, reaching its 1983 level again in 1988.

In terms of the commodity composition of Canada–U.S. trade, both import and export value shares by major product category have remained relatively constant throughout the 1980s. For instance, roughly half the value of U.S. exports to Canada consists of machinery and transport equipment (Category 7 of Schedules E and A of the U.S. Trade Classification Code).[6] Much of this trade is in the form of motor vehicle bodies and chassis shipped to Canada for final assembly and fully assembled passenger cars. Other products that have consistently ranked in the top ten (by value) of U.S. exports to Canada in the 1980s include piston engines, computers, and business machines.

The United States imports a wide variety of products from Canada. The largest share by value (roughly 40 percent) during the 1980s has been machinery and transport equipment. Passenger cars and motor vehicles have invariably ranked in the top three product categories. Other important Canadian exports include paper, petroleum, and wood products.

Japan

The United States has maintained a trade deficit with Japan since the 1960s. Through 1975 this deficit was relatively small. Since 1976 the deficit has grown almost every year, narrowing slightly in 1979 and 1988. By 1988 it stood at $53 billion, over 40 percent of the total U.S. deficit. From 1980 through 1985 U.S. exports to Japan were essentially flat. U.S. imports from Japan were also relatively constant between 1981 and 1983. Since 1983, however, U.S. imports from Japan have exploded, doubling in value in three years. By 1986 Japan had become the United States' largest (single-nation) source of imports.

Three major product categories account for almost equal parts of half of U.S. exports to Japan. These are food and live animals (mostly corn, meat, and fish); crude materials (wood, oilseeds, and pulp and waste paper); and machinery and transport equipment (aircraft, office machines, and computers). More than 80 percent of U.S. imports from Japan are concentrated in two categories: manufactured goods and machinery and transport equipment. The single largest product is passenger cars ($22 billion in 1987, up from $11 billion in 1983). Other major imports include phonographs and televisions ($4 billion in 1987), telecommunications equipment ($4 billion), computers ($3.6 billion), radios ($2.2 billion), and office machines ($1.7 billion).

Western Europe

As a region, Western Europe is the largest market for U.S. exports and the second largest source of U.S. imports. U.S.–Western European trade has several unique features. First, from 1967 to 1983 the United States tended to run a small surplus with Europe. The surplus rose to its maximum of over $20 billion in 1980. This became a deficit, however, exceeding $30 billion by 1986. Since that time, the deficit has begun to shrink, reaching $15 billion in 1988.

The United States' two largest trading partners in Europe are West Germany and the United Kingdom. Combined, these countries purchase more than 35 percent of U.S. exports to Europe and supply about 45 percent of U.S. imports from Europe. More than half of U.S. trade with West Germany on both the export and the import side again is in Category 7, machinery and transport equipment. This category also accounts for more than half of U.S. exports to the United Kingdom. British exports to the United States include a wide variety of manufactured goods as well as petroleum.

U.S. imports from Europe have followed a linear trend, except for the recession years in the early 1970s and 1980s. U.S. exports have been considerably more volatile. Between 1967 and 1978 exports tracked imports. In 1978 exports accelerated, rising by 75 percent in two years. Then a period of export deterioration and stagnation set in. Exports fell by about $13 billion between 1980 and 1983, and then remained relatively constant from 1983 to 1986.

Contrasting these patterns with those of Canada and Japan offers some interesting comparisons. First, export deterioration in the early 1980s vis-à-vis Europe preceded and was far more severe than that encountered in either Canada or Japan. But the export stagnation that followed in the mid-1980s was very similar for both Western Europe and Japan. Exports to Canada, however, resumed their earlier growth pattern after only a one-year downturn in 1982. Imports from all three areas followed similar patterns, with the steepest growth occurring between 1983 and 1986.

Latin America

Most of U.S. trade with Latin America involves only three countries: Mexico, Brazil, and Venezuela. Commodity flows tend to be along classic comparative advantage lines, with the United States exchanging manufactured products for food (coffee, bananas, etc.), raw materials (bauxite, copper, etc.), low-technology manufactures (shoes), and petroleum. Of late, however, there has been a strong growth in manufactured imports from Mexico, reflecting the growing use by multinational corporations of assembly plants in that country. For instance, automobile imports have risen from $13 million in 1983 to $1.2 billion in 1987. Brazilian exports to the United States have also shifted toward manufactured goods, with machinery and transport equipment accounting for a 25 percent share in 1987, up from 12.5 percent in 1983.

Until recently, U.S.–Latin American trade flows have tended to move together quite closely. Between 1967 and 1982 merchandise imbalances were very small, despite an eightfold increase in the value of trade. In general, during this era imports and exports followed a step function, rising sharply in 1973 and in the late 1970s. These dates coincide with major shocks to the commodity markets, including substantial increases in petroleum and coffee prices. Apparently, as commodity prices and therefore Latin American export earnings rose, these revenues were used to purchase U.S. manufactures.

U.S. export sales to Latin America peaked in 1981 and then fell by almost 50 percent in a two-year period. Historical events seem to explain the downturn well, since 1982 marked the onset of the Latin American debt crisis. The fall in the value of U.S. imports between 1984 and 1986 clearly was related to the fall in petroleum and other commodity prices, combined with (short-run) inelastic demand for these products. And, as noted above, the recent upswing in U.S. expenditures on goods from this region is comprised of manufactured goods.

Other Developing Countries

Trade with African and (especially) Asian developing countries has become increasingly important for the United States. Imports from these countries grew at a very rapid rate between 1973 and 1980, rising in value by 700 percent. Imports during that era were dominated by petroleum from Africa (Nigeria and Libya) and the Middle East. With falling oil prices and the advent of new sources of supply, U.S. imports from Africa have plummeted since 1981, falling by more than 50 percent in value. At the same time, imports from the East Asian NICs have more than tripled. Imports from the rest of Asia have remained roughly constant, although within this group imports from Indonesia (mostly petroleum) have fallen, while Malaysian and Thai exports to the United States have exhibited strong growth.

In a pattern that should seem familiar by now, U.S. exports to these countries rose throughout the 1970s, peaked in 1981, and then stagnated, falling slightly each year after 1981 until 1986. For the past two years, exports to this area have boomed, rising by more than 60 percent over their 1986 level. In 1988 alone, exports rose by $18 billion, with Hong Kong, Korea, and Taiwan responsible for roughly half of the increased U.S. sales.

As in all other areas of the world, exports of machinery and transport equipment lead all product categories in total value. However, no single product dominates within this category. Major manufactured exports include (in no particular order) aircraft, electronic components and parts, business machines parts, and computers. The United States also exports significant amounts of crude materials (e.g., hides, pulp and waste paper, oilseeds, and cotton) to this region. Imports from Africa and the Middle East are dominated by petroleum and food (cocoa and coffee). Imports from Asia are increasingly weighted toward miscellaneous manufactures (textiles, apparel, household goods, shoes, consumer and office electronics). Korea's leading export, by value, in 1987 was passenger cars ($2.2 billion—up from $5.4 million in 1984).

ECONOMETRIC ANALYSIS

In this section I turn to an econometric exploration of U.S. bilateral trade flows. My purpose is to see how well simple models of trade flows fit the recent data. That is, there is a considerable econometric literature related to the analysis of trade flows.[7] The question pursued in this section is whether "standard" models from this empirical literature capture the changes in U.S. bilateral trade patterns observed in the 1980s.

The model employed in this exercise assumes that real imports *(M)* depend on real economic activity in the importing country *(A)* and the domestic currency relative price of imports *(RP)*. Lags in the influence of these variables as well as in the past level of real imports are allowed to enter the specification. The relationship between the independent variables is assumed to be multiplicative so that the equation to be estimated is linear in logarithms. Thus a representative model of real import demand is given by (13.1):

$$\ln M_t = \kappa + \sum_{i=0}^{l} \delta_i \ln RP_{t-i} + \sum_{j=0}^{m} \eta_j \ln A_{t-j} + \sum_{k=1}^{n} \mu_k \ln M_{t-k} \quad (13.1)$$

When the lags on the right-hand variables are set equal to zero, the model is standard excess demand equation, and the coefficients on *RP* and *A* represent constant elasticities of price and activity respectively. When lags are included, the coefficients on the contemporaneous variables have traditionally been thought of as short-run elasticities, while long-run elasticities are obtained from sums of current and lagged coefficients weighted by one minus the sum of the coefficients on lagged imports.

The introduction of lags in models such as (13.1) has been suggested in the empirical literature on import demand going back at least as far as Orcutt (1950). These lags have been invoked to capture the effects of delivery lags, adjustment costs, and other frictions that may exist in the real world. Until recently, the theoretical underpinnings of the distributed lag specifications such as (13.1) have not been well established. In a series of papers with Tryphon Kollintzas, I have shown that models such as (13.1) can be thought of as unrestricted reduced form solutions to a dynamic optimization problem faced by a forward-looking importer with rational expectations who faces adjustment and inventory holding costs in handling imports.[8] These papers demonstrate that the coefficients on the right-hand variables are nonlinear functions of underlying structural parameters, related to tastes and/or technology, and expectations formation parameters.

There are two implications to this result. First, statistical models based on specifications such as (13.1) are useful means of organizing data on trade flows, even when they are estimated in their unrestricted form, as is the case in this chapter. However, estimates from unrestricted reduced form specifications are difficult to interpret because statistical criteria (such as statistical significance) rather than theoretical considerations have been used to spell out the model explicitly. Second, unrestricted estimates from models such as (13.1) are subject to the well-known Lucas critique of econometric modelling. That is, such models should not be used for prediction or policy evaluation purposes, since the coefficients are not insensitive to changes in the economic environment.

A statistical model based on equation (13.1) was estimated for bilateral trade flows between the United States and Canada, Japan, the United Kingdom, the original European Community (EC6), Latin America (LAM), and the African and Asian developing countries (DCs), respectively. The model used annual data for the period 1967 to 1987. Data on trade flows were taken from the *Survey of Current Business,* published by the U.S. Department of Commerce; data on prices and exchange rates were obtained from *International Financial Statistics,* published by the International Monetary Fund. Data on domestic activity and some exchange rates were taken from *World Tables,* published by the World Bank.

Real U.S. exports (foreign real imports) to various locations were generated by deflating nominal flows by the U.S. export unit value index. Real U.S. imports from various sources were created by deflating nominal flows by exchange rate-adjusted foreign export unit values.[9] Real economic activity in each area was defined as total domestic absorption (i.e., $C + I + G$) divided by that area's consumer price index (CPI).[10] U.S. real import prices were calculated as exchange rate-adjusted foreign export prices relative to the U.S. CPI. Foreign real import prices were constructed using an exchange rate-adjusted measure of the U.S. export unit value index relative to that country's (or region's) CPI. The exchange rate used throughout was the average annual value of the foreign currency price of the U.S. dollar.

Because annual data were employed, lag lengths were restricted to one period. This seems sufficient to capture much of the dynamics reported in studies such as Wilson and Takacs (1979). It also encompasses as special cases the "standard" partial adjustment model, in which the only lagged variable in the specification is real imports, and the Houthakker and Magee (1969) specification involving one lag of each of the right-hand variables. These two specifications performed the best (in the sense of passing specification error tests) in

Table 13.2
Trade Flow Equation Estimates

U.S. Imports from:	RP_t	RP_{t-1}	A_t	A_{t-1}	M_{t-1}	R^2	DW (h)
Canada	-.59 (.23)	.38 (.21)	1.77 (.37)	-.96 (.65)	.60 (.24)	.99	1.96 (und)
Japan	-1.33 (.19)		3.90 (.15)			.98	1.61
U.K.	-.55 (.56)	.77 (.25)	1.83 (.86)	-1.62 (1.53)	.82 (.30)	.95	1.83 (und)
EC6	-.66 (.16)	-.42 (.16)	1.24 (.50)	1.12 (.50)		.97	2.05
LAM	-.47 (.05)		1.70 (.16)			.89	2.10
DC*	-.74 (.35)		.47 (1.44)		.96 (.11)	.97	2.28 (.71)

U.S. Exports to:	RP_t	RP_{t-1}	A_t	A_{t-1}	M_{t-1}	R^2	DW (h)
Canada	-.18 (.44)		.94 (.23)		.28 (.23)	.96	1.77 (und)
Japan	-.28 (.28)		1.23 (.28)			.93	1.51
U.K.	-.19 (.36)		.90 (.33)		.54 (.16)	.88	1.63 (1.18)
EC6	-.33 (.11)		.63 (.21)		.43 (.14)	.93	1.96 (.11)
LAM	-.41 (.25)	.14 (.29)	1.59 (.32)	-1.01 (.39)	.43 (.23)	.95	1.43 (und)
DC**	-.17 (.46)		.39 (.16)		.46 (.20)	.96	1.78 (.26)

(Standard errors in parentheses); (h)=Durbin h statistic; und=undefined

* Equation included an interaction term between time trend and A.
** Equation estimated using a correction for first order autocorrelation.

a recent study of specification error in import demand modelling (see Thursby and Thursby 1984).

Because of problems of potential endogeneity and/or errors in variables in the measurement of unit values, an instrumental variables estimator, two-stage least squares, was employed in the regressions.[11] Results from the "best" model for each of the bilateral flows as well as some summary statistics are presented in Table 13.2.[12]

Several points emerge from an examination of the figures in the Table. First, simple import demand models explain the data rather well. Most variables are statistically significant with plausible signs and magnitudes; R^2 are uniformly

Table 13.3
Selected Data

Real U.S. Import Prices
1980-1987

Year	Canada	Japan	U.K.	EC6	LAM	D.C.
1980	100.0	100.0	100.0	100.0	100.0	100.0
1981	93.9	95.9	85.2	88.3	112.1	113.0
1982	86.8	84.3	74.8	85.2	110.5	110.5
1983	84.3	79.8	68.0	81.3	98.4	100.7
1984	80.4	76.5	62.0	77.0	95.4	101.2
1985	74.9	73.0	60.5	77.3	91.8	97.9
1986	69.7	85.7	64.9	96.2	51.0	85.4
1987	71.0	90.6	72.6	111.9	65.1	96.5

Real U.S. Export Prices (in foreign currency)
1980-1987

Year	Canada	Japan	U.K.	EC6	LAM	D.C.
1980	100.0	100.0	100.0	100.0	100.0	100.0
1981	101.7	101.3	112.9	125.9	92.2	102.9
1982	99.7	112.5	120.9	131.4	118.3	105.5
1983	97.4	106.4	134.6	136.3	124.1	106.2
1984	99.7	105.5	147.3	148.9	124.2	107.5
1985	101.5	103.0	143.5	147.6	120.0	111.7
1986	103.4	73.0	122.7	110.6	140.9	114.4
1987	97.9	63.7	107.2	96.5	143.8	113.1

Real Domestic Absorption (in local currency)
1980-1987

Year	U.S.	Canada	Japan	U.K.	EC6	LAM	D.C.
1980	100.0	100.0	100.0	100.0	100.0	100.0	100.0
1981	101.4	105.2	100.4	97.9	97.1	103.8	107.1
1982	99.4	101.6	102.4	99.1	96.2	99.6	117.8
1983	104.3	107.7	103.4	104.0	96.6	87.1	124.9
1984	112.3	113.0	106.5	106.6	98.1	91.0	130.3
1985	115.6	119.9	110.0	109.1	99.8	94.7	128.1
1986	120.2	127.9	113.2	114.5	103.6	93.3	127.4
1987	123.6	135.2	118.7	120.3	107.6	102.7	136.3

Source: Calculated by author (see text).

high; and, in most cases, autocorrelation does not appear to be a problem. Second, interpreting the coefficients as elasticities leads to the presumption that U.S. imports are more responsive to both changes in price and in domestic economic activity than foreign imports of U.S. goods. In particular, with the exception of the *DC* equation, point estimates of short-run elasticities of U.S. import demand with respect to changes in absorption all exceed unity, and in several cases are significantly different from one. Counterpart elasticities in the foreign import demand equations are typically smaller than unity.

Table 13.3 presents data on real domestic absorption (in local currency) and real bilateral import prices (also in local currency) for the period 1980–87. Using the values from this table and the parameter estimates in Table 13.2, an explanation of the growth in U.S. bilateral trade deficits becomes readily apparent. U.S. domestic absorption has grown relatively rapidly, especially in 1983 and 1984, and especially when compared with domestic demand growth in Japan, Europe, and Latin America. Due largely to a strong dollar throughout much of the 1980s, real U.S. import prices fell on goods from all sources between 1981 and 1985. At the same time, the real price of U.S. goods in all foreign markets except Canada rose above their 1980 levels.

Recent reductions in the U.S. trade deficit have come about because of a reversal in the forces described above. With the depreciation in the dollar, most U.S. export prices have begun to fall. This has not been the case, however, with Latin America or most of the rest of the developing countries. In Latin America, rampant inflation has fueled exchange rate depreciation relative to the U.S. dollar. And until recently, the Asian NICs maintained essentially fixed exchange rates vis-à-vis the United States, even as the dollar depreciated against the currencies of the industrialized nations. In addition, real domestic demand in foreign countries has started to grow faster than demand growth in the United States.

CONCLUSION

This chapter has sought to analyze the recent behavior of the U.S. trade balance by exploring patterns of bilateral trade between the United States and its major trading partners. A number of interesting points emerge from the study.

First, the 1980s are unique, at least in the recent history of the United States. Prior to this decade, trade was relatively in balance bilaterally and hence over-all, even as trade volumes grew. In the late 1970s the United States experienced an historically large trade deficit. This deficit occurred mainly with the developing countries and can be explained by commodity price shocks. Trade with the industrialized countries, as a group, remained in balance. The large external deficits that appeared during this decade are different. Most of the U.S. trade deficit now is with the industrialized countries and hence involves trade in manufactured goods.

Second, the bilateral deficits that have emerged over the past five years are no mystery. Moreover, there is no evidence that they are due to unfair trade policies of foreign governments. Statistical analysis shows that U.S. bilateral trade flows are well explained by simple import demand models. The estimates from these models suggest that U.S. imports are more sensitive to changes in real domestic demand and relative prices than are foreign counterpart demands. In addition, these relationships appear to be very stable.

Between 1982 and 1985, when overall trade imbalances were expanding most rapidly, U.S. real domestic demand growth was much stronger than that experienced in most of the rest of the world. Moreover, during this period the strong U.S. dollar acted to encourage further U.S. imports and to discourage exports. During the mid- and late 1980s, U.S. demand growth remained strong overall but slowed relative to most trading partners, and the dollar depreciated against the currencies of the industrialized countries. Foreign demand growth has stimulated U.S. exports. Dollar depreciation has begun to show in the price data, again especially with the industrialized countries. This should slow the growth in demand for goods coming from these countries. Working against this effect is the fact that a growing proportion of manufactured goods imports are obtained from developing countries, including Brazil and Mexico, where the dollar has continued to appreciate over the entire decade.

In sum, the United States today finds itself with large and persistent deficits in its external accounts. These deficits are a product of a series of economic conditions, including a surging economy at home and a strong dollar in world markets, that are clearly part of the Reagan economic legacy. Reversing these imbalances is not likely to happen on its own, although there has been some movement in that direction in the past two years. What may be required is a set of policies designed to slow growth and raise domestic savings rates (i.e., expenditure-reducing policies). Whether or not the Bush administration should implement such policies, or for that matter engage in any policies aimed at altering the U.S. external position, is beyond the scope of this chapter. What is clear, however, is that expenditure-reducing policies are not politically popular, and in fact may not even be politically feasible. Thus it seems safe to predict that the Reagan trade deficits will be part of the U.S. economic picture for some time to come.

NOTES

I would like to thank Jim Cassing and Russell Boyer for several helpful comments. The usual proviso applies.

1. Real net exports are defined as exports of goods and services (in constant dollars) minus imports of goods and services (in constant dollars), both measured on a national income and products account basis.

2. See, for instance, Marris (1985); Bryant, Holtham, and Hooper (1988); Krugman and Baldwin (1987); and Bryant and Holtham (1987) for a representative example of this work.

3. See, for instance, Hooper (1989a; 1989b); Helkie and Hooper (1989); and Sachs (1988).

4. A major exception to this statement is the relatively large number of studies focused on U.S. trade with Japan and the Asian NICs. See, for instance, Chou and Shih (1988), Reinhart (1986), Nolle and Pigott (1986), Sakamoto (1988), and Ueda (1988).

5. See, for instance, Council of Economic Advisors (1987), Hutchinson and Pigott (1987), and Truman (1989).

6. The source for this discussion and the commodity composition of trade discussion in the material that follows is *U.S. Foreign Trade Highlights,* published annually by the Department of Commerce.

7. For an excellent survey of the recent literature in this area, see Goldstein and Khan (1985).

8. See, for instance, Husted and Kollintzas (1984: 1987); and Kollintzas and Husted (1984).

9. In cases in which the foreign source is a region rather than a country, export unit values were generated as a weighted sum of export unit values (or their proxies) of major countries within the region. In particular, the EC6 export unit value index was a weighted sum of the indices of France, Germany, Italy, and the Netherlands; the LAM index involved data from Brazil, Mexico, and Venezuela. The DC index used data from Korea, Nigeria, Saudi Arabia, Singapore, and Thailand. Weights were constructed based on trade shares of the countries within each group with the United States. The information required to generate these weights in turn was obtained from the *Direction of Trade Yearbooks,* published by the International Monetary Fund. Export unit values were used for each country except Mexico, Venezuela, Saudi Arabia, and Nigeria, where oil prices were used, and Singapore, where the consumer price index was employed.

10. As was the case for export prices, in cases involving regional trade, aggregates were constructed as trade-weighted sums of statistics for representative countries. The countries involved in these calculations are given in note 9.

11. The instruments used in the estimation were wholesale price and nominal wage indices. These data were obtained from various issues of *International Financial Statistics.* For a discussion of the problems inherent in the use of unit value indices in empirical studies of trade flows, see Goldstein and Khan (1985).

12. In addition to the results reported to Table 13.2, several models were estimated that allowed for intercept shifts and/or changes in price and income elasticities in the 1980s. In general, these new variables added little explanatory power to the model and had no effect on the remaining coefficient estimates.

"Trade Policy of the Reagan Years" and "The Reagan Trade Deficit": *Comment*

Russell S. Boyer

Chapters 12 and 13 are useful contributions in that they deal with some aspects of U.S. trade during the last decade that have not been studied directly before. In particular, Deardorff deals with the administration of U.S. trade law during the Reagan years, while Husted considers bilateral trade patterns since 1967, with special emphasis on how the 1980s differed from earlier years.

The best aspect of these chapters is their presentation of relatively raw data that hammer home points that might otherwise go unnoticed. In this regard, Deardorff's chronology of major trade policy events and his table of Trade Actions Filed (Table 12.2) put the subject in a clear perspective. Similarly, Husted's data on bilateral trade flows in dollar terms from 1970 to 1988 (Table 13.1) and in real terms for the 1980s (Table 13.3) spell out specifically how trade patterns have developed. There are no major surprises here, but these tables force us to keep in mind that there have been tremendous changes over this period, and there are likely to be many more in the future. The questions remain as to whether these changes are merely apparent, and whether the Reagan years represent any sort of major break in this evolution.

What is not so satisfying about these chapters is the sense that they leave that all the action is really elsewhere, that they are dealing with rather minor issues. Thus, Deardorff's concluding sentence states that the most damage to the liberal trading system during the Reagan years "may have been done . . . by the macroeconomic policies . . . that were not . . . intended to affect trade at all." Husted's chapter is stronger on this criterion in that he makes clear in the introduction and conclusion that the force that generated U.S. trade imbalances with each individual country is an example of the overall mechanism that generated the enormous trade deficits. But here too there is only limited discussion of this underlying mechanism; since this mechanism continues to be controversial, a lengthier analysis of it would have been justified.

These years are and will continue to be challenging ones to analyze, but the task is made more difficult by the authors taking the view that the United States is a relatively closed economy, so that microeconomic tools can be used for assessing trade policy. This is true of the Deardorff chapter in that he looks at trade laws without assessing the macroeconomic backdrop against which their administration took place; and of the Husted chapter in that his focus is on individual bilateral trading relations, once again with the aggregate picture being virtually absent. These authors were unaware that these macroeconomic effects would not be covered elsewhere in the volume, and they should not be held directly responsible for this omission.

A contribution that dealt with these broader issues would have come to grips with the macroeconomic policies that were put in place in the early 1980s, and the effects that they had on GNP, the exchange rate, and the trade balance. Canadians have been well aware, since at least 1958, of the effects of macroeconomic policies (in particular, tight monetary policy) on an open economy with high capital mobility. That same period shows that developments in the foreign sector provide a useful scapegoat for the government in order to draw attention away from its own policies, which may be inappropriate. In the 1958–61 period, such motivation was apparent as the head of the Bank of Canada, Governor Coyne, was a strong advocate of protectionist policies in order to boost output and employment. He failed to acknowledge (or, perhaps, realize) that the policy over which he had direct control could be reversed in order to accomplish the same purpose.

While the discussion of these macroeconomic issues would have been desirable in a volume such as this, I will review them on their own terms, dealing first with Deardorff's chapter. On reading the body of his contribution one is disappointed to find that the chronology set out in his tables is not reflected fully in the discussion. Instead, one gets the impression from the text that all the Reagan years were alike, and were possibly different from those that preceded them. Thus, the chapter suggests that the foreign-currency value of the U.S. dollar rose and stayed up the whole decade. In fact, the bulk of the appreciation to the 1985 peak came after mid-1982. The failure of imports to surge in the early 1980s is therefore not surprising. Furthermore, even the simplest macro models recognize that output has an important, independent influence on import demand, and with an elasticity greater than unity, as Husted's results show. Since output moved irregularly during this period (for example, contracting in 1982), it is not surprising that the ratio of imports to GNP did as well. For this reason, the volume of imports should not be taken as an accurate measure of protectionist pressure during that time period. In presenting his trade data, Deardorff does deflate by GNP, and this is a useful graphical device that Husted could have employed to tame what looks like a runaway explosive trade deficit in his Figure 13.1.

Deardorff's assertion that alterations in U.S. trade law were not as important as was the change in their administration, certainly rings true in the Canadian context. For example, a popular book on the Canada-U.S. Free Trade Agreement, edited by John Crispo (1988: 194) describes the irritations with U.S. trade policy in the following terms:

The problem has arisen from the unfair administration and interpretation of these U.S. laws over the last half-dozen years. An example of this transformation is the softwood-lumber case, which Canada won on essentially the same evidence only three years before it lost it. In the interval the United States drifted away from a basically economic approach toward a more political one in its countervail and anti-dumping decisions.

Now Deardorff claims that protectionism is a micro policy without direct effects on the value of the exchange rate. While this is true of minor trade restrictions, the observation fails to take account of the fact that the general level of trade barriers is often seen as an important influence on the foreign-exchange value of a currency (as in Britain in 1932; Canada in 1962, and many LDCs today). Thus, if a small industry is successful in its bid for protectionist legislation, the effect on the exchange rate is certainly negligible. However, when a large number of major industries seek protection, as in the Omnibus Trade Bill, the resulting strengthening of the U.S. dollar cannot be ignored.

The conventional Canadian view of this process (dating at least from 1961, when Mundell formalized the argument) is that a general tariff under flexible exchange rates has limited real costs (or benefits) for the economy. Instead, the view is that the exchange rate's value is just such as to offset the tariff so that in relative price terms the economy is precisely as it would have been without the tariff's imposition. Thus a 10 percent rise in the general tariff on imports and an equal percentage rise in subsidies on exports cause a 10 percent rise in the foreign-exchange value of the currency, which alters some nominal values in the economy but has no effect on real magnitudes.

Deardorff makes the useful distinction between current protectionism and fear of future protectionism. Interestingly, this same Canadian view finds that the fear of future protectionism can have major costs for the economy. The reason is that this fear will have the immediate effect of strengthening the domestic currency, and thereby make domestic industry less competitive. This competitive disadvantage will last until the legislation is passed and implemented. Specifically, in the context of the 1982–84 period, the surging U.S. dollar provided a strong argument on the part of the lobbyists for protectionist legislation. Clearly, this mechanism has the potential for generating an explosive movement of the exchange rate, and economists should draw greater attention to this threat.

Turning now to Husted's chapter, one is led initially to believe that perhaps a host of special factors is necessary to analyze the bilateral trade balances between the United States and other countries. Thus Husted provides a detailed description of the structure of commodities traded on both the import and the export side for each of the five countries/regions he considers. Furthermore, there is a year-by-year description of the way in which this trade has changed over time. One comes to the conclusion that each region should be analyzed separately from every other because of the specific factors that affect it.

The reader is therefore quite surprised to learn that these bilateral trade balances can be explained easily (R^2 over 0.9), using a short list of explanatory variables with only a single lag for each. None of the special factors mentioned is entered in the regression equations. The only complication is that two-stage least squares must be employed, with wholesale price and nominal wage indices used as instruments.

Now it seems to me that with such outstanding success in fitting the model to the data it would have been worthwhile spending some time comparing the fitted values to the actual values, with the country-specific special factors being brought in only insofar as there was a major discrepancy between these two values. Furthermore, it would have been useful to make a specific comparison between standard import demand functions describing the movement of the aggregate U.S. trade account, and the numbers that arose from these bilateral regressions. This would have provided some interesting insights and hinted at why aggregation problems limit the success of a similar treatment of the total trade balance. The underlying theory in essence is based on the analysis of a representative country. One is pleased to see that it works in that context.

Husted says that his equations are stable and it would have been helpful if the results of formal tests of stability had been reported. Instead, we are assured in a footnote that the introduction of intercept shifts and/or changes in price and income elasticities in the 1980s added little explanatory power and had no effect on the remaining coefficient estimates. The conclusion must be then that the 1980s were no different from the preceding decades except insofar as income grew differently or relative prices (presumably due to the movement of the exchange rate or primary commodity pricing) behaved somewhat atypically.

In a sense, then, Husted's conclusions amount to a denial of the importance of trade restrictions for understanding trade flows between the United States and other countries; or, at least, they provide very few avenues through which such trade barriers might have worked. As noted above, Deardorff's concluding sentence is in essence an admission of this: that the major part of the U.S. trade story was due to macroeconomic factors, with the change in trade law administration being a response to their effects.

Any remaining inconsistency in the conclusions of these two chapters is perhaps a desirable aspect of a volume about the policies of the Reagan years. Surely two of the most important changes in Washington economic policymaking during that era were a decline in the level of candor in policy discussions, and less directness in policy implementations. Deardorff has noted the discrepancy between rhetoric and action in the area of trade policy, but we should acknowledge that this is only one example of a general development in policymaking. The confusion that was thereby engendered will persist for years to come, making any assessment of this era difficult and controversial.

14

Exchange Rates during the Reagan Years

Craig S. Hakkio

The exchange value of the dollar (as measured by the International Monetary Fund (IMF)) rose 48 percent between 1980 and the first quarter of 1985; since then it has fallen 48 percent. In addition, exchange rate volatility remained high in the 1980s. Partly as a result of these facts, many analysts say we should fix the exchange rate, or at least set a target range for exchange rates. Furthermore, the associated rise in the trade deficit has increased the pressure for protection. Moreover, the exchange rate is increasingly important in the decision to tighten or loosen monetary policy. Finally, the role of foreign exchange market intervention has changed over the last nine years. During President Reagan's first term, the authorities seldom intervened in foreign exchange markets; during his second term, they intervened much more frequently. For these reasons, explaining the behavior of the dollar in the 1980s has been an important area of research.

The behavior of the dollar exchange rate in the 1980s raises several questions. First, was the behavior "unusual"? Exchange rate behavior can be unusual from a historical perspective, or from a cross-country perspective. Second, why did the dollar rise and fall so much? Two explanations are typically given: the change to anti-inflationary monetary policy and the increase in the budget deficit. Third, what is the proper role of the exchange rate in setting macroeconomic policy? And should the government actively intervene in foreign exchange markets? While all three questions are important, this chapter answers the first question, and provides part of the answer to the second question.

This study concludes that the dollar exchange rate in the 1980s was not unusual, given that we were in a flexible exchange rate regime; the dollar exchange rate was unusual when compared with fixed exchange rate regimes.

Stated more starkly, flexible exchange rate regimes are different from fixed exchange rate regimes, and all flexible exchange rate regimes are the same. At first glance, this appears obvious. However, several papers (see Lucas 1982 and Obstfeld and Stockman 1985) argue that the behavior of the real exchange rate should not depend on the nominal exchange rate regime. Mussa (1986) calls this "the nominal exchange rate regime neutrality" hypothesis. The results in this chapter, then, provide evidence against the nominal exchange rate regime neutrality hypothesis.

Four observations characterize the behavior of the dollar exchange rate in the 1980s: (1) the swings were large; (2) the real exchange rate followed a random walk (more accurately, had a unit root); (3) the correlation between the nominal and real exchange rate was large; and (4) the volatility was great. These observations reflect various aspects of the time series distribution of the dollar exchange rate. The first two observations refer to the mean value of the exchange rate, the third observation refers to a bivariate relationship, and the fourth observation refers to the (time-varying) variance of the exchange rate.

This characterization of the dollar exchange rate in the 1980s is not controversial. Consequently, this chapter examines whether this behavior was unusual from a historical perspective and from a cross-currency perspective. Whether the dollar exchange rate in the 1980s was unusual is an important first step in explaining its behavior in the 1980s. If the dollar exchange rate behaved unusually, we need to determine in what ways the 1980s were unusual. Alternatively, if the dollar exchange rate and, say, the German exchange rate were similar in the 1980s, then stories that are essentially "U.S. stories" may not be appropriate. In addition, if the dollar exchange rate in the 1980s is similar to the dollar exchange rate in other flexible exchange rate periods, we need to explain why flexible exchange rate regimes differ from fixed exchange rate regimes.

The next four sections of this chapter examine the four observations that characterize the dollar exchange rate in the 1980s. Each section looks first at the pound/dollar exchange rate since 1914 and then at the G-7 exchange rates during the floating rate period (post-1973 and post-1980) to see whether the behavior of the dollar exchange rate in the 1980s was unusual.[1] The IMF indices for the G-7 currencies are used because their calculation is consistent across currencies. The data used in the text are discussed in Appendix A. The IMF dollar exchange rate index is always used when discussing the dollar in the 1980s.

WERE SWINGS IN THE DOLLAR EXCHANGE RATE LARGE?

Swings in the value of the dollar were large during the 1980s. The nominal value of the dollar rose 46 percent from 1980 to its peak, then fell 50 percent from its peak to the end of 1988; the real value of the dollar rose and fell by similar amounts. Since the real exchange rate measures the deviations from purchasing power parity (PPP), we conclude that deviations from PPP were large and persistent.

The rest of this section shows that these swings in the dollar were not unusual when compared with other floating exchange rate periods or when compared with other currencies during the current floating exchange rate period. The pound/dollar exchange rate since 1914 is examined first. Then, the G-7 exchange rate indexes are examined. Finally, the implications of these findings for explaining the swings in the dollar are discussed.

The Pound/Dollar Exchange Rate Since 1914

The pound/dollar exchange rate (real and nominal) is the only exchange rate that is readily available monthly since 1914. Therefore, analyzing exchange rates over a long historical period is limited. However, it is hoped that this exchange rate is representative.[2] Since 1914 there have been three floating-rate periods and two fixed-rate periods. The floating-rate periods were (1) July 1919 to March 1925; (2) September 1931 to August 1939; and (3) March 1973 to the present. The fixed-rate periods were (1) April 1925 to August 1931; and (2) January 1947 to February 1973. The periods 1914 to 1918 and 1939 to 1945 were war years.

Figure 14.1 shows the monthly exchange rate between the dollar and the pound from 1916 to the end of 1988. The solid line is the real exchange rate and the dashed line represents the nominal exchange rate. The vertical axis is a log-scale, with the values being the actual pound/dollar exchange rate. A log scale is used because the exchange rate is now about four times larger than in the 1920s.

The figure shows quite vividly that the pound/dollar exchange rate underwent large changes during floating-exchange rate periods. Changes in the pound/dollar exchange rate—as measured by the standard deviation or the average absolute value of the 12-month percent change—were about the same (but perhaps slightly larger) during the current floating-rate period than during the earlier floating-rate periods. However, some changes were larger in the earlier period. For example, the dollar depreciated by 45 percent between November 1932 and November 1933; the largest annual change in the 1980s was 28 percent (between September 1980 and September 1981).

Even though the evidence presented so far suggests that swings in the dollar during the 1980s were not unusual, other evidence suggests that some things were unusual in the 1980s. In particular, the first jump in the dollar in 1919 was quite rapid: The dollar rose 35 percent from February 1919 to February 1920. The second jump in the dollar was also rapid: The dollar rose 36 percent from June 1931 to December 1931. In contrast, in the 1980s, it took the dollar almost three years to rise the same 35 percent (February 1980 to December 1982), and it took five years to go from the trough to the peak.

Figure 14.1
Real and Nominal Pound/Dollar Exchange Rates

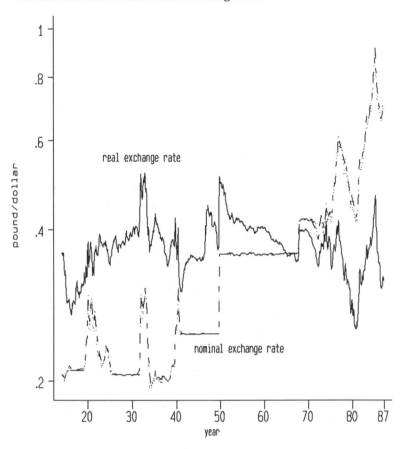

Other Exchange Rates in the 1980s

Figure 14.2 plots the IMF exchange rate indices for the U.S. dollar and the other G-7 currencies. As in Figure 14.1, the solid line represents the real exchange rate index and the dashed line is the nominal exchange rate index. To allow comparisons across panels, the vertical axis is the same in all panels. In addition, each index was normalized so that the average value over the 1975 to 1989 period is 100.

The Figure indicates that although the nominal appreciation and depreciation of the dollar was large, it was not large relative to the Japanese yen or Italian lira. For example, the Japanese yen appreciated over the entire 1980s, with its total appreciation greater than the dollar appreciation. Furthermore, the lira depreciated over the entire period, but much of the depreciation reflected higher

Figure 14.2
Real and Nominal Exchange Rates

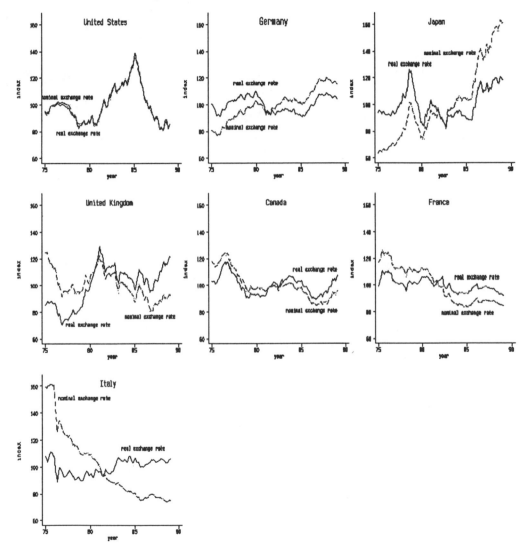

inflation in Italy. Notice that although the German mark also appreciated over most of the period, the appreciation was small.

The implication of Figure 14.2—that exchange rate indices exhibited large swings—is not an artifact of using indices instead of bilateral exchange rates. For example, between 1980 and February 1985, the dollar rose 87 percent against the French franc, while the yen rose 73 percent. In addition, between February 1985 and December 1988 the dollar fell 63 percent against the German mark, while the yen rose 62 percent against the Canadian dollar. Even though other currencies rose (or fell) a large amount, it is still true that changes in the dollar (bilateral and effective rates) were generally larger than those in other currencies. [3]

Implications for Exchange Rate Expansions

There are three simple conclusions to be drawn from this section:

- Swings in the pound/dollar exchange rate are large during flexible exchange rate regimes, and small during fixed exchange rate regimes.
- Swings took longer in the 1980s.
- Swings in all exchange rates are large during flexible exchange rate periods.

An implication of this section is that any explanation of the large swings in the dollar exchange rate during the 1980s cannot be simply a U.S. story: Either it must be a world story, or it must explain why events in the United States were transmitted to other currencies. Moreover, any accounting should explain why exchange rates exhibit large changes during flexible exchange rate periods. Before continuing, a discussion of the conventional explanations is useful.

U.S. monetary and fiscal policy contributed to the dollar's appreciation during the early 1980s. [4] The shift in monetary policy from perceived ease in the late 1970s to an anti-inflationary stance spurred the dollar's early advance, and the tightening of monetary policy that began in early 1984 may have pushed the dollar up farther in 1984. In addition, higher U.S. real interest rates—due to changes in tax laws and rising budget deficits (in an expanding economy)— may have attracted foreign capital, which tended to push up the value of the dollar. Finally, the strong recovery in the United States relative to most other industrial countries and a sense of renewed confidence in the U.S. economy led to further dollar appreciation.

A partial reversal of the monetary and fiscal policies that contributed to the dollar's appreciation also contributed to its depreciation. U.S. monetary policy eased in late 1984. Furthermore, the Tax Reform Act of 1986 raised the effective tax rate on capital investment in the United States, reducing the attractiveness of U.S. assets. The deceleration in U.S. growth may also have contributed to the dollar's decline. Finally, the Plaza Agreement of September 1985, which announced the intention of the G-5 countries to seek a lower dollar, probably hastened the dollar's fall.[5]

The evidence in this section is consistent with the importance of monetary and fiscal policy in explaining the appreciation and subsequent depreciation of the dollar. Since exchange rates involve two currencies, the differences in monetary and fiscal policy are obviously important. By the early 1980s most industrial countries recognized that macro policy should focus on medium-term objectives, such as reducing inflation and government budget deficits. Beginning in October 1979, the objective of U.S. monetary policy turned toward reducing inflation (CPI inflation in December 1979 was 13 percent from December of the previous year). Anti-inflation policies later took hold in most industrial countries. That is, the timing of changes in monetary policy is consistent with the rise and subsequent fall of the dollar.

Similarly, changes in tax policy are also consistent with the timing of the rise and fall of the dollar. As indicated above, changes in U.S. tax policy contributed to the dollar's rise and subsequent fall. Following the U.S. example, most industrial countries reduced marginal income tax rates in the 1980s. This reduction in foreign tax rates, in conjunction with the Tax Reform Act of 1986, increased the attractiveness of foreign assets. That is, the reduction in U.S. tax rates contributed to the dollar's rise; the subsequent increase in U.S. tax rates and the decrease in foreign tax rates contributed to the dollar's fall.

DO REAL EXCHANGE RATES FOLLOW A RANDOM WALK?

The second characteristic of the real and nominal values of the dollar in the 1980s is that they followed a random walk (or, more accurately, they had a unit root).[6] This result is consistent with real and nominal shocks being nonstationary. In addition, a nonstationary real exchange rate means that there is no tendency for purchasing power parity to hold in the long run. Several authors have examined this issue and found that real exchange rates are close to a random walk. This subsection tests whether the real pound/dollar exchange rate followed a random walk during the period 1914 to 1986, and whether other real exchange rate indices followed a random walk during the post-Bretton Woods era.

The Pound/Dollar Exchange Rate since 1914

Table 14.1 presents the augmented Dickey-Fuller statistic for testing whether the pound/dollar exchange rate (nominal and real) is a random walk. Two statistics are calculated: one including a constant and one including a constant and time trend in the Dickey-Fuller regression (the time trend was generally significant). The null hypothesis is that the variable follows a random walk (with drift or with drift and trend). Therefore, a "small" test statistic means that we

Table 14.1
Do Exchange Rates Follow a Random Walk?

	Augmented Dickey-Fuller Statistic			
	Real Exchange Rate		Nominal Exchange Rate	
Period or Country	Constant	Time	Constant	Time
	Floating Rate Periods			
Pound/Dollar exchange rate:				
1919:7 - 1925:3	-2.824 [2]**	-2.665 [2]	-1.403 [2]	-3.149 [2]
1931:9 - 1939:8	-2.186 [4]	-2.223 [2]	-2.504 [4]	-1.760 [4]
1973:3 - 1986:12	-1.666 [2]	-1.682 [2]	-1.363 [2]	-1.662 [2]
1980:1 - 1986:12	-1.421 [2]	-0.848 [2]	-1.301 [2]	-1.019 [2]
G-7 exchange rates (January 1980 - February 1989):				
United States	-0.928 [2]	-1.216 [2]		
Germany	-1.539 [2]	-2.913 [2]		
Japan	-1.149 [3]	-1.589 [2]		
United Kingdom	-2.337 [2]	-2.361 [2]		
Canada	-1.005 [2]	-0.979 [2]		
France	-1.790 [2]	-2.308 [2]		
Italy	-2.183 [3]	-2.185 [3]		
	Fixed Exchange Rate Periods			
Pound/dollar exchange rate:				
1925:4 - 1931:8	-1.966 [2]	-3.580 [2]*	-3.319 [2]*	-3.340 [2]**
1947:1 - 1973:2	-2.548 [3]	-3.888 [3]*	-2.653 [4]**	-2.775 [4]

Note: The number in brackets denotes the number of lagged dependent variables included in the Dickey-Fuller regression. "Constant" means a constant was included; and "Time Trend" means a constant and a time trend were included.

The null hypothesis is nonstationarity. Therefore, a "large" negative statistic means reject a random walk, and accept the alternative of stationarity; a "small" negative statistic (or positive) means "accept" the null of a random walk. Critical values are:

	5 percent		10 percent	
Sample size	constant	time	constant	time
50	-2.93	-3.50	-2.60	-3.18
100	-2.89	-3.45	-2.58	-3.15
250	-2.86	-3.43	-2.57	-3.13

* denotes significant at the 5 percent level (reject a random walk);
** denotes significant at the 10 percent level (reject a random walk).

cannot reject a random walk, while a "large" test statistic means that we can reject a random walk, and conclude that the variable is stationary, or stationary around a time trend.

The evidence presented in Table 14.1 suggests that the random walk behavior of the pound/dollar exchange rate depends on the exchange rate regime. This conclusion is based on two observations: (1) the pound/dollar exchange rate (real and nominal) follows a random walk during flexible exchange rate periods; and (2) the pound/dollar exchange rate (real and nominal) does not follow a random walk during fixed exchange rate periods.[7] This result is quite striking and is further evidence against the nominal exchange rate neutrality hypothesis.

Did Other Real Exchange Rates Follow a Random Walk in 1980?

Table 14.1 also indicates that random walk behavior for real exchange rates during flexible exchange rate periods is a universal finding. The table reports the results for testing whether the IMF's real exchange rate index for the G-7 currencies followed a random walk during the 1980s. As above, two Dickey-Fuller test statistics were calculated. The results are clear: Each real exchange rate appears to follow a random walk. (More specifically, we cannot reject the null hypothesis that each real exchange rate had a unit root.)

In a highly integrated capital market, exchange rates should be viewed as a vector process, rather than independent processes as in Table 14.1 While each of the seven real exchange rates had a unit root, it is possible that there are actually fewer than seven unit roots when viewed as a vector process. In other words, some of the exchange rates may share a unit root (or, equivalently, have a common trend). For example, if there is a single, nonstationary world shock, then all real exchange rates would share a common unit root. Alternatively, if each country had its own nonstationary shock, then each real exchange rate would have its own unit root. Or, to express this idea in reverse form, the number of unit roots tells us something about the number of nonstationary shocks hitting the world economy.[8]

Determining the number of unit roots is a multivariate generalization of the notion of cointegration: If two series share a unit root, they are said to be cointegrated. Seven series may have anywhere from seven unit roots to one unit root. (One unit root would correspond to one common trend.)

Evidence suggests that there are as many unit roots as there are exchange rates.[9] First, exchange rates were tested for pairwise cointegration; only two pair of exchange rate indices were cointegrated (the DM and yen indices, and the franc and lira indices).[10] Second, exchange rates were tested for joint cointegration: We could not reject the null of no cointegration (that is, that the six exchange rate indices are not cointegrated). Finally, we used the Stock-Watson procedure to test for the number of common trends—unit roots—in the six exchange rates; we could not reject the hypothesis of six unit roots.

Implications for Explaining the Dollar Exchange Rate in the 1980s

Two conclusions can be drawn from this section:

- Exchange rates (real and nominal) are random walks (have unit roots) during flexible exchange rate periods, but not during fixed exchange rate periods.

- In the 1980s, the six exchange rates possessed six unit roots.

These conclusions must remain tentative because tests for a random walk do not have a great deal of power (when p is close to 1).

Strong implications follow from a nonstationary real exchange rate. If the real exchange rate follows a random walk, there is no tendency for it to return to a long-run level, it will take arbitrarily large values with probability one. While this may be plausible for a nominal exchange rate (with positive inflation), it is difficult to accept for a relative price such as the real exchange rate. Also, a nonstationary real exchange rate suggests that the real exogenous shocks that hit the economy are nonstationary. The reason is simple: Nonstationary shocks will likely be passed through to relative prices such as the real exchange rate. However, this explanation is not fully satisfactory since consistency with the data would require stationary shocks during fixed exchange rate periods and nonstationary shocks during flexible exchange rate periods. For these reasons, this result must be further investigated.

The second conclusion suggests that there are six sources of nonstationarity in the six countries. This result is consistent with two possible explanations: Either each country has its own nonstationary disturbance, or there are six nonstationary world disturbances that affect all exchange rates. At this level of analysis, it is not possible to distinguish between these alternatives.

IS THE CORRELATION BETWEEN REAL AND NOMINAL EXCHANGE RATES LARGE?

The real and nominal exchange values of the dollar were highly correlated in the 1980s. In this section, we look at the correlation between the real and nominal pound/dollar exchange rate since 1914, and the correlation between real and nominal effective exchange rates for each of the G-7 currencies. Three types of evidence are brought to bear on this question: graphical, regression estimates, and cointegration tests.

The Real and Nominal Pound/Dollar Exchange Rate since 1914

Figure 14.1 shows that over the entire sample period (1914–86) the real and nominal pound/dollar exchange rates were not highly correlated.[11] During the whole period, the nominal exchange rate ranged from 0.19 to 0.91, the real exchange rate ranged from 0.25 to 0.52, and the ratio of the ranges was 2.7. Even if we exclude the 1980s, the ratio was 1.7. The evidence shown in Figure 14.1 is consistent with Mussa's finding (1986) that real and nominal exchange rates (pound/dollar) were highly correlated in the current flexible exchange rate period, but not in the fixed exchange rate period (Bretton-Woods). Figure 14.1 extends Mussa's analysis by examining the pound/dollar exchange rate in other fixed and flexible exchange rate periods.

Since a figure may not provide strong evidence, Table 14.2 provides some statistical evidence. The table reports the result of regressing the log of the

Table 14.2
The Relationship between the Real and Nominal Exchange Rates
$$\ln(e_t) = \alpha + \beta \ln(q_t) + e_t$$

Period or Country	α	β	R^2	D-F statistic
		Floating Exchange Rate Periods		
Pound/Dollar exchange rate:				
1919:7 - 1925:3	-1.740	-0.300	0.02	-1.743 [2]
	(0.772)	(0.753)		
1931:9 - 1939:8	-0.518	1.094	0.80	-1.361 [2]
	(0.181)	(0.196)		
1973:3 - 1986:12	0.138	0.695	0.19	-1.140 [4]
	(0.508)	(0.470)		
1980:1 - 1986:12	0.929	1.294	0.85	0.551 [2]
	(0.239)	(0.215)		
G-7 exchange rates (January 1980 - February 1989):				
United States	-0.077	1.017	1.00	-2.530 [3]
	(0.042)	(0.010)		
Germany	-0.102	1.015	0.99	-2.002 [4]
	(1.490)	(0.319)		
Japan	-3.889)	1.815	0.83	-1.316 [3]
	(1.444)	(0.308)		
United Kingdom	-0.242	1.052	0.46	0.363 [4]
	(2.000)	(0.431)		
Canada	1.149	0.753	0.50	-1.508 [2]
	(1.351)	(0.294)		
France	-4.700	2.028	0.81	-2.305 [2]
	(1.431)	(0.310)		
Italy	13.171	-1.844	0.53	-2.308 [2]
	(2.355)	(0.512)		
		Fixed Exchange Rate Periods		
Pound/Dollar exchange rate:				
1925:4 - 1931:8	-1.593	-0.012	0.03	-3.488 [2]
	(0.027)	(0.028)		
1947:1 - 1973:2	-1.386	-0.375	0.05	-2.800 [4]
	(0.339)	(0.364)		

Note: The number in parentheses below each coefficient is the West-standard error (using 20 lags). The "D-F statistic" is the augmented Dickey-Fuller statistic for testing whether the real and nominal pound/dollar exchange rates are cointegrated; the number in brackets next to the D-F statistic is the number of lagged dependent variables used in calculating the augmented Dickey-Fuller statistic. The 5 percent critical value is -3.17. A "large" negative statistic means reject the null hypothesis of no-cointegration, and accept the alternative of cointegration; a "small" negative statistic (or positive) means "accept" the null of no-cointegration.

nominal exchange rate on the log of the real exchange rate for the various floating and fixed exchange rate periods. The coefficient estimates are reported in the table, along with the standard errors.[12]

Two conclusions can be drawn from Table 14.2. First, there is no simple, uniform relationship between real and nominal exchange rates. Over the entire period (including war years), there is no relationship—the slope coefficient is insignificantly different from zero and the R^2 is zero. Furthermore, during the two fixed-rate periods, the estimated slope coefficient is negative (but insignificantly different from zero). During the first floating-rate period (June 1919 to March 1925), there is also no relationship. However, during the other two floating-rate periods (September 1931 to August 1939 and the 1980s) the relationship between real and nominal exchange rates is much stronger. In both cases the slope is insignificantly different from one (and significantly different from zero), and the R^2 is large.

The second conclusion is that even though real and nominal exchange rates appear to be highly correlated, they are not cointegrated. The last column in Table 14.2 reports the augmented Dickey-Fuller statistic for testing whether the nominal and real pound/dollar exchange rates are cointegrated during the various subperiods. Given the small size of the D-F statistic, we cannot reject the null hypothesis of no-cointegration. As a result, the difference in the log of the price levels must be nonstationary.

Real and Nominal Exchange Rates in the 1980s

The evidence on whether other real and nominal exchange rates have been highly correlated during the current flexible exchange rate period is mixed. The evidence shown in Figure 14.2 is striking: The correlation between the real and nominal values of the dollar is strong, but the correlation is much weaker— though positive—for all other currencies. Notice, too, that the real French franc and the real Italian lira have been reasonably constant since 1973. The French experience probably reflects a sharp deceleration in inflation between 1980 and 1985; the high inflation in the mid- to late 1970s contributed to the depreciation of the franc since 1975.

Table 14.2 confirms the visual evidence presented in Figure 14.2. The relationship between real and nominal exchange rates was strongest for the United States, where "strongest" means the R^2 was large and the slope coefficient was close to one. Although not reported, the coefficient on the real exchange rate index was insignificantly different from zero for Germany, Japan, and Italy for the period beginning in 1975. However, for the period beginning in January 1980, the slope coefficient is significantly different from zero in all cases. (In the Italian case, the slope coefficient is significantly negative.) In addition, in three cases—the United States, Germany, and Canada—the slope coefficient is insignificantly different from one.

The Table also shows the results of testing whether the real and nominal exchange rate indices are cointegrated. As with the pound/dollar, we find that real and nominal exchange rate indices are not cointegrated (or, more accurately, we cannot reject the hypothesis of no-cointegration).

Implications for Exchange Rate Behavior

Four general conclusions can be drawn from this section:

- Real and nominal exchange rates are correlated during flexible exchange rate periods.
- The relationship is weaker for currencies other than the dollar.
- Real and nominal exchange rates are not highly correlated during fixed exchange rate periods.
- Although real and nominal exchange rates appear highly correlated, they are not cointegrated during fixed or flexible exchange rate periods.

Mussa (1986) argued that sticky prices were the major reason that real exchange rates were more variable during flexible exchange rate regimes than during fixed regimes. If prices are sticky, then real exchange rates will be "noisy" proxies for nominal exchange rates, and so real and nominal exchange rates should be highly correlated. If this explanation were true, one would expect that real and nominal exchange rates for other countries would also be highly correlated; however, they are not.[13]

The results in the last two sections suggest that there are many kinds of nonstationary shocks. The six real exchange rates having six unit roots means there are six real nonstationary shocks. In addition, the fact that real and nominal exchange rates are not cointegrated implies that nominal shocks (which affect national price levels) are also nonstationary.

DID EXCHANGE RATE VOLATILITY INCREASE IN THE 1980s?

It is well known that exchange rate volatility increased following the move to flexible exchange rates. With hindsight, this was not surprising: Exchange rates are asset prices (set in auction markets) that quickly respond to new information. It is also true, however, that volatility did not decrease in the 1980s. Therefore, the volatility in the mid-1970s is probably not the result of a transition period from fixed to flexible exchange rates.

Although volatility can be measured in several ways, we used a measure of volatility based on regression results and similar to Engle's ARCH process.[14] The procedure is described in Schwert (1988). Simply put, monthly rates of depreciation are regressed against 12 lags, and 12 monthly dummies. Then, a twelfth order autoregression is estimated for the absolute value of the errors from the above regression (12 monthly dummies are again included). Finally, the fitted values from the last regression are the estimates of volatility used by Schwert (1988). These estimates were then smoothed using a robust nonlinear compound smoother. There are three steps in smoothing the data. First, a five-period centered median was calculated. Then, a three-period centered median was calculated. Finally, a three-period weighted average was calculated, with weights equal to 0.25, 0.50, and 0.25. The smoothed estimates are the estimates of volatility used in this chapter.

Volatility of the Pound/Dollar Exchange Rate since 1914

The top part of Figure 14.3 shows the volatility of the real pound/dollar exchange rate since 1914. The figure shows that volatility in the 1980s was slightly greater than in the 1970s. For example, volatility in the 1980s averaged 2.8, but was only 2.1 during the 1973 to 1980 period.

In addition, volatility in the current floating rate period was only slightly greater than in other flexible exchange rate periods. For example, volatility

Figure 14.3
Volatility of Real Exchange Rates

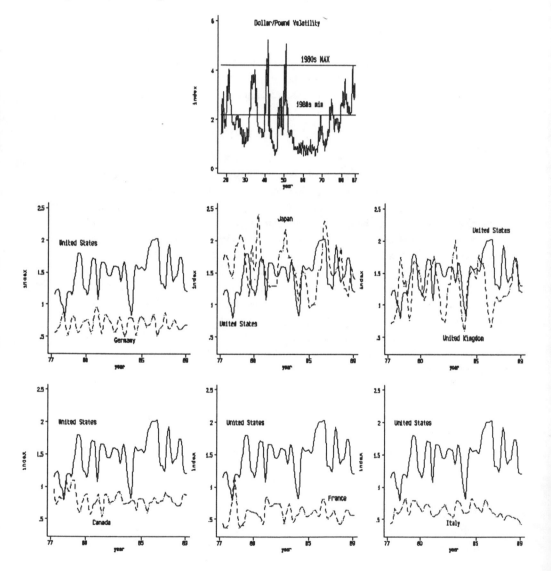

averaged 2.5 during the 1973 to 1988 period, which is not very different from the volatility during the 1919 to 1924 period (1.6) or the 1932 to 1939 period (2.4).

Figure 14.3 also makes the obvious point that volatility is greater during flexible exchange rate periods than fixed exchange rate periods. Volatility of real exchange rates is about twice as great in flexible-exchange rate periods as in fixed exchange rate periods.

Volatility of Other Exchange Rates in the 1980s

Volatility of real exchange rates (percentage change) was greater in the United States than in Germany, Canada, France, and Italy; volatility in the United States, Japan, and the United Kingdom was approximately the same. The basis for this statement is shown in the bottom part of Figure 14.3.

Economic theory can provide some reasons for the increase in exchange rate volatility in the 1980s. Various theories of exchange rate determination suggest that exchange rates depend on the money supply, income, and prices. Therefore, it is reasonable to expect that exchange rate volatility depends on volatility of these same variables. Unfortunately, preliminary analysis suggests that volatility of inflation, growth of industrial production, and growth of money provide little information about exchange rate volatility.

Implications for Exchange Rate Volatility

Four conclusions can be drawn from this section:

- Volatility of the dollar is greater during flexible exchange rate periods than during fixed exchange rate periods.
- Volatility of the dollar in the 1980s is about the same as volatility of the dollar during the other flexible exchange rate periods.
- Volatility in the (real) dollar in the 1980s was only slightly greater than volatility in other (real) exchange rates.
- No simple explanation for (real) exchange rate volatility exists.

CONCLUSIONS

The evidence presented in this chapter can be summarized by saying: (1) exchange rates (real and nominal) behave differently during flexible and fixed exchange rate regimes; and (2) the dollar exchange rate is like other exchange rates (in most respects) during flexible exchange rate regimes.

Exchange rates in floating and fixed exchange rate regimes are different in at least four ways. (This conclusion is based on the pound/dollar exchange rate.) First, swings are larger during floating regimes than during fixed regimes.

Second, exchange rates are a random walk during floating regimes but not during fixed regimes. Third, real and nominal exchange rates are correlated during floating regimes but not during fixed regimes. And finally, exchange rates are more variable during floating regimes than during fixed regimes.

These results are therefore inconsistent with the nominal exchange rate regime neutrality hypothesis, which predicts that real exchange rates should behave the same during fixed and flexible exchange rate regimes. Since this result is based on the pound/dollar exchange rate since 1914, it would be useful to extend these results (if true) to other exchange rates.

The important question now becomes: In what ways are flexible and fixed exchange rate regimes different? Mussa (1986) argues that since prices are sticky, real exchange rates are simply noisy measures of nominal exchange rates. And since nominal exchange rates behave differently in flexible and fixed exchange rate regimes, so do real exchange rates. Stockman (1988), however, argues that trade policy is different in flexible and fixed exchange rate regimes; therefore, real exchange rates behave differently in the two regimes. Based on the pound/dollar exchange rate experience, we cannot distinguish between these two hypotheses.

However, the second conclusion of the chapter—that the dollar exchange rate is like other exchange rates (in most respects) during flexible-exchange rate regimes—may help to distinguish between these two hypotheses. All exchange rates (dollar and non-dollar) during the 1980s exhibited large swings, followed random walks, and were highly volatile. But while the correlation between real and nominal exchange rates was positive during the 1980s for all currencies, the correlation was weaker for currencies other than the dollar.

If Mussa's argument that sticky prices explain the greater volatility of real exchange rates during flexible-exchange rate regimes is correct, we would expect real and nominal exchange rates to be highly correlated during flexible exchange rate regimes. But the evidence for currencies other than the dollar contradicts this presumption. Therefore, if price levels are sticky in all countries, this lack of correlation is evidence against Mussa's argument.

The evidence presented in this chapter suggests that there are several nonstationary shocks in the world economy. The random walk behavior of real exchange rates suggest the presence of nonstationary real shocks. In addition, the six unit roots (in the six exchange rates) suggest multiple sources of real nonstationarity. This explanation is not fully satisfactory, however, since real exchange rates appear stationary during fixed exchange rate regimes. This would mean that the exchange rate regime determines whether real shocks are stationary or nonstationary. Finally, the fact that real and nominal exchange rates are not cointegrated suggests that nominal shocks (which affect price levels) are also nonstationary.

The evidence in the chapter also suggests that the long swings in the dollar—not the short-run volatility—were unusual. While the pound/dollar exchange rate exhibited large changes during earlier flexible-exchange rate periods, they occurred quickly. During the 1980s, the swings took much longer. In addition, the swings were larger in the 1980s, but not significantly larger. Finally, short-run volatility was about the same during all flexible exchange rate periods.

NOTES

I thank Dodd Snoddgrass for his research assistance. I also thank Sean Becketti, Jon Faust, Bryon Higgins, Doug Joines, and participants at the Federal Reserve Bank of Kansas City seminar for helpful comments. The views expressed herein are solely those of the author and do not necessarily reflect the views of the Federal Reserve Bank of Kansas City or of the Federal Reserve System.

1. A longer version of this chapter, Hakkio (1989), "Exchange Rates in the 1980s," examines these same issues in greater detail. In particular, additional charts and tables are presented.

2. Grilli and Kaminsky (1988:1) state: "Nevertheless, we believe that the properties of this rate are quite representative of the general historical properties of real exchange rates."

3. The longer version of this chapter shows the percentage changes in all bilateral exchange rates among the G-7 currencies during the 1980s.

4. Several papers discuss the rise and fall of the dollar. Rather than provide an extensive list, two representative studies are cited: *The Economic Report of the President, 1988* (Council of Economic Advisors, February 1988, chapter 3) and "The U.S. External Deficit: Its Causes and Persistence," by Hooper and Mann (1989).

5. It should be noted that the dollar actually began falling in February 1985, seven months before the Plaza Agreement.

6. Although it is a misuse of terminology, I will often use the expression "follows a random walk" to mean "has a unit root." To see the distinction, consider the difference in the variable x_t. If x_t is a random walk, its difference is a zero mean serially uncorrelated random variable. If x_t has a unit root, however, its difference is only stationary (as opposed to serially uncorrelated), it may have a nonzero mean, and it may have a deterministic time trend.

7. Grilli and Kaminsky (1988) also test for whether the real pound/dollar exchange rate is a random walk. Since the data used in Table 14.2 are the same as their data, both results should match. (They do not report the actual Dickey-Fuller statistics, so a direct comparison is not possible. They also use slightly different sample periods.) They summarize their results (p. 14) as: "Both real exchange rates [based on PPI and CPI] seem to be stationary when the whole period January 1985–December 1986 is analyzed. However, once we consider specific subperiods, we discover that in general we cannot reject the unit-root hypothesis."

8. The terms "number of common trends" and "number of unit roots" are often used synonymously. However, "number of unit roots" is more precise and leads to less confusion. For example, in the case of three variables, the term "three unit roots" makes sense, but the term "three common trends" is confusing. Therefore, in this chapter I will refer to the number of unit roots.

9. The longer version of this chapter provides the details of the tests discussed in the text.

10. Edison and Fisher (1989:15) found that European Monetary System (EMS) nominal exchange rates were not cointegrated.

11. Real exchange rates are calculated using Producer Price Indexes (PPIs). The data were provided by Professor Grilli (Grilli and Kaminsky 1988).

12. Since the real and nominal exchange rates may have a unit root, conventional Ordinary Least Squares standard errors are incorrect. Therefore, we use the standard errors suggested by West (1987).

13. Mussa actually argues that real exchange rates are more variable during flexible exchange rate periods than in fixed exchange rate periods. However, this argument also implies that real and nominal exchange rates should be highly correlated during flexible exchange rate periods. Stockman (1988) argues that countries are more likely to adopt protectionist policies during fixed exchange rate regimes, which implies that real exchange rates are more variable during flexible exchange rate periods than in fixed exchange rate periods.

14. The longer version of this chapter showed that the results in this section are not sensitive to the definition of volatility. In that paper, five different measures of volatility were calculated.

"Exchange Rates during the Reagan Years": *Comment*

Jay H. Levin

In September 1985, around the time of the famous Plaza Agreement, a Pulitzer Prize–winning editorial cartoonist for the *Miami News,* Don Wright, published a cartoon that is very relevant for this discussion. It showed Ronald Reagan sitting in the Oval Office at his desk. On the front was a sign reading, "The Buck Drops Here." This sign, which President Bush presumably has already turned upside down, raises an important question: Has the behavior of the dollar been unusual in the 1980s? This is precisely the question that Craig Hakkio has investigated in his excellent chapter.

Let me first summarize the four major findings in Chapter 14 as I see them. Then I will discuss each of them in turn.

1. In the 1980s medium-run swings in the dollar were large, but not unusually large when compared with other flexible exchange rate periods or with other currencies.

2. As a tentative conclusion, the nominal and real exchange rates on the dollar followed a random walk in the 1980s. This preliminary finding also applies to other flexible exchange rate periods and to other currencies.

3. Real and nominal exchange rates on the dollar were highly correlated in the 1980s. This correlation is stronger than in earlier floating-rate periods and for other currencies.

4. The short-run volatility of the nominal exchange rate on the dollar in the 1980s was not unusual as compared with other floating-rate periods. It increased somewhat relative to the 1970s. Also, the volatility of the real dollar exchange rate was somewhat greater than for the other Group of Seven real exchange rates, except in Japan and the United Kingdom.

Now let's consider each of these propositions. First, concerning the medium-run swings in the dollar, Craig's evidence is certainly convincing. He also

appears to accept conventional explanations for these swings. These include
changes in the monetary–fiscal policy mix in the United States over this period
relative to other countries, as well as other factors, such as changes in U.S. tax
laws affecting the rate of return on capital investment in the United States, and
perhaps the Plaza Agreement to which I have already referred. I would add
that a sharp relative decline in U.S. inflation after 1981 may have contributed
to the period of appreciation. In addition, expectations of increased fiscal restraint in the United States due to Gramm-Rudman may have contributed to the
subsequent period of depreciation.

Let us now turn to the finding that the dollar followed a random walk. This
is a subject on which Craig is probably the world's leading expert, and so I am
going to approach this as gingerly as possible. Craig's econometric evidence is
based on Dickey-Fuller test statistics. But why are his conclusions tentative?
One reason is that tests for a random walk have low power, as Craig taught us
in a paper published in 1986. In addition, I would add that when one considers
very long time periods, some studies have shown that the real exchange rate
regresses to purchasing power parity (see Edison 1987 and Frankel 1986). So
I believe the jury is still out on the random walk hypothesis as far as real
exchange rates are concerned.

Craig's third finding is the high correlation between the real and nominal
exchange rates on the dollar in the 1980s. This is borne out by the simple
regression of the nominal rate on the real rate in his Table 14.2, which also
contains regressions for the other Group of Seven countries. The R^2 for the
United States is the highest, and the slope coefficient is close to 1. Since Craig
is concerned with the slope coefficient as well as the R^2 for all of these countries, I would suggest that it might also be useful to regress the real exchange
rate on the nominal exchange rate. The reason is that according to the asset
market approach, a movement in the nominal exchange rate, due, say, to a
monetary disturbance, leads to a movement in the real exchange rate because
goods prices are sluggish. I realize that both the nominal and real rates are
endogenous, but if there is any cause and effect here, it runs from the nominal
rate to the real rate under this approach. This might be important because the
slope coefficients are not reciprocals of each other whenever R^2 differs from 1.
In practice, however, the results may not change because the product of the
slope coefficients will equal R^2, and from inspection the alternative coefficients
seem to tell the same story as Craig's.

I would also like to note that the evidence on the nominal–real exchange
rate relationship for other countries may be a bit muddy. In a recent study,
Richard Marston (1988:84) found that the standard deviations of monthly percentage changes of nominal and real effective exchange rates were almost identical for the G-5 countries over the period July 1973–December 1985. He concludes that "real exchange rates are volatile primarily because nominal exchange
rates are volatile. That is, the relative stability of price levels means that nominal exchange rate volatility translates into real exchange rate volatility." Given

Marston's findings and those reported here by Craig, it appears that there are conflicting results that remain to be resolved for the other currencies.

Finally, we come to Craig's findings about the short-run volatility of the dollar in the 1980s. Why should we be concerned with the issue of volatility? Presumably because exchange rate risk is linked to volatility, and higher volatility might therefore impair international trade and investment. Craig's evidence is that the volatility of the dollar increased in the 1980s, but unfortunately he is unable to obtain a statistical explanation for the increase based on current theories of exchange rate determination. Perhaps these results are not surprising. After all, empirical models of exchange rate determination themselves have been a dismal failure, so one should not expect much from these models for explaining exchange rate volatility. On a more technical level, sticky price monetary models of the exchange rate contain a short-term interest rate variable that Craig does not consider. This variable is designed to capture the amount of exchange rate overshooting in response to a monetary disturbance. It is possible that by introducing interest rates into his regressions, the increase in volatility of the dollar might be related to an increase in interest rate volatility, if the latter did indeed occur. Nevertheless, I would be surprised if this change improved the results materially. Finally, on the entire issue of volatility, I would add that most empirical evidence that I have seen suggests that volatility has not impeded international trade flows. However, there are well-known exceptions to these findings, and I do not believe the issue has yet been settled.

I will conclude with a reminder that Craig's chapter is concerned solely with the important issue of the behavior of the dollar in the 1980s. There are, of course, many other issues pertaining to the floating exchange rate system. Has speculation been stabilizing or destabilizing? Is exchange market intervention useless? Are there speculative bubbles, like the one alleged to have occurred in February 1985? Are exchange rates excessively volatile in some sense? Perhaps at some future date Craig will provide us with answers to these questions. In the meantime, we have learned a great deal from his chapter already.

NOTE

I am grateful to my colleague An-Loh Lin for helpful discussions in preparing this comment.

Part VI

An Alternative Theoretical Synthesis

15

The Reagan Legacy: Unwarranted Optimism or Unfolding Opportunities?

Roger C. Kormendi

The title of this book, *The Economic Legacy of the Reagan Years: Euphoria or Chaos?*, reflects a fundamental uncertainty about what the Reagan legacy has been and will be. Economic growth since 1983 has been good, but some of it may have been recovery from the preceding recession. Inflation has been low, but real interest rates have been high. Income tax rates are lower, but the budget deficit continues to be large. Moreover, we have been running large current account deficits, financed by borrowing from abroad and by foreign purchases of U.S. capital, a situation Senator Lloyd Bentsen characterized in his now-famous 1988 vice-presidential debate as "selling America on the cheap."

A list such as the above certainly seems to have a chaotic character to it. Yet many believe that the U.S. economy is basically on the right track, poised for sustained economic growth well into the 1990s. Although concerned about budget deficits, they see them as coming down. They believe that lower tax rates, in particular, and the rollback in government intervention, more generally, will unleash individual initiative, entrepreneurial effort, and private sector productivity. They are confident that renewed strength in foreign policy will result in economic benefits emerging from both superpower and Third World relations. They believe they see at work President Reagan's vision of the "unlimited potential of the human mind" rather than President Carter's "era of limited resources."

Webster's dictionary defines "euphoria" as "a feeling of vigor and well-being," but one that may be "exaggerated and without obvious cause." Certainly, the Reagan era was characterized by a rebirth of optimism about the future of America. The fundamental question, however, is whether that optimism has been warranted or not. Is the Reagan legacy one of false euphoria, with the chaos of high interest rates, budget deficits, and current account deficits ultimately undermining the future? Or is the optimism in fact warranted? Will the 1990s reveal the Reagan legacy to be an unfolding set of opportunities?

Those who believe that the Reagan legacy is one of unwarranted optimism point to the large budget and current account deficits and high real interest rates as evidence of a troubled economic future of America. President Reagan, however, argued that high real interest rates are a reflection of the rebirth of the U.S. economy, that capital inflows from Japan and elsewhere reveal foreign confidence in that economy, and that the budget deficit poses no fundamental problem to a rapidly growing economy as long as government spending is controlled.

In the discussion that follows, I present a brief analysis of the debate in the context of a simple two-period Fisherian model that incorporates the key issues at stake. The purpose of the model is not to resolve the debate, but to analyze it in a systematic way. I have found this model—derived from Irving Fisher's *Theory of Interest* (1930), which is also the basis for modern finance theory— to be especially useful as a means of characterizing many issues in macroeconomics relating to intertemporal resource allocation. Jack Hirshleifer's *Investment, Interest and Capital* (1970) contains a good exposition of this theory. The 1981 article by Sachs in the *Brookings Papers on Economic Activity* was perhaps the first to introduce international considerations into Fisherian theory.

MODEL SET-UP

Consider a simple two-period model of intertemporal resource allocation, where c_1 denotes "current period" consumption and c_2 denotes future consumption. The model economy is open with respect to international capital flows, but may, like the United States, be large enough to affect world interest rates. All discussion relates to Figure 15.1, in which the economy is modeled in terms of a "representative individual" so that all analysis is on a per capita basis.

The point of departure is the "endowment" denoted by point E. At E, current period income is y_1^e and future income is y_2^e. This intertemporal flow of income derives from the current period total capital stock (including physical, human, and resource-base capital) assuming no capital-augmenting (net) investment, but sufficient maintenance investment to offset depreciation.

The intertemporal transformation opportunities are given by the convex curve *ETA*. Moving from point E to a point like T represents net investment that increases the capital stock. The convex shape of *ETA* reflects diminishing returns to investment.

The world rate of interest relevant for borrowing and lending in international capital markets is given by r^w, and hence the slope of the capital market budget constraint is $-(1+r^w)$. The wealth-maximizing choice for investment involves investing up to the point at which the slope of the intertemporal transformation

Figure 15.1
Fisherian Analysis of the Reagan Legacy

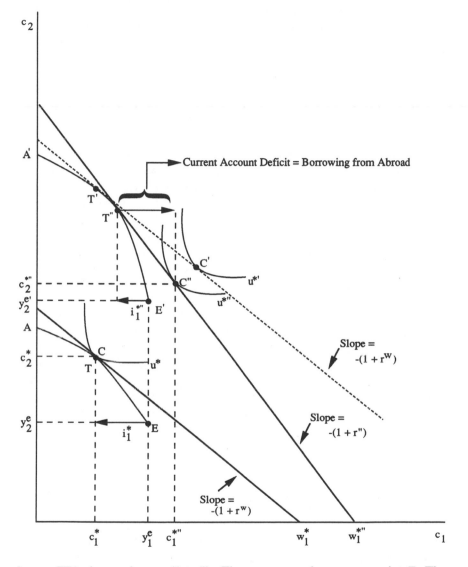

locus, *ETA*, is equal to $-(1+r^w)$. That occurs at the tangent point T. The amount of investment is shown as i_1^*, the length of the arrow starting at E. The present value of the income flow associated with T is given by w_1^* on the horizontal axis. That is also the maximized market value of the economy's total capital stock.

Depending on preferences, the representative individual can choose any point along the intertemporal budget constraint given by the straight line tangent at

T. A point between T and w_1^* represents borrowing on world capital markets. A point to the upper left of T represents lending. The preferences shown in Figure 15.1 indicate a choice point C lying right on top of T, which involves c_1^* current period consumption and c_2^* future consumption. At this point, the representative individual is neither borrowing nor lending abroad and is consuming exactly the income left over after investment, $c_1^* = y_1^* - i^*$. In this special case, no net imports of capital are needed, so that the current account is balanced.

EXPECTATIONS OF A BETTER FUTURE

Consider now the question: What would be the predicted effects on the economy, depicted in Figure 15.1, of improved expectations of future opportunities? The question at this point is not whether those expectations are correct, but rather what the observable consequences would be of such improved expectations.

I model the change in expectations as an increase in the future productivity both of total capital currently in place and of additions to the capital stock (i.e., investment). For total capital in place, the enhanced expectations would result in a shift in the endowment point from E to E'. This corresponds to a higher expected future income flow, $y_2^{e'} > y_2^e$. For new investment, the enhanced expectations involve a higher expected return, manifested as a steeper slope at each point on the new intertemporal opportunity locus $E'T'A'$.

At the original world rate of interest r^w; the wealth-maximizing decision would involve investing up to the point of tangency with the new intertemporal opportunity locus, which would occur at T'. If the economy were fully open and small enough not to affect world interest rates, this would be the optimum investment decision, and the intertemporal budget constraint would be the dotted line tangent to T'. If both current and future consumption are normal goods, the tangency point would be at a point like C'. To achieve this consumption point requires net imports in the current period, that is, a current account deficit, since current period consumption plus investment would exceed current period income. The net imports would be paid for by foreign borrowing.

If the economy in question is large, the borrowing from abroad necessary to move from T' to C' may increase world, and hence domestic, interest rates. Alternatively, if the economy were only partially open to international capital markets, then domestic interest rates would be bid up above the world rate r^w, due to increased domestic borrowing. Either or both of the scenarios may apply to the United States, and so the equilibrium at C'' features a domestic interest rate r'' greater than r^w.

The wealth-maximizing intertemporal transformation point is now where $E'T'A'$ is tangent to the line with slope $-(1 + r'')$. This occurs at T'', which implies investment in the amount $i_1^{*''}$ indicated by the arrow starting at E'. Note that, in the case illustrated, investment $i_1^{*''}$ is less than i_1^*. This effect

Table 15.1
Contrasting Predictions for the Reagan Legacy: Fisherian Theory vs. "Crowding Out"

Observable	Prediction from Figure 1	Prediction from "Crowding Out"
1. real interest rates	higher	higher
2. consumption/GNP	higher	higher
3. investment/GNP	lower	lower
4. current account deficit	larger	larger
5. stock market value	higher	lower
6. consumer debt/GNP	larger	smaller
7. corporate debt/GNP	larger	smaller
8. (future) economic growth	greater	smaller

occurs because the interest rate increase from r^w to r'' more than offsets the increased return to new investment. The size of the positive "wealth effect" on current consumption drives this result.

Given r'', the new consumption optimum will be a point such as $C^{*''}$. Despite the higher r'', the wealth effect dominates the substitution effect, yielding higher current consumption $c_1^{*''}$. The borrowing from abroad necessary to support the movement from T'' to $C^{*''}$ is explicitly labeled and is equal to the current account deficit. Given the increase in the rate of interest from r^w to r'', the market value of the total capital stock is now given by $w_1^{*''}$, which is shown as greater than w_1^*.

UNDERSTANDING THE REAGAN LEGACY

From the preceding analysis, we can draw a number of observations that derive from expectations of better future opportunities (see Table 15.1). Also summarized are predictions from theories that presume that large government budget deficits "crowd out" private sector investment and drive up interest rates. Again, these predictions require a large or partially closed economy as well.

The key predictions are those that distinguish between the two. Under the "crowding out" theory, as real rates are driven up by the government budget deficit, without expectations of increased future income, (1) the current market value of the private sector capital stock should be lower; (2) both consumers and corporations will reduce their indebtedness; and (3) future economic growth will be smaller (due to reduced investment). Thus we can see whether actual data conform better to the predictions of the "optimism" theory or the "crowding out" theory.

Table 15.2 presents the evidence comparing 1976–79 with 1983–88. Interestingly, the data in Table 15.2 conform directly to the predictions from Figure 15.1. In particular, the value of the stock market (a subset of $w_1^{*''}$) has in-

Table 15.2
Some Evidence on the Contrasting Predictions in Table 15.1

		1976-79	1983-88
1.	Ex ante Real Rate of Interest[a]	.7%	3.2%
2.	Consumption Expenditures[b]	.637	.664
3.	Gross Private Investment Excluding Inventories[b]	.167	.154
4.	Current Account Deficit[b]	-.001	-.026
5.	Real value of the S&P 500 as of the end of the period (12/31/25 = 1)	6.65	26.40
6.	Consumer Indebtedness[b]	.531	.617*
7.	Business Indebtedness[b]	.675	.785*
8.	Growth rate of real GDP[a]	3.9%	4.3%

*1983-7
[a]Average annual values.
[b]Average annual value as a fraction of GDP.

Sources: All data are annual. Row 1: Barro, R. J., *Macroeconomics,* 3rd ed., Table 7-3, col. 5. Rows 2–4, 8: *U.S. Dept. of Commerce, Survey of Current Business,* July 1987 and 1989, and *National Income and Product Accounts of the U.S.: Historical Tables. 1929– 82.* Row 5: Ibbotson Associates, *Stocks, Bonds, Bills and Inflation: 1989 Yearbook.* Real values computed using the implicit deflator for GDP. Rows 6–7: Board of Governors of the Federal Reserve System, *Balance Sheets for the U.S. Economy,* Release C.9, "Sector Balance Sheets with Tangible Assets at Current Costs." Indebtedness is taken from the row labeled "Total Liabilities."

creased, as have consumer and corporate debt. All sectors appear to have been borrowing in expectation of a better future. In this context, government sector borrowing appears to be part of an overall increase in borrowing. The higher real interest rates do not appear to have crowded out either consumer or corporate debt; neither have higher rates adversely affected the stock market (or the housing market, for that matter). The one prediction that we have yet to observe is of a more prosperous economic future. We have experienced a somewhat higher rate of economic growth over 1983–88 than over 1976–79. Yet the difference is hardly large, and in any case, the jury is still out.

Thus we return to the title of this chapter. Are the expectations of a better future that appear to explain the data in Table 15.2 unwarranted and overly optimistic (that is, euphoric)? Or is the "longest sustained peacetime recovery" the front end of an unfolding set of improved future opportunities? Will the future economic benefits of world peace and the democratization that are currently taking place in Eastern Europe and elsewhere be the realization of these expectations? Will world economic integration and an accelerating pace of technological advance ultimately lead to mutually beneficial economic gains for all countries, including the United States?

The analysis here does not answer these questions, of course. But it does reveal that high real interest rates, large current account deficits, and even large budget deficits are not necessarily fundamental problems hanging over our economy, a legacy of chaos from the Reagan era. Rather, when viewed as a whole, they are the natural consequences of expectations of an improved future.

NOTE

I wish to thank Mack Ott and Philip Meguire for conversations that benefited this chapter. Meguire also developed the calculations in Table 15.2.

References

Aho, C. Michael, and Jonathan David Aronson. *Trade Talks: America Better Listen!* New York: Council on Foreign Relations, 1985.

Alm, James. "Uncertain Tax Policies, Individual Behavior, and Welfare." *American Economic Review*, March 1988, 237–45.

Almon, Shirley. "The Distributed Lag between Capital Appropriations and Expenditures." *Econometrica*, January 1965, 178–96.

Anderson, G., W. Shughart, and R. Tollison. "Adam Smith in the Customhouse." *Journal of Political Economy*, August 1985, 740–59.

Ando, Albert K., Franco Modigliani, Robert Rasche, and Stephen J. Turnovsky. "On the Role of Expectations of Price and Technological Change in an Investment Function." *International Economic Review*, June 1974, 384–414.

Auerbach, Alan J. "Wealth Maximization and the Cost of Capital." *Quarterly Journal of Economics*, August 1979, 433–46.

———. "Corporate Taxation in the United States." *Brookings Papers on Economic Activity*, 1983, 451–505.

———. "Taxes, Firm Financial Policy, and the Cost of Capital: An Empirical Analysis." *Journal of Public Economics*, February–March 1984, 27–57.

———. "The Dynamic Effects of Tax Law Asymmetries." *Review of Economic Studies*, April 1986, 205–25.

——— and Dale W. Jorgenson. "Inflation-proof Depreciation of Assets." *Harvard Business Review*, September–October 1980, 113–18.

——— and Laurence J. Kotlikoff. *Dynamic Fiscal Policy.* New York: Cambridge University Press, 1987.

Axilrod, S. H. "Defining the Issues: Monetary Aggregates and Monetary Policy in a Deregulated Financial World." *Asilomar Conference on Interest Rate Deregulation and Monetary Policy.* San Francisco: Federal Reserve Bank of San Francisco, 1982.

Baldwin, Robert E. "The Political Economy of Protection." In Jagdish Bhagwati, ed., *Import Competition and Response*. Chicago: University of Chicago Press, 1982.

——— and J. David Richardson, eds. *Issues in the Uruguay Round*. Cambridge, Mass.: National Bureau of Economic Research, 1988.

Ballard, Charles L., and Lawrence H. Goulder. "Consumption Taxes, Foresight, and Welfare: A Computable General Equilibrium Analysis." In J. Piggot and J. Whalley, eds., *New Developments in Applied General Equilibrium Analysis*. New York: Cambridge University Press, 1985.

———, Don Fullerton, John B. Shoven, and John Whalley. *A General Equilibrium Model for Tax Policy Evaluation*. Chicago: University of Chicago Press, 1985.

Beach, Charles M., and James G. MacKinnon. "A Maximum Likelihood Procedure for Regression With Autocorrelated Errors." *Econometrica*, January 1978, 51–58.

Becketti, Sean, and Gordon Sellon. "Has Financial Market Volatility Increased?" *Economic Review*, Federal Reserve Bank of Kansas City, June 1989, 17–30.

Bennett, B. A. " 'Shift Adjustments' to the Monetary Aggregates." *Economic Review*, Federal Reserve Bank of San Francisco, Spring 1982.

Berle, Adolph A., and Gardiner C. Means. *The Modern Corporation and Private Property*. New York: Macmillan, 1932.

Bernanke, Ben, Henning Bohn, and Peter C. Reiss. "Alternative Non-Nested Specification Tests of Time-Series Investment Models." *Journal of Econometrics*, March 1988, 293–326.

Berndt, E. R., and L. R. Christensen. "The Translog Production Function and the Substitution of Equipment, Structures, and Labor in U.S. Manufacturing 1929–69." *Journal of Econometrics*, March 1973, 81–114.

Birnbaum, Jeffrey H., and Alan S. Murray. *Showdown at Gucci Gulch: Lawmakers, Lobbyists, and the Unlikely Triumph of Tax Reform*. New York: Random House, 1987.

Bischoff, Charles W. "A Model of Nonresidential Construction in the United States." *American Economic Review Proceedings*, May 1970, 10–17.

———. "The Effect of Alternative Lag Distributions." In Gary Fromm, ed., *Tax Incentives and Capital Spending*. Washington, D.C.: The Brookings Institution, 1971a.

———. "Business Investment in the 1970s: A Comparison of Models." *Brookings Papers on Economic Activity*, 1971b:1, 13–63.

Blanchard, Oliver J., and Lawrence H. Summers. "Perspectives on High World Real Interest Rates." *Brookings Panel on Economic Activity*, 1984:2, 273–324.

Board of Governors of the Federal Reserve System. *A Review and Evaluation of Federal Margin Regulations*. Study by the Staff, December 1984.

———. "The Impact of the Payment of Interest on Demand Deposits." Study by the Staff, January 31, 1977 (mimeo).

Boskin, Michael J. "Taxation, Saving, and the Rate of Interest." *Journal of Political Economy*, April 1978, S3–S27.

Bosworth, Barry P. *Tax Incentives and Economic Growth*. Washington, D.C.: The Brookings Institution, 1984.

Bradford, David F. "The Incidence and Allocation Effects of a Tax on Corporate Distributions." *Journal of Public Economics*, February 1981, 1–22.

Breen, Dennis A. "The Potential for Tax Gains as a Merger Motive." Federal Trade Commission, Bureau of Economics, July 1987.

Bryant, Ralph, and Gerald Holtham. "The External Deficit: Why? Where Next? What Remedy?" *Brookings Review,* Spring 1987, 28–36.

────── and Peter Hooper, eds. *External Deficits and the Dollar.* Washington, D.C.: The Brookings Institution, 1988.

Buchanan, J. "Politics without Romance." In James Buchanan and Robert Tollison, eds., *The Theory of Public Choice-II.* Ann Arbor: The University of Michigan Press, 1984.

──────. "Our Times: Past, Present and Future." In Martin Anderson, ed., *The Unfinished Agenda.* London: Institute for Economic Affairs, 1986a.

──────. "Quest for a Tempered Utopia." *The Wall Street Journal,* Friday, November 14, 1986b.

──────. "Political Economy and Social Philosophy." In James Buchanan, ed., *Liberty, Market and State.* New York: New York University Press, 1986c.

──────. "Post-Reagan Political Economy." In Alan Peacock, ed., *Reaganomics and After.* London: Institute for Economic Affairs, 1989.

──────, Robert Tollison, and Gordon Tullock, eds. *Toward a Theory of the Rent-Seeking Society.* College Station: Texas A&M University Press, 1980.

Burtless, Gary. "The Work Response to a Guaranteed Income." In Alicia Munnell, ed., *Income Maintenance Experiments.* Boston, Mass.: Federal Reserve Bank of Boston, 1987.

Buser, Stephen A., and Patrick J. Hess. "Empirical Determinants of the Relative Yields on Taxable and Tax-Exempt Yields." *Journal of Financial Economics,* 1986, 335–55.

Cargill, T. F., and G. G. Garcia. *Financial Reform in the 1980s.* Stanford, Calif.: Hoover Institution Press, 1985.

Chang, R. R., and D. E. Wildasin. "Randomization of Comodity Taxes: An Expenditure Minimization Approach." *Journal of Public Economics,* December 1986, 329–45.

Chirinko, Robert S. "Business Tax Policy, The Lucas Critique, and Lessons from the 1980s." *American Economic Review Proceedings,* May 1988, 206–10.

────── and Robert Eisner. "Tax Policy and Investment in Major U.S. Macroeconomic Econometric Models." *Journal of Public Economics,* March 1983, 139–66.

Chou, W. L., and Y. C. Shih. "Trade, Determinants, and Causality: A Case of Hong Kong's Exports to the United States." *International Economic Journal,* Winter 1988, 21–33.

Clarida, Richard H., and Benjamin M. Friedman. "Why Have Short-Term Interest Rates Been so High?" *Brookings Papers on Economic Activity,* 1983:2, 553–78.

Clark, John Maurice. "Business Acceleration and the Law of Demand: A Technical Factor in Business Cycles." *Journal of Political Economy,* March 1917, 217–35.

Clark, Peter K. "Investment in the 1970s: Theory, Performance, and Prediction." *Brookings Papers on Economic Activity,* 1979:1, 73–113.

Cline, William R. *The Future of World Trade in Textiles and Apparel.* Washington, D.C.: Institute for International Economics, 1987.

Cooper, Richard N. "What Future for the International Monetary System?" Paper prepared for the Fourth International Conference, "The Evolution of the International Monetary System: How Can Efficiency and Stability be Attained?" Sponsored by the Institute for Monetary and Economic Studies, the Bank of Japan, May 30–June 1, 1989.

Council of Economic Advisors. *Economic Report of the President.* Washington, D.C.: U.S. Government Printing Office, February 1986.

———. *Economic Report of the President.* Washington, D.C.: U.S. Government Printing Office, January 1987.

———. *Economic Report of the President.* Washington, D.C.: U.S. Government Printing Office, February 1988.

———. *Economic Report of the President.* Washington, D.C.: U.S. Government Printing Office, January 1989.

Cowen, T., ed. *The Theory of Market Failure.* Fairfax: George Mason University Press, 1988.

Crispo, John. *Free Trade: The Real Story.* Toronto: Gage Educational Publishing, 1988.

Davis, R. G. "Monetary Targeting in a 'Zero Balance' World." *Asilomar Conference on Interest Rate Deregulation and Monetary Policy.* San Francisco: Federal Reserve Bank of San Francisco, 1982.

Deardorff, Alan V. "Why Do Governments Prefer Nontariff Barriers?" *Carnegie-Rochester Conference Series on Public Policy,* Spring 1987, 191–216.

——— and Robert M. Stern. "Economic Effects of the Tokyo Round." *Southern Economic Journal,* January 1983, 605–24.

———. *Methods of Measurement of Non-Tariff Barriers.* New York: United Nations Conference on Trade and Development, UNCTAD/ST/MD/28, January 1985.

Derthick, M., and P. Quirk. *The Politics of Deregulation.* Washington, D.C.: Brookings Institution, 1985.

Dickey, David A., and Wayne A. Fuller. "Distribution of the Estimators for Autoregressive Time Series with a Unit Root." *Journal of the American Statistical Association,* June 1979, 427–31.

DiLorenzo, T. "Classroom Struggle: The Free-Market Takeover of Economic Textbooks." *Policy Review,* Spring 1987.

Dolde, Walter. "Issues and Models in Empirical Research on Aggregate Consumer Expenditure." *Carnegie-Rochester Conference Series on Public Policy,* 1980, 161–205.

Economist. "Assessing Reaganomics: The Trouble with Theories." January 21, 1989, 74–75.

Edison, Hali. "Purchasing Power Parity in the Long Run: A Test of the Dollar/Pound Exchange Rate (1890–1978)." *Journal of Money, Credit, and Banking,* August 1987, 376–87.

——— and Eric Fisher. "A Long-Run View of the European Monetary System." *International Finance Discussion Papers,* Federal Reserve Board, no. 339, January 1989.

Eisner, Robert. "Divergences of Measurement and Theory and Some Implications for Economic Policy." *American Economic Review,* March 1989, 1–13.

Engle, Robert F., and C. W. Granger. "Cointegration and Error Correction: Representation, Estimation, and Testing." *Econometrica,* March 1987, 251–76.

——— and Byung Sam Yoo. "Forecasting and Testing in Co-Integrated Systems." *Journal of Econometrics,* May 1987, 143–59.

Feldstein, Martin. "On the Theory of Tax Reform." *Journal of Public Economics,* July–August 1976, 77–104.

————. "Will the Good Times Last Through '84?" *U.S. News & World Report*, March 5, 1984.

————. "We are Going to Need More Revenue." *U.S. News & World Report*, December 31, 1984.

————. "American Economic Policy and the World Economy." *Foreign Affairs*, Summer 1985, 995–1008.

Fisher, Irving. *The Theory of Interest*. New York: Macmillan, 1930.

Fosu, A. K. "Labor Force Participation by Married Women: Evidence for 1980." Unpublished paper, 1989.

————. "Cost of Living and Labor Force Participation of Married Women in Urban Labor Markets." Unpublished paper, 1990.

Frankel, Jeffrey. "International Capital Mobility and Crowding-Out in the U.S. Economy: Imperfect Integration of Financial Markets or of Goods Markets?" In R. Hafer, ed., *How Open is the U.S. Economy?* Lexington: Lexington Books, 1986.

Friedman, B. M. "Monetary Policy without Quantity Variables." *American Economic Review*, May 1988, 440–45.

————. "Lessons on Monetary Policy from the 1980s." *Economic Perspectives*, Spring 1988b, 51–72.

Fuller, Wayne A. *Introduction to Statistical Time Series*. New York: John Wiley & Sons, 1976.

Fullerton, Don, Robert Gillette, and James Mackie. "Investment Incentives under the Tax Reform Act of 1986." In Office of Tax Analysis, Department of the Treasury, *Compendium of Tax Research 1987*. Washington, D.C.: U.S. Government Printing Office, 1987.

———— and Yolanda K. Henderson. "Incentive Effects of Taxes on Income from Capital: Alternative Policies in the 1980s." In Charles R. Hulten and Isabel V. Sawhill, eds., *The Legacy of Reaganomics*. Washington, D.C.: The Urban Institute Press, 1984.

———— and Yolanda K. Henderson. "Long-Run Effects of the Accelerated Cost Recovery System." *Review of Economics and Statistics*, August 1985, 363–72.

———— and Yolanda K. Henderson. "A Disaggregate Equilibrium Model of the Tax Distortions among Assets, Sectors, and Industries." *International Economic Review*, May 1989, 391–413.

————, Yolanda K. Henderson, and James Mackie. "Investment Allocation and Growth under the Tax Reform Act of 1986." In Office of Tax Analysis, Department of the Treasury, *Compendium of Tax Research 1987*. Washington, D.C.: U.S. Government Printing Office, 1987, 173–201.

———— and Andrew B. Lyon. "Tax Neutrality and Intangible Capital." In L. Summers, ed., *Tax Policy and the Economy*, vol. 2. Cambridge, Mass.: MIT Press, 1988.

————, John B. Shoven, and John Whalley. "Replacing the U.S. Income Tax with a Progressive Consumption Tax: A Sequenced General Equilibrium Approach." *Journal of Public Economics*, February 1983, 3–23.

Gilson, Ronald J., Myron Scholes, and Mark Wolfson. "Taxation and the Dynamics of Corporate Control: The Uncertain Case for Tax-Motivated Acquisitions." In J. Coffee, Jr., L. Lowenstein, and S. Rose-Ackerman, eds., *Knights, Raiders, and Targets: The Impact of the Hostile Takeover*. New York: Oxford University Press, 1988.

Goldstein, Morris, and Mohsin S. Khan. "Income and Price Effects in Foreign Trade." In Ronald Jones and Peter B. Kenen, eds., *Handbook of International Trade*. Amsterdam: North-Holland, 1985.

Gordon, Robert J. *Macroeconomics,* 4th ed. Boston: Little, Brown, 1987.

Gordon, Roger H., James R. Hines, and Lawrence H. Summers. "Notes on the Tax Treatment of Structures." In M. Feldstein, ed., *The Effects of Taxation on Capital Accumulation*. Chicago: University of Chicago Press, 1987.

Goulder, Lawrence H., and Barry Eichengreen. "Savings Promotion, Investment Promotion, and International Competitiveness." Working Paper no. 2635. Cambridge, Mass.: National Bureau of Economic Research, 1988.

——, John B. Shoven, and John Whalley. "Domestic Tax Policy and the Foreign Sector." In M. Feldstein, ed., *Behavioral Simulation Methods in Tax Policy Analysis*. Chicago: University of Chicago Press, 1983.

Granger, Clive W. J., and Robert F. Engle. "Co-Integration and Error Correction: Representation, Estimation, and Testing." *Econometrica,* March 1987, 251–76.

Gravelle, Jane G. "The Social Cost of Nonneutral Taxation: Estimates for Nonresidential Capital." In C. R. Hulten, ed., *Depreciation, Inflation, and the Taxation of Income from Capital*. Washington, D.C.: The Urban Institute Press, 1981.

——. "Tax Policy and Rental Housing: An Economic Analysis." Congressional Research Service Report no. 87 536E. Washington, D.C.: Library of Congress, 1987.

—— and Laurence J. Kotlikoff. "The Incidence and Efficiency Costs of Corporate Taxation When Corporate and Noncorporate Firms Produce the Same Good." *Journal of Political Economy,* August 1989, 749–80.

Greenspan, Alan. "1989 Monetary Policy Objectives." Washington, D.C.: Board of Governors of the Federal Reserve System, February 21, 1989.

Greider, W. "The Education of David Stockman." *Atlantic,* December 1981.

Grilli, Vittorio, and Graciela Kaminsky. "Nominal Exchange Rate Regimes and the Real Exchange Rate Evidence from the U.S. and Britain, 1885–1986." Discussion paper no. 19, International Economics Research Center, Department of Economics, University of Pennsylvania, October 1988.

Hakkio, Craig S. "Does the Exchange Rate Follow a Random Walk? A Monte Carlo Study of Four Tests for a Random Walk." *Journal of International Money and Finance,* June 1986.

——. "Exchange Rates During the 1980s." Federal Reserve Bank of Kansas City Working Paper, RWP 89-04, August 1989.

Hall, Robert E. "Investment, Interest Rates, and the Effects of Stabilization Policies." *Brookings Papers on Economic Activity,* 1977:1, 61–121.

—— and Dale W. Jorgenson, "Tax Policy and Investment Behavior." *American Economic Review,* June 1967, 391–414.

—— and Dale W. Jorgenson. "Application of the Theory of Optimum Capital Accumulation." In Gary Fromm, ed., *Tax Incentives and Capital Spending*. Washington, D.C.: The Brookings Institution, 1971.

Hardouvelis, Gikas. "Margin Requirements and Stock Market Volatility." *FRBNY Quarterly Review,* Summer 1988a, 80–89.

——. "Margin Requirements, Volatility, and the Transitory Component of Stock Prices." First Boston Working Paper Series, FB 88-38, November 1988b.

Hausman, Jerry A. "Labor Supply." In Henry Aaron and Joseph Pechman, eds., *The*

Effect of Taxes on Economic Activity. Washington, D.C.: The Brookings Institution, 1981a.

———. "Income and Payroll Tax Policy and Labor Supply." In Lawrence H. Meyer, ed., *The Supply-Side Effects of Economic Policy.* Boston, Mass.: Kluwer-Nijhoff, 1981b.

———. "Stochastic Problems in the Simulation of Labor Supply." In Martin Feldstein, ed., *Behavioral Simulation Methods in Tax Policy Analysis.* Chicago, Ill.: University of Chicago Press, 1983.

Haveman, Robert H. "How Much Have the Reagan Administration's Tax and Spending Policies Increased Work Effort?" In Charles R. Hulten and Isabel V. Sawhill, eds., *The Legacy of Reaganomics: Prospects for Long-Term Growth.* Washington, D.C.: Urban Institute Press, 1984.

Hayek, F. A. "The Intellectuals and Socialism." In Friedrich A. Hayek, ed., *Studies in Philosophy, Politics and Economics.* Chicago: University of Chicago Press, 1967.

———. *The Counter-Revolution of Science.* Indianapolis: Liberty Classics, 1979.

Helkie, William, and Peter Hooper. "U.S. External Adjustment: Progress and Prospects." *International Finance Discussion Papers,* no. 345, Board of Governors of the Federal Reserve System, Washington, D.C., March 1989.

Hendershott, Patric H. "Tax Reform and Financial Markets." *Economic Consequences of Tax Simplification.* Conference Series no. 29, Federal Reserve Bank of Boston, 1985.

———. "Tax Reform, Interest Rates, and Capital Allocation." In J. Follain, ed., *Tax Reform and Real Estate.* Washington, D.C.: The Urban Institute Press, 1986a.

———. "Debt and Equity Returns Revisited." In B. Friedman, ed., *Financing Corporation Capital Structure.* Chicago: University of Chicago Press, 1986b.

——— and Stephen A. Buser. "Spotting Prepayment Premiums." *Secondary Mortgage Markets,* August 1984.

——— and Joe Peek. "Treasury Bill Rates in the 1970s and 1980s." NBER Working Paper, July 1989.

——— and Robert Van Order. "Integration of Mortgage and Capital Markets and the Accumulation of Residential Capital." *Regional Science and Urban Economics,* May 1989, 189–210.

Higgs, R. *Crisis and Leviathan.* New York: Oxford University Press, 1987.

Hirshleifer, J. *Investment, Interest and Capital.* Englewood Cliffs: Prentice Hall, 1970.

Hoaglin, David, Frederick Mosteller, and John W. Tukey. *Understanding Robust and Exploratory Data Analysis.* New York: John Wiley & Sons, 1983.

Hoffman, D., and R. H. Rasche. "Long-Run Income and Interest Elasticities of Money Demand in the United States." *Review of Economics and Statistics,* forthcoming (1991).

Hooper, Peter. "Exchange Rates and U.S. External Adjustment in the Short Run and the Long Run." *International Finance Discussion Papers,* no. 346, Board of Governors of the Federal Reserve System, Washington, D.C., March 1989a.

———. "Macroeconomic Policies, Competitiveness, and U.S. External Adjustment." *International Finance Discussion Papers,* no. 347, Board of Governors of the Federal Reserve System, Washington, D.C., March 1989b.

——— and Catherine L. Mann. In Albert E. Burger, ed., *U.S., Trade Deficit: Causes, Consequences and Cures,* Proceedings of the Twelfth Annual Economic Policy

Conference Federal Reserve Bank of St. Louis. Boston: Kluer Academic Publishers, 1989.

Houthakker, Hendrik, and Stephen Magee. "Income and Price Elasticities in World Trade." *Review of Economics and Statistics,* May 1969, 111–25.

Howard, H., and K. H. Johnson. "Financial Innovation, Deregulation, and Monetary Policy: The Foreign Experience," *Asilomar Conference on Interest Rate Deregulation and Monetary Policy,* San Francisco: Federal Reserve Bank of San Francisco, 1982.

Howry, E. Philip, and Saul H. Hymans. "The Measurement and Determination of Loanable Funds Saving." *Brookings Papers on Economic Activity,* 1978, 655–85.

Hulten, Charles R., and Frank C. Wykoff. *Tax Changes and Substitution Elasticities."* Washington, D.C.: The Urban Institute, 1981a.

——— and Frank C. Wykoff. "Economic Depreciation and Accelerated Depreciation: An Evaluation of the Conable-Jones 10-5-3 Proposal." *National Tax Journal,* March 1981b, 45–60.

——— and Frank C. Wykoff. "The Measurement of Economic Depreciation." In Charles R. Hulten, ed., *Depreciation, Inflation and the Taxation of Income from Capital.* Washington, D.C.: The Urban Institute Press, 1981c.

Husted, Steven, and Tryphon Kollintzas. "Import Demand with Rational Expectations: Estimates for Bauxite, Cocoa, Coffee, and Petroleum." *Review of Economics and Statistics,* November 1984, 608–18.

——— and Tryphon Kollintzas. "Rational Expectations Equilibrium Laws of Motion for Selected U.S. Commodity Imports." *International Economic Review,* October 1987, 651–70.

Hutchison, Michael, and Charles Pigott. "Real and Financial Linkages in the Macroeconomic Response to Budget Deficits: An Empirical Investigation." In Sven Arndt and David Richardson, eds., *Real-Financial Linkages among Open Economies.* Cambridge: The MIT Press, 1987.

Jarrell, Gregg A., James A. Brickley, and Jeffry M. Netter. "The Market for Corporate Control: The Empirical Evidence Since 1980." *Journal of Economic Perspectives,* Winter 1988, 49–68.

Jensen, Michael C. "Agency Costs of Free Cash Flow, Corporate Finance, and Takeovers." *American Economic Review,* May 1986, 323–39.

———. "Takeovers: Their Causes and Consequences." *Journal of Economic Perspectives,* Winter 1988, 21–48.

——— and Richard Ruback. "The Market for Corporate Control: The Scientific Evidence." *Journal of Financial Economics,* April 1983, 5–50.

Jorgenson, Dale W. "Anticipations and Investment Behavior." In James S. Duesenberry, Gary Fromm, Lawrence R. Klein, and Edwin Kuh, eds., *The Brookings Quarterly Econometric Model of the United States.* Chicago: Rand McNally, 1965.

——— and Martin A. Sullivan. "Inflation and Corporate Capital Recovery." In Charles R. Hulten, ed., *Depreciation, Inflation and the Taxation of Income from Capital.* Washington, D.C.: The Urban Institute Press, 1981.

Judd, J. P., and J. L. Scaddings. "Financial Change and Monetary Targeting in the United States." *Asilomar Conference on Interest Rate Deregulation and Monetary Policy.* San Francisco: Federal Reserve Bank of San Francisco, 1982.

Kahn, Alfred. *The Economics of Regulation: Principles and Institutions.* New York: John Wiley and Sons, 1970.

———. "The Road to More Intelligent Telephone Pricing." *Yale Journal of Regulation,* 1984, 139–57.

Kaplan, Steven. "Management Buyouts: Evidence on Taxes as a Source of Value." Working paper, University of Chicago, 1988a.

———. "Sources of Value in Management Buyouts." Working paper, University of Chicago, 1988b.

Keynes, J. *The General Theory of Employment, Interest and Money.* New York: Harcourt Brace Jovanovich, 1964.

King, Mervyn A. *Public Policy and the Corporation.* London: Chapman and Hall, 1977.

Kolko, Gabriel. *The Triumph of Conservatism: A Reinterpretation of American History, 1900–1916.* New York: The Free Press, 1963.

Kollintzas, Tryphon, and Steven Husted. "Distributed Lags and Intermediate Good Imports." *Journal of Economic Dynamics and Control,* December 1984, 302–28.

Kopcke, Richard W. "The Behavior of Investment Spending during the Recession and Recovery, 1973–76." *New England Economic Review,* November–December 1977, 5–41.

———. "Forecasting Investment Spending: The Performance of Statistical Models." *New England Economic Review,* November–December 1982, 13–35.

———. "The Determinants of Investment Spending." *New England Economic Review,* July–August 1985, 19–35.

Kotlikoff, Laurence J. "Deficit Delusion." *The Public Interest,* Summer 1986.

Krugman, Paul, and Richard Baldwin. "The Persistence of the U.S. Trade Deficit." *Brookings Papers on Economic Activity,* 1:1987, 1–43.

Laffer, Arthur B. "Government Exactions and Revenue Deficiencies." *Cato Journal,* Spring 1981, 1–21.

Lehn, Kenneth, and Annette Poulsen. "Leveraged Buyouts: Wealth Created or Wealth Redistributed?" In Murray Weidenbaum and Kenneth Chilton, eds., *Public Policy Towards Corporate Takeovers.* New Brunswick: Transaction Publishers, 1988.

Levy, Frank. "The Labor Supply of Female Heads, or AFDC Work Incentives Don't Work Too Well." *Journal of Human Resources,* Winter 1979, 76–97.

Lichtenberg, Frank, and Donald Siegel. "The Effects of Leveraged Buyouts on Productivity and Related Aspects of Firm Behavior." *NBER Working Paper,* no. 3022, June 1989 (mimeo).

Lucas, Robert E., Jr. "Econometric Policy Evaluation: A Critique." In Karl Brunner and Allan H. Meltzer, eds., *The Phillips Curve and Labor Markets,* Carnegie-Rochester Conference Series on Public Policy. Amsterdam: North-Holland Publishing Co., 1976.

———. "Interest Rates and Currency Prices in a Two-Country World." *Journal of Monetary Economics,* November 1982, 335–59.

Lyon, Andrew B. *Understanding Investment Incentives under Parallel Tax Systems: An Application to the Alternative Minimum Tax.* College Park: University of Maryland Press, 1989.

Mackie, James B. *Two Essays on Capital Taxation.* Ph.D. dissertation, University of Virginia, 1985.

Macris, Robert N. "Leveraged Buyouts: Federal Income Tax Considerations." Paper presented at the Conference on Management Buyouts, New York University Graduate School of Business Administration, May 20, 1988.

Maggenheim, E., and D. Mueller. "On Measuring the Effect of Mergers on Acquiring Firm Shareholders." In John Coffee et al., eds., *Knights, Raiders, and Targets.* New York: Oxford University Press, 1987.

Manne, Henry. "Mergers and the Market for Corporate Control." *Journal of Political Economy,* April 1965, 110–20.

Marais, Laurentius, Katherine Schipper, and Abbie Smith. "Wealth Effects of Going Private for Senior Securities." Working paper, University of Chicago, June 1988.

Marris, Robin. "A Model of the Managerial Enterprise." *Quarterly Journal of Economics,* May 1963, 185–209.

Marris, Stephen. *Deficits and the Dollar: The World Economy at Risk.* Washington, D.C.: Institute for International Economics, 1985.

Marston, Richard C. "Exchange Rate Policy Reconsidered." In Martin Feldstein, ed., *International Economic Policy Coordination.* Chicago: University of Chicago Press, 1988.

McCloskey, D. *The Rhetoric of Economics.* Madison: University of Wisconsin Press, 1985.

McCormick, R., W. Shughart, and R. Tollison. "The Disinterest in Deregulation." *American Economic Review,* December 1984, 1075–79.

McCraw, Thomas. "Kahn and the Economist's Hour." In Thomas K. McCraw, ed., *Prophets of Regulation.* Cambridge, Mass.: Belknap Press of Harvard University Press, 1984.

McIntyre, Robert S., and Robert Folen. *Corporate Income Taxes in the Reagan Years: A Study of Three Years of Legalized Corporate Tax Avoidance.* Washington, D.C.: Citizens for Tax Justice, 1984.

McLure, Charles E. *Must Corporate Income Be Taxed Twice?* Washington, D.C.: The Brookings Institution, 1979.

Mitchell, Mark, and Kenneth Lehn. "Do Bad Bidders Become Good Targets?" *Journal of Political Economy,* forthcoming.

Moffitt, Robert A. "A Problem With the Negative Income Tax." *Economics Letters,* 1985, 261–65.

Mohr, M. F. "The Long-Term Structure of Production, Factor Demands, and Factor Productivity in U.S. Manufacturing Industries." In J. W. Kendrick and B. N. Vaccara, eds., *New Developments in Productivity Measurement and Analysis.* Chicago: The University of Chicago Press, 1980.

Moore, G. R., R. D. Porter, and D. H. Small. "Modeling the Disaggregated Demands for M2 and M1 in the 1980s: the U.S. Experience." *Financial Sectors in Open Economies: Empirical Analysis and Policy Issues.* Washington, D.C.: Board of Governors of the Federal Reserve System, 1990.

Mussa, Michael. "Nominal Exchange Rate Regimes and the Behavior of Real Exchange Rates: Evidence and Implications." In Karl Brunner and Allan H. Meltzer, eds., *Real Business Cycles, Real Exchange Rates and Actual Policies.* Carnegie-Rochester Conference Series on Public Policy, Autumn 1986.

Mutti, John, and Harry Grubert. "The Taxation of Capital Income in an Open Economy: The Importance of Resident-Nonresident Tax Treatment." *Journal of Public Economics,* August 1985, 291–309.

Neubig, Thomas S., and Martin A. Sullivan. "Implications of Tax Reform for Banks Holding Tax-Exempt Securities." *National Tax Journal,* September 1987, 403–18.

Niskanen, W. *Reaganomics.* New York: Oxford University Press, 1988.

Nolle, Daniel, and Charles Pigott. "The Changing Commodity Composition of U.S. Imports from Japan." *Federal Reserve Bank of New York Quarterly Review,* Spring 1986, 12–18.

Obstfeld, Maurice, and Alan Stockman. "Exchange-Rate Dynamics." In Ronald W. Jones and Peter B. Kenen, eds., *Handbook of International Economics.* New York: North-Holland, 1985.

Officer, R. R. "The Variability of the Market Factor of the New York Stock Exchange." *Journal of Business,* July 1973, 434–53.

Orcutt, Guy. "Measurement of Price Elasticities in International Trade." *Review of Economics and Statistics,* May 1950, 117–32.

Pearson, Charles S. *Free Trade, Fair Trade: The Reagan Record.* Lanham, Md.: The University Press of America, 1989.

Pechman, Joseph A. *Federal Tax Policy,* 5th ed. Washington, D.C.: The Brookings Institution, 1987.

Peltzman, S. "Toward a More General Theory of Regulation." *Journal of Law and Economics,* August 1976, 211–40.

———. "The Economic Theory of Regulation After a Decade of Deregulation." In Martin Baily and Clifford Winston, eds., *Brooking Papers on Economic Activity: Microeconomics.* Washington, D.C.: Brookings Institution, 1989.

Penner, Rudolf G. "Public Policy and Aggregate Saving." *Business Economics,* March 1983, 1–10.

Poole, Robert. "Airline Deregulation and Implications for Europe 1992." Paper presented at conference on "Le Libéralisme à L'Européenne," at the Université D'Eté des Nouveaux Economistes, Aix-en-Provence, France, August 28–September 2, 1989.

Poole, W. "Monetary Policy Lessons of Recent Inflation and Disinflation." *Economic Perspectives,* Summer 1988, 73–100.

Porter, M. "From Competitive Advantage to Corporate Strategy." *Harvard Business Review,* May–June 1987, 43–59.

Poterba, James M., and Lawrence H. Summers. "Dividend Taxes, Corporate Investment, and 'Q'." *Journal of Public Economics,* November 1983, 135–67.

——— and Lawrence H. Summers. "The Economic Effects of Dividend Taxation." In Edward I. Altman and Marti G. Subrahmanyam, eds., *Recent Advances in Corporate Finance.* Homewood, Ill.: Richard D. Irwin, 1985.

Prakken, Joel. "The Macroeconomics of Tax Reform." In Charles E. Walker and Mark A. Bloomfield, eds., *The Consumption Tax: A Better Alternative?* Cambridge: Ballinger, 1987.

Presidential Task Force on Market Mechanisms. *Report of the Presidential Task Force on Market Mechanisms.* Washington, D.C.: U.S. Government Printing Office, January 1988.

Rasche, R. H. "M1 Velocity and Money Demand Functions: Do Stable Relationships Exist?" *Carnegie-Rochester Conference Series on Public Policy,* 1987, 9–88.

——— and J. M. Johannes. *Controlling the Growth of Monetary Aggregates.* Boston: Kluwer Academic Publishers, 1987.

Ravenscraft, D., and F. Scherer. "Life After Takeover." *Journal of Industrial Economics,* December 1987, 147–56.

Reagan, R. *America's New Beginning: A Program for Economic Recovery,* part II. Washington, D.C.: The White House, February 18, 1981.

———. *Public Papers of the Presidents of the United States, 1981.* Washington, D.C.: U.S. Government Printing Office, 1982.

Reinhart, Vincent. "Macroeconomic Influences on the U.S.–Japan Trade Imbalance." *Federal Reserve Bank of New York Quarterly Review,* Spring 1986, 6–11.

Roll, R. "The International Crash of October 1987." *Financial Analysts Journal,* September–October 1988, 19–35.

Ryngaert, Michael, and Jeffry M. Netter. "Shareholder Wealth Effects of the Ohio Anti-takeover Law." *Journal of Law, Economics, and Organization,* Fall 1988, 373–83.

Sachs, Jeffrey. "Global Adjustments to a Shrinking Trade Deficit." *Brookings Papers on Economic Activity,* 1988, 639–67.

———. "The Current Account and Macroeconomic Adjustment in the 1970s." *Brookings Papers on Economic Activity,* 1981:1, 201–68.

Sakamoto, Tomohiko. "The Japan–U.S. Bilateral Trade." *Economic Review,* Federal Reserve Bank of San Francisco, Spring 1988, 3–14.

Sawhill, Isabel V. *The Legacy of Reaganomics: Prospects for Long-Term Growth.* Washington, D.C.: Urban Institute Press, 1984.

Schipper, Katherine, and Abbie Smith. "Corporate Income Tax Effects of Management Buyouts." Working paper, University of Chicago, July 1986.

Schumann, Lawrence. "State Regulation of Takeovers and Shareholder Wealth: The Case of New York's 1985 Takeover Statutes." *Rand Journal of Economics,* Winter 1988, 557–67.

Schwert, G. W. "The Causes of Changing Stock Price Volatility." Working paper, University of Rochester, 1987.

———. "Why Does Stock Market Volatility Change Over Time?" NBER Working Paper no. 2798, December 1988.

Securities and Exchange Commission, Office of the Chief Economist. "Institutional Ownership, Tender Offers, and Long-Term Investments." 1985.

Semmens, John, and Dianne Kresich. "Deregulation, Privatization and Air Travel Safety." *A Heartland Policy Study,* May 12, 1989.

Sen, A. *On Ethics and Economics.* New York: Basil Blackwell, 1987.

Shleifer, A., and L. Summers. "Hostile Takeovers as Breaches of Trust." Working paper, National Bureau of Economic Research, 1987.

Shoven, John B. "The Tax Consequences of Share Repurchases and Other Non-Dividend Cash Payments to Equity Owners." In L. Summers, ed., *Tax Policy and the Economy.* Cambridge, Mass.: MIT Press, 1987.

Simons, Henry. *Personal Income Taxation.* Chicago: University of Chicago Press, 1938.

Skinner, Jonathan. "The Welfare Cost of Uncertain Tax Policy." NBER Working Paper no. 1947, 1986.

Smith, Abbie. "Corporate Ownership Structure and Performance: The Case of Management Buyouts." Working paper, University of Chicago, 1988.

Stigler, G. "The Theory of Economic Regulation." *Bell Journal of Economics and Management Science,* Spring 1971, 3–21.

————, ed. *Chicago Studies in Political Economy*. Chicago: University of Chicago Press, 1988.

Stiglitz, Joseph E. "Utilitarianism and Horizontal Equity: The Case for Random Taxation." *Journal of Public Economics*, June 1982, 1–33.

Stock, James H., and Mark W. Watson. "Testing for Common Trends." *Journal of the American Statistical Association*, December 1988, 1097–107.

Stockman, Alan C. "Real Exchange Rate Variability Under Pegged and Floating Nominal Exchange Rate Systems: An Equilibrium Theory." NBER Working Paper no. 2565, April 1988.

Stockman, David. *The Triumph of Politics*. New York: Harper and Row, 1986.

Summers, Lawrence H. "Capital Taxation and Accumulation in a Life Cycle Growth Model." *American Economic Review*, September 1981, 533–44.

————. "Should Tax Reform Level the Playing Field?" *Proceedings of the National Tax Association-Tax Institute of America*. Meetings of November 1986, 1987, 119–25.

Survey of Current Business, December 1983 and August 1988.

Tarr, David G. *A General Equilibrium Analysis of the Welfare and Employment Effects of US Quotas in Textiles, Autos and Steel*. Washington, D.C.: Federal Trade Commission, 1989.

Thompson, Aileen. "A Study of the United States–Canadian Free Trade Agreement." Mimeo, 1989.

Thursby, Jerry, and Marie Thursby. "How Reliable Are Simple, Single Equation Models of Import Demand?" *Review of Economics and Statistics*, February 1984, 120–28.

Tobin, James, and Murray Weidenbaum, eds. *Two Revolutions in Economic Policy*, Cambridge, Mass.: MIT Press, 1988.

Travlos, Nickolaos G., and Marcia H. Millon. "Going Private Buyouts and Determinants of Stockholders' Returns." Working paper, Southern Methodist University, April 1987.

Truman, Edwin. "Approaches to Managing External Equilibria: Where We Are, Where We Might Be Headed, and How We Might Get There." *International Finance Discussion Papers*, no. 342, Board of Governors of the Federal Reserve System, Washington, D.C., February 1989.

Ueda, Kazuo. "Perspectives on the Japanese Current Account Surplus." In Stanley Fischer, ed., *Macroeconomics Annual 1988*. Cambridge, Mass.: MIT Press, 1988.

U.S. Bureau of the Census. *Money Income of Households, Families, and Persons in the United States: 1987*. Washington, D.C.: U.S. Government Printing Office, 1988.

U.S. Congress, Committee on Ways and Means, U.S. House of Representatives. *Background Material and Data on Programs within the Jurisdiction of the Committee on Ways and Means*. Washington, D.C.: U.S. Government Printing Office, 1989.

U.S. Department of Commerce, Bureau of Economic Analysis. *Fixed Reproducible Tangible Wealth in the United States 1925–85*. Washington, D.C.: U.S. Government Printing Office, June 1987.

U.S. Trade Representative (USTR). "Administration Statement on International Trade Policy," September 23, 1985.

Warren, M., and K. Chilton. "The Regulatory Legacy of the Reagan Revolution."

OP72, Center for the Study of American Business, Washington University, May 1989.

Weinstein, James. *The Corporate Ideal in the Liberal State, 1900–1918*. Boston: Beacon Books, 1968.

West, Kenneth D. *Asymptotic Normality, When Regressors have a Unit Root*. Unpublished manuscript, Princeton University, March 1987.

Wilcox, James A. "Why Real Interest Rates Were so Low in the 1970s." *American Economic Review*, March 1983, 44–53.

Wilson, John, and Wendy Takacs. "Differential Responses to Price and Exchange Rate Influences in the Foreign Trade of Selected Industrial Countries." *Review of Economics and Statistics*, May 1979, 267–79.

Working Group on Financial Markets. *Interim Report of the Working Group on Financial Markets*. Washington, D.C.: U.S. Government Printing Office, May 1988.

Zodrow, George. "Implementing Tax Reform." *National Tax Journal*, December 1981, 401–18.

Index

About the Contributors

CHARLES W. BISCHOFF is associate professor of economics at the State University of New York at Binghamton. His publications include articles in *American Economic Review, Applied Economics, Brookings Papers on Economic Activity, Journal of Forecasting, Proceedings of the National Tax Association,* and *Review of Economics and Statistics.*

PETER J. BOETTKE is an assistant professor of economics at New York University and the author of *The Political Economy of Soviet Socialism: The Formative Years, 1918–1928* (1990). He has published essays and reviews in various professional journals, including *The Journal of Economic Perspectives, The Southern Economics Journal, Research in the History of Economic Thought and Methodology, Critical Review,* and *Market Process.*

KENNETH D. BOYER is professor of economics at Michigan State University. In addition to articles on industry definitions and the effects of advertising, he has written numerous papers on the transportation industries, and has published in such journals as the *Rand Journal of Economics.*

RUSSELL S. BOYER is professor of economics at the University of Western Ontario. He has published many articles in scholarly journals, including *American Economic Review* and *Journal of Political Economy.*

GARY BURTLESS is an economist and senior fellow at the Brookings Institution in Washington, D.C. He is coauthor of *Can America Afford to Grow Old? Paying for Social Security,* editor of *A Future of Lousy Jobs? The Changing Structure of U.S. Wages,* and *Work, Health and Income among the Elderly,* and the author of numerous articles on the effects of social security, welfare, unemployment insurance, and taxes.

JEFFRY DAVIS is deputy chief economist of the Securities and Exchange Commission. He has authored or coauthored articles and SEC publications on market structure and regulatory issues.

ALAN V. DEARDORFF is professor of economics and public policy at the University of Michigan. He is coauthor, with Robert M. Stern, of *The Michigan Model of World Production and Trade* and *Computational Analysis of Global Trading Arrangements*. He has also published numerous articles on various aspects of international trade theory and policy, with special emphasis on the theory of comparative advantage.

RONALD C. FISHER is professor and chairperson of the Department of Economics at Michigan State University. His publications include *State and Local Public Finance* and numerous professional articles and research reports on public finance topics.

AUGUSTIN KWASI FOSU is associate professor of economics at Oakland University. He has published numerous articles in scholarly journals, especially in the areas of fringe benefits, unions, labor economics of minorities and women, and open economies.

DON FULLERTON is professor of economics at the University of Virginia, a research associate at the National Bureau of Economic Research, and a nonresident senior fellow at the Brookings Institution. He is a coauthor of *The Taxation of Income from Capital: A Comparative Study of the United States, United Kingdom, Sweden, and West Germany* and *A General Equilibrium Model for Tax Policy Evaluation*.

CRAIG S. HAKKIO is an assistant vice president and economist at the Federal Reserve Bank of Kansas City. He has published a number of articles on international macroeconomic issues.

PATRIC H. HENDERSHOTT is a professor of finance and public policy and holder of the John W. Galbreath Chair in Real Estate at Ohio State University. He has written widely in the areas of financial markets, taxes, and real estate.

STEVEN HUSTED is associate professor of economics at the University of Pittsburgh. He is the coauthor (with Michael Melvin) of *International Economics* and coeditor (with James Cassing) of *Capital, Technology, and Labor in the New Global Economy*. He has published articles in areas related to international trade, international finance, and monetary economics.

ROBERT T. KLEIMAN is assistant professor of finance at Oakland University. He has published extensively in the areas of inflation and asset returns, corporate restructuring activity, and the impact of regulation on stock market returns in such journals as the *Quarterly Review of Economics and Business,* the *Journal of Applied Corporate Finance,* and *Financial Services Review.* He is the coauthor of four finance books for the American Management Association as well as a research associate of the Heartland Institute.

EDWARD C. KOKKELENBERG is associate professor of economics and finance at the State University of New York at Binghamton. His publications include *Expectations and Factor Demands, Interrelated Factor Demands under Certainty,* and *Measuring Plant Capacity Utilization and Technical Change.* He is a member of the American Statistical Association's Committee on Energy Statistics and is on the editorial board of the *Journal of Productivity Analysis.*

ROGER C. KORMENDI is professor of business economics and public policy at the University of Michigan. He is also cofounder and research director of the Mid-America Institute for Public Policy Research (Chicago). Professor Kormendi has authored or edited four books including *Black Monday and the Future of Financial Markets* (1988) and *Crisis Resolution in the Thrift Industry* (1989). He has published numerous articles on issues related to budget policy, monetary policy, economic growth and development, and financial markets and institutions.

KENNETH LEHN is chief economist of the U.S. Securities and Exchange Commission. His publications include articles on corporate control that have appeared in the *Journal of Political Economy, The Journal of Finance,* the *Journal of Financial Economics,* and the *Journal of Law and Economics.*

JAY H. LEVIN is professor of economics at Wayne State University. His publications include numerous articles in the field of international monetary economics.

JAMES B. MACKIE is a financial economist in the Office of Tax Analysis of the U.S. Treasury Department. His publications include articles analyzing the 1986 Tax Reform Act.

LAURENCE H. MEYER is a professor of economics at Washington University (St. Louis) and president of Laurence H. Meyer & Associates, an economic consulting firm specializing in forecasting and policy analysis. He has published in the *Southern Economics Journal* with Anandi Sahu and Raghbendra Jha and in *Carnegie-Rochester Conference on Public Policy* with Charles Webster, and is author of *Macroeconomics: A Model Building Approach.* He is editor of

The Economic Consequences of Budget Deficits and *The Supply-Side Effects of Economic Policy.*

THOMAS GALE MOORE is a senior fellow at the Hoover Institution and was a member of Ronald Reagan's Council of Economic Advisers from 1985 to 1989. His publications include *The Economics of the American Theater, Trucking Regulation: Lessons from Europe, Freight Transportation,* and numerous articles in professional journals.

KEVIN J. MURPHY is associate professor of economics at Oakland University. His publications include articles in the *Review of Economics and Statistics, Economic Inquiry,* the *Journal of Regional Science,* and the *Journal of Macroeconomics.*

JOE PEEK is a professor of economics at Boston College and visiting economist at the Federal Reserve Bank of Boston. His articles have appeared in the *American Economic Review, Journal of Money, Credit, and Banking, The Review of Economics and Statistics, The Journal of Finance, Journal of Business and Economic Statistics,* and *New England Economic Review.*

JOEL L. PRAKKEN is vice president and cofounder of Laurence H. Meyer & Associates, a private consulting firm based in Saint Louis and specializing in macroeconomic forecasting and policy analysis. He is also an adjunct assistant professor of economics at Washington University (Saint Louis). His recent publications include "The Federal Deficit," "National Saving and Economic Performance," and "The Macroeconomics of Tax Reform."

ROBERT H. RASCHE is professor of economics at Michigan State University. He is coauthor of *Controlling the Growth of Monetary Aggregates* and has published articles on the demand for money and monetary policy. He is a member of the Shadow Open Market Committee.

ANANDI P. SAHU is assistant professor of economics at Oakland University. He has published articles in academic and professional journals.

MARTHA SEGER is the longest-serving member of the Board of Governors of the Federal Reserve System. In addition to her monetary policymaking duties, she represents the Board on the National Women's Business Council and is chairman of the board of directors of the Neighborhood Reinvestment Corporation.

RALPH A. TERREGROSSA is an assistant professor in the Department of Economics and Finance at St. John's University.

RONALD L. TRACY is an associate professor and chairperson of the Department of Economics at Oakland University. He has published numerous articles about monetary and macroeconomic policy as well as econometrics.

CHRIS P. VARVARES is vice president of Laurence H. Meyer & Associates. In addition, he is an adjunct instructor at Washington University (Saint Louis).